T0319870

China's Urbanization and the World Economy

For Yuping and Lisa

China's Urbanization and the World Economy

Fan Zhang

National School of Development, Peking University, China

Edward Elgar
Cheltenham, UK • Northampton, MA, USA

Published by
Edward Elgar Publishing Limited
The Lypiatts
15 Lansdown Road
Cheltenham
Glos GL50 2JA
UK

Edward Elgar Publishing, Inc.
William Pratt House
9 Dewey Court
Northampton
Massachusetts 01060
USA

A catalogue record for this book
is available from the British Library

Library of Congress Control Number: 2013957769

This book is available electronically in the ElgarOnline.com
Economics Subject Collection, E-ISBN 978 1 78100 188 2

ISBN 978 1 78100 187 5

Typeset by Servis Filmsetting Ltd, Stockport, Cheshire
Printed and bound in Great Britain by T.J. International Ltd, Padstow

Contents

Preface

This is a tale of two Chinas, of rural China versus urban China. Urbanization is a process ending the urban–rural segregation, which means equal treatment of all Chinese, and equal opportunities for every resident, no matter where they live. If it is completed, this great event will set the foundation of a peaceful, united, and equalized China in the twenty-first century, a Chinese version of the liberalization of serfs, just like the emancipation of the slaves in the United States in the nineteenth century.

This book tries to depict an original picture of China's urbanization, explaining the fundamentals and details of what has happened in China and the logic behind urbanization, and bringing vital aspects of China's urbanization into clearer view. The book will explore how urbanization raised the ordinary citizen's real income ten times from 1978 to 2011, and reallocated wealth among individuals in the past three decades. This book provides a forecast of China's economic growth and estimations for important products up to 2030. I will simulate the decision-making of the leadership about China's urbanization, explaining how crisis imposes choices between tough alternatives.

By evaluating China's urbanization in a global environment, this book tries to treat domestic and international affairs as connected subjects, placing China's urbanization within a broader global context. This book estimates the size of China's domestic market, and the future demands for major products and services in domestic and world markets. This book also probes the costs and benefits of China's urbanization from the viewpoint of both China and the rest of the world.

The scale of China's urbanization is wholly without precedent in human history. It includes issues that no twentieth-century government had faced. The challenges are in keeping a group of intertwined factors under control and accomplishing correlated works virtually all at once. The difficulty is in incorporating the migrants and containing the dangerous features of a mass urban society at the same time.

Acknowledgements

I would like to thank Mr Edward Elgar for inviting me to write this book. He went to Beijing in May 2011, meeting me at the National School of Development, Peking University, discussing my plan for this book. To my surprise, he came, without any assistant accompanying him, from another school to my office, a 15-minute walk, with a large bag of papers and books. After discussing the writing plan, we walked along the Weiming Lake, talking about the construction and history of Peking University. At an entrance to the university I found a taxi for Edward, but the driver refused to carry him, probably because he cannot speak Chinese. After a while, we finally found a taxi that would take him to his hotel. Ironically, this was the origin of this book. We will further discuss taxi drivers refusing to drive or selecting customers in Chinese cities in Chapter 8.

I could not have finished this book without the help of my daughter, Lisa Zhang, who did a close-read edit of my first drafts. I would like to thank my research assistants, Yunlei Qi and Junxiao Bu of Peking University, for their excellent information collecting and model building. I would also like to thank Emily Mew, Laura Mann, Victoria Nicols, Madhubanti Bhattacharyya, and Emma Gribbon from Edward Elgar Publishing, for helping me to improve the text. Finally, my greatest debt is to my wife, Yuping Li, who always supports my work, especially during the hot days in the summer of 2013 when I was finishing this book.

Introduction

Urbanization in China and technology innovation in the United States are two major events in contemporary times, which will have enormous impact on the future development of human history.

Urbanization is a process of transformation from rural life to a life in cities. It has been an engine of the growth in China since the economic reform started in 1978 and will be a crucial driving force of the economic and social changes in the twenty-first century. China was a rural society until the recent past. About 80 percent of the population were still living in the countryside in the late 1970s, not much different from the late Qing Dynasty (1616–1911). A rapid change has happened since then. Hundreds of millions of peasants poured into the cities over the past 30 years and over half of the population live in urban areas now. The suddenness of the change seems to defy some economists' belief that 'nature does not take great leaps' (Mokyr 2000; Darwin 1859).

How did this happen? What is the driving force of this process? What are the obstacles to this process? What is the meaning of this urbanization to China and the world? This book is an attempt to answer these questions. To do so, urbanization is put in a larger framework of the economic growth in China and in the world. The role of urbanization in this growth process will be located and the linkages between urbanization and the stages of growth will be analyzed.

In particular, I will argue that China has two stages of development: the first is overseas market-oriented, and the second is domestic market-oriented. China is in a process of transformation from the first to the second, and urbanization is the key link between the two. China's first stage of development since late 1970s has been export-oriented, targeting the overseas market. An export-oriented manufacturing and trade sector was set up, using foreign capital and domestic rural labor, which is largely separated from the domestic market, importing raw materials, processing and re-exporting to the world market. This is the take-off stage of the Chinese economy in the late twentieth century. However, this first stage of China's economic development is not sustainable. A large country, such as China or the United States, needs to root its industry in its own market in the long run. How can China transform from an export-oriented economy to a domestic market-oriented one? The answer is urbanization.

Urbanization allows the foundation of a domestic market, with two sub-stages: city building (construction) and the formation of a domestic market. The first sub-stage started in the late 1990s, and has made much progress. A large number of buildings have been built in the old and new urban areas. However, not much progress has been made with the second sub-stage, the building of the domestic consumption market. The construction of the cities has created a large demand for raw materials and investment goods, which impacted the world market. If China can overcome the obstacles of domestic consumer market building in the near future, it will be one of the world's central markets and be able to overthrow the existing world economic order. The Chinese economy will become domestic market-oriented and the exports to China will be extremely important for other countries. The main obstacle toward this is institutional, including the income distribution and residency regulation. To overthrow these obstacles, China needs to relax the residency regulation and give the rural immigrants country-wide citizenship in the next decade. 'Liberation of the peasants' will be the next target in the near future, which will create a huge domestic market.

Government plays an important role in China's urbanization. Since ancient times, Chinese cities have been the administration centers of the government system, as well as the economic and cultural centers. Cities are at the administrative level in the current political structure. In this system, some cities are at higher administrative levels than the other cities. However, urban society has been less developed compared to the state and its administrative system. The future of Chinese cities is thus decided in a game played between the central government and its local counterparts. Successful urbanization in China means finding a proper relationship between state and society, between government and market. The objectives should be to keep government power in check, while maintaining internal solidarity and security in the process.

A large number of books and papers deal with the issue of China's urbanization, in English and in Chinese, for example Vernon Henderson's (2009) paper on China's urbanization, and Yan Song and Chengri Ding's (2007) book on urbanization in China. More research can be found in Chinese, for example: China Development Research Foundation (2010), Gu et al. (2008), Wan and Cai (2012), Chen et al. (2009), Chen (2012) and Tong (2011). These provide detailed analyses of all the important aspects of China's urbanization, and provide their suggestions on how China is achieving its urbanization.

Some books are more general urban economic textbooks, for example

McDonald and McMillen (2011) and O'Sullivan (2009); or focused on China, for example Hu (2005). These books provide general principles of urban economics and/or a detailed analysis on China's urbanization.

Other research is about certain special fields related to China's urbanization, for example: Ren (2012; the housing market), Chung and Lam (2004; government administrative system), Kim and Nangia (2008; infrastructure), EIA (2011, 2012; environment), Dong (2004; history of construction in Chinese cities), Hui and Huo (2007; rural labor transfer), Hu and Guo (2010; grain demand), and many more. These researches provide knowledge and analyses of the special fields, which are needed in estimating the future of China's market and its impacts on the world economy. See also Cai et al. (2009), Chan and Zhang (n.d.), Cheng (2007), Fleisher and Yang (2006), Hua (2013), Lin (2012), National Bureau of Statistics (2009e).

Professor Qiren Zhou, Professor Zhaofeng Xue, Professor Janguo Xu, Professor Lixing Li and Professor Min Wang of the National School of Development (NSD), Peking University, did a lot of field surveys and policy research on China's land market, property rights and land reform, transferring first-hand materials into theory and policies. Guoqing Song, Feng Lu, Yiping Huang, Miaojie Yu and other colleagues of mine at NSD, led a large-scale research on China's international macroeconomic relations, from which I benefited a lot while writing this book. In general, the research of Professor Justin Yifu Lin, Professor Yang Yao, Professor Xiaobo Zhang, Professor Shuanglin Lin, Professor Hemao Wu, and many other colleagues at the NSD on economic development and the Chinese economy also made a significant impact on this book. Professor Barry Naughton, a leading China specialist, emphasizes the complexity and difficulties in achieving China's urbanization on many occasions in his published work, from which I benefited a lot (Naughton 2006).

Chinese names are given throughout the volume in a style that has been used in the West for a long time: the given name without a comma followed by the family name (i.e. Xiaoping Deng). Commas are to be used only to invert the author's name (or name of first author if more than one) in the References list (i.e. Deng, Xiaoping).The book uses simple economic theory, for example, factor allocation, transaction costs and scale economy, and illustrates some basic points with statistics, charts and case studies. Part I of the book deals with the urbanization itself, discussing the trend and current status of urbanization in China, industrialization and urbanization, the massive migration from rural areas, construction and the housing market, and the social problems caused by urbanization. Part II focuses on the impact of China's urbanization on the world market, discussing the raw material markets, consumer markets and production-factor markets. Part III is about the policymakers' decisions, including relating to the trade-off facing China and the world, to give the reader a more realistic idea of how complex the problem is and what challenges the leaders are facing.

PART I

China's urbanization

Urbanization has been a long process since the birth of cities in China. This process speeded up only in the past century. China's official urbanization rate has grown more than 1 percentage point annually in the past 20 years (National Bureau of Statistics 2012a).

The official statistical category of 'urban population' has changed a lot. The 1964 and 1982 censuses counted the population with non-agricultural *Hukou* registration as the urban population. As the scale of migration increased, this statistical caliber could not accurately calculate the urban population. The 1990 census first used the term 'resident population', which includes the population living in a place for more than one year. In the 2000 census, a person only needed to live in a place for six months to be considered as a resident. As a result, the official statistics of the urban population before 2000 do not include all migrant workers who live in cities, while after 2000 they include a large portion of population who do not have an urban *Hukou* (Wan and Cai 2012, p.148).

According to the China Urban Development Report issued by the China Mayors Association in July 2013 (*Jinghua Times* 2013), China's official urbanization rate reached 52.57 percent in 2012. However, according to data from the Ministry of Public Security, the non-agricultural population with urban resident ID was only 34.17 percent, which means that China's actual urbanization rate is about 15 percentage points lower than the official urbanization rates shown in Table I.1 (*Jinghua Times* 2013).

The high population density of an urban area facilitates contact among people and economic activities. Currently in China, a city is an administrative division, created by the order of a higher level in government. The cities are divided into three types: (1) centrally administered cities; (2) deputy-province-level and prefecture-level city; and (3) county-level city (Table I.2). A city is officially defined as: (1) an 'extra-large' city when the population is greater than 1 million; (2) a 'large' city when the population is between 500 000 and 1 million; (3) a 'medium' city when the population is between

Table I.1   China's population and urbanization rate (10000)

	Total population (year end)	Urban	%	Rural	%
1949	54167	5765	10.6	48402	89.4
1978	96259	17245	17.9	79014	82.1
1990	114333	30195	26.4	84138	73.6
2000	126743	45906	36.2	80837	63.8
2010	134091	66978	49.9	67113	50.1
2011	134735	69079	51.3	65656	48.7

Note: Urban population includes population without residential ID. This is an official estimate by the National Bureau of Statistics of China.

Source: Based on National Bureau of Statistics (2012a, table 3-1).

Table I.2   Number of cities, China, by administrative level

	1949	1978	2010
Centrally administered cities	12	3	4
Deputy-province-level and prefecture-level cities	54	98	283
County-level cities	66	92	370

Sources: Chung and Lam (2004); National Bureau of Statistics (2011b, p. 23).

Table I.3   Size distribution of Chinese cities, 2007

Population	Number of cities
>1 million	58
0.5–1 million	82
0.2–0.5 million	232
< 0.2 million	283
Total	655

Sources: Ministry of Housing and Construction, Bureau of Planning (2007); China Development Research Foundation (2010, p. 12).

200000 and 500000; and a 'small' city when the population is between 100000 and 200000.

The size distribution of Chinese cities is closely correlated to the distribution of administrative levels (Table I.3).

According to the National Bureau of Statistics of China, in 2011, 691 million people were living in cities and towns, and of them 398 million were living in prefecture cities, deputy-province-level cities and centrally administered cities (National Bureau of Statistics 2012a, pp. 101, 386). Others are living in county-level cities, counties and towns.

1. China's urbanization: history and facts

1.1 A QUICK REVIEW

China's urbanization can be traced back thousands of years, when large human settlements appeared in central China, although opinions vary on whether any particular ancient settlement can be considered to be a city. Urbanization in China begins at Banpo (4800–3750 BC) on the Zhongyuan plain of the Yellow River (in Shangqiu, Shandong province today). Banpo grew from a typical Yangshao village in both size and organization until the construction of the Great City Hall in 4000 BC. Banpo was composed of 200 round pit houses and the Great Hall occupying 5 hectares and surrounded by a ditch. These pit houses were sited for solar gain by aligning the door to face south (Wikipedia n.d.-d).

Based on archaeological discoveries, many of the earliest Chinese cities were established during the Shang Dynasty, in the second millennium BC. Ao was one of these ancient Chinese cities. At the site of Ao, large walls were erected in the fifteenth century BC that had dimensions of 4–8 meters in width at the base and enclosed an area of 1600–1900 m squared (Dong 2004, p.9).

Cities of significant scale appeared in the Han, Tang and Song dynasties. Chang'an (today known as Xi'an, in Shaanxi province, middle-west China) is a capital city of more than ten dynasties. During the Han Dynasty (206 BC to AD 220), Chang'an had a population of 300 000–400 000. The city's population increased to 1 million in the Tang Dynasty (AD 618–907), with a city wall of 36 km long and 8 m wide at the base (China Development Research Foundation 2010, p.8; Dong 2004, pp.31, 47). The city was in the form of an irregular rectangle. Eleven streets and 14 avenues divided the city into 109 walled wards (Dong 2004, p.53). Bianjing, the capital city of the Song Dynasty (AD 960–1279) and now known as Kaifeng, was surrounded by three rings of city walls and had a civilian population between 1.1 million and 1.3 million in the eleventh century. It is believed that Bianjing was the largest city in the world at that time (Dong 2004, p.81). As the capital of the southern Song Dynasty (AD 1127–1279), Hangzhou was a city with over 1 million people and vast amounts of commerce and busy river and canal traffic.

The invasion of the Mongolians ended the prosperity in central China in the twelfth century, and big cities disappeared until the twentieth century. The sizes of many Chinese cities were trivial at the end of the nineteenth century, much smaller than their size in Tang Dynasty, about 1000 years before.

In the late nineteenth century, China gradually opened the door to the Western powers. The British established a concession in Shanghai after China lost the First Opium War. The French, Americans and Japanese soon followed the British in establishing territories in Shanghai. Before and after the establishment of the Republic of China in 1912, urbanization gradually progressed. Modern commercial and industrial cities appeared in China, especially in the eastern coastal area. Shanghai became the most important port in Asia, and the world's largest trading and banking firms set up houses along the Bund. It became the most modern city in Asia. The Second World War and the Civil War in the 1930s and 1940s ended this wave of urbanization and the Communist government came to power in 1949.

1.2   SOME BACKGROUND OF THE CHINESE POLITICAL AND ECONOMIC SYSTEM

The Chinese Communists installed a Soviet-type planned economic system in the early 1950s, in which decisions regarding production and investment are embodied in a plan formulated by the central government. Under this system, the government controls and regulates production, distribution, prices, and so on. Most of the large enterprises were state-owned and located in the cities, while the peasants were organized in communes in the countryside. The government adopted a system of food rationing to feed the urban residents through state-owned retail stores, while collecting grain from communes in the countryside. After turning over their grain requirement, the peasants were allowed to consume the surplus. The performance of the planned system in China was poor, mainly due to the government's lack of information and the workers' lack of incentive. The economic reform started in December 1978 by reformists within the Communist Party of China (CPC), and led by de facto leader Xiaoping Deng, is also known as the Reform and Opening Up. The reform first decollectivized agriculture and set up a Household Responsibility System, which divided the land of the people's communes among the peasants. This move increased agricultural production and improved the living standards of the peasants. In urban areas, large-scale privatization occurred in 1990s, in which all state enterprises, except a few large monopolies, were sold to private investors.

1.3   URBANIZATION IN THE PLANNED PERIOD, 1949–1977

China's urban population was 57.7 million and its urbanization ratio was 10.6 percent in 1949 (National Bureau of Statistics 2012a, table 3-1). This low level of urbanization was a result of the Second World War and the Civil War in the 1940s. After the founding of the People's Republic in 1949, China's urbanization level increased gradually during the planned period and the early period of economic reform and opening up to the world.

Statistics: Definition of Urban Population

Before reviewing the history, the definitions of the urban population set by the Chinese government need to be identified. From 1949 to 1958, the urban population was defined as residents living in the urban area, which is no different from that in other countries. In 1958, the *Hukou* Registration Regulation was established, designed to control migration between rural and urban areas. Under the 1958 regulation, the urban population was defined as the sum of the people who had an urban *Hukou* registration. This means anyone living in the urban area without an urban *Hukou* would not be counted as an urban resident. After the economic reform started in the late 1970s, large numbers of peasants moved into the city. The definition of urban population based on *Hukou* could not reflect this great change and the urban population was underestimated. In 1999, the National Bureau of Statistics and other government agencies published regulations designating urban and rural areas. In 2006, these agencies published a revised regulation addressing this issue. The new system counts urban population based on actual residence, not based on the records in the *Hukou* system (Wan and Cai 2012, p.128).

Hukou is a residency registration system which officially identifies a person as a resident of an area. It is a term that will be used frequently in this book. Under the *Hukou* system, each household has a registration record which usually includes the names, births, deaths, marriages, divorces and moves for each member of the household. A *Hukou* book is kept in the household, while the police station in each area keeps a copy of it. *Hukou* can be traced back to ancient China, and exists in some other East Asian countries, but no other government controls residency more tightly than the modern Chinese government. There are fundamental differences between an urban *Hukou* and a rural *Hukou*, in terms of the holders' rights. The Chinese government promulgated the *Hukou* system to control the movement of people between urban and rural areas. More details about *Hukou* will be discussed in Chapter 4.

Most of the statistics used in this book are those published by Statistics Bureau of the People's Republic of China, which includes the population and urbanization data of Mainland China only, excluding Taiwan, Macau and Hong Kong.

Stages of China's Urbanization Under the Planned System

In China, under the planned system and before the economic reform started in 1978, all cities were set up by the government's bureaucratic system. A city was an administrative division of the government system. The mayor of a city was actually nominated by the upper-level government and was responsible for reporting to the upper-level government. Local application for setting up a city needed to be approved by the upper-level government. This is quite different from the system prevailing in the West. The history of urbanization in China is actually one of a series of decisions made by the government, and the people's reactions to these decisions.

After the founding of the People's Republic of China by the Communists in 1949, urbanization revived for a short period of time. In 1951, about one-tenth of the people lived in urban areas. Supported by technological and financial aid from the Soviet Union, industrialization in China increased rapidly. A total of 156 major industrial and defense projects were constructed and large number of peasants moved into the cities as new workers. Eight million people migrated from the countryside to cities in the 1950s as a by-product of industrialization (Chen et al. 2009, p.21). In 1957, China's urban population increased to 99.5 million and the urbanization ratio reached 15.4 percent. The number of cities increased from 136 in 1949 to 176 in 1957 (China Development Research Foundation 2010, p.9).

The urbanization process experienced large fluctuations during the period between 1958 and 1965. In the first half of this period, large numbers of people moved into the cities due to the Great Leap Forward, a political and economic campaign that aimed to use the large population to speed up China's economy to catch up with the economies of the US and UK within a short period of time. The urban population rose to 130.7 million in 1960, an increase of 31.2 million from 1957. The urbanization ratio increased to 19.8 percent, and 44 new cities were established in a short period of time. As a result of neglecting harvests in autumn 1958, with farmers forced to produce iron and steel, and the spread of public dining rooms (an attempt to destroy families by political force), the Great Famine (1959–1961) immediately followed the Great Leap Forward in the spring of 1959. The government did not have enough food to feed the urban population and therefore removed a large number of cities from the maps. Thirty million people or 26 percent of the urban population were forced to move back to the countryside. The urbanization ratio was reduced and the number of cities reduced from 179 in 1957 to 169 in 1965 (China Development Research Foundation 2010, p.9).

The urbanization process in China was frozen during the Great Proletarian Cultural Revolution, from 1966 to 1978. Zedong Mao, then Chairman of the Communist Party, initiated the Cultural Revolution to remove capitalist and traditionalist culture from Chinese society. During the Cultural Revolution, Mao mobilized the masses to remove the government officials who did not follow Mao's instructions. The movement paralyzed the activities of the government and society. The production slowed down, the government ceased to function, and schools closed for several years. At the end of the Cultural Revolution, urban youths were sent to live and work in the countryside. The urban population grew slowly from 1966 to 1976. By 1978, only 17.9 percent of the Chinese population was living in the cities and towns. There were 193 cities existing in China in 1978 (calculated based on Hu 2005 and National Bureau of Statistics 2000–2012-a).

Overall, in Mao's mind, China should be a great rural society, in which cities played a minor role. Mao's policy was to ruralize China rather than to urbanize it. The official policy was anti-urbanization. *Hukou* was used to keep the peasants on the land. However, against Mao's wishes, the process of urbanization restarted immediately after his death in 1976.

1.4 RAPID DEVELOPMENT IN URBANIZATION DURING ECONOMIC REFORM

Economic performance was poor under the planned system from 1952 to 1978, compared to other East Asian countries or regions, such as Japan and Korea. The central planning system was riddled with inefficiencies. Everyone, from an ordinary worker to a high-ranking official, was hurt by the Revolution and learned a lesson from it. Reform became common sense and Xiaoping Deng, the leader[1] of the Communist Party and the designer of the reform, was widely supported by the Communist Party officials and ordinary citizens.

At the end of the 1970s, China began an economic reform towards a market economy. The Communist Party's Central Committee held a conference in December 1978, which formally launched the economic reform. More decision-making responsibilities shifted from central to local government. Agriculture was decollectivized and the Household Responsibility System was carried out, under which farmland was divided into private lots. The urban industries were allowed to sell products above the planned quota. A dual price system was introduced, in which commodities were sold at both planned and market prices. Shortages were avoided since consumers could buy products on the market if the planned products were not available. The policy shift was based on economic and social considerations, including reducing rural poverty and hunger. From the late 1970s to the early twenty-first century, by the Chinese government's standards, which is lower than international standards, the number of people living in poverty fell dramatically from 250 million to 28 million.

Urbanization experienced a period of recovery in the early 1980s. The urban population increased slightly, from 163.4 million in 1976 to 250.9 million in 1985. There was a jump in the number of cities during the same period, which increased to 324 in 1985. The urbanization ratio rose to 23.7 percent in 1985.

In 1986, the National People's Congress passed the Seventh National Development Plan, which announced a revision of the urban development policy. The revision emphasized the development of middle-sized and small cities, instead of large cities, to avoid overcrowding in the large cities. At the same time, the State Council reduced the standard for setting up towns from a population of 100000 to 60000,[2] and allowed the peasants to work and live in towns with their own food rations. This was one way to allow rural residents who did not have urban food rations to work and live in cities. China's urban population reached 331.7 million in 1993, with an urbanization ratio of 28 percent, and the number of cities increased to 570 by 1993, from 324 in 1985.

The administrative structure of Chinese cities saw an 'inflated urbanization' in the 1980s and 1990s, when the number of cities increased from 193 in 1978 to 463 in 1991, and then to 677 in 2001. The increase in the number of cities in China refers to the rise in administrative designation rather than to the natural development in population and area. During the planned period, cities, which had jurisdiction over small spaces, were placed under rural-based administrative entities since urban areas were rated as much less important than governing the rural areas. It was not the cities or prefectures but the counties that really held the power. In the reform years, the administrative measures used to expend the number of cities include three types: turning prefectures into cities (*Di Gai Shi*); designating rural counties as cities (*Xian Gai Shi*); and transforming suburban counties into urban districts (*Xian Shi Gai Qu*). The process was mainly by the endorsement of what had happened at the local level by the central government. The local government has tremendous incentives to upgrade its administrative level, because: (1) it improves prefecture-level cities' budgetary position when it becomes a formal independent fiscal regime; (2) county-level cities sell temporary *Hukou* to raise revenue; (3) it helps administration in the suburbs of the cities; and (4) it helps the central government to cut down the number of government units and staff numbers (Chung and Lam 2004).

Li (2008) examines a distinctive mechanism of providing incentives for local governments that upgrade from counties to 'cities'. Using a large panel data set covering all counties in China during 1993–2004, Li investigates the determinants of upgrading and finds that economic growth rate plays a key role in obtaining city status. The findings are consistent with the hypothesis that the central government uses upgrading to reward local officials for high growth, as well as aligning local interests with those of the central government.

Urban development in China has taken place at an unprecedented pace and scale since the 1990s. Although the number of cities was stable (there were 660 in 2003 and 655 in 2008), population and the extent of built-up areas soared (National Bureau of Statistics 2009, in Hu 2005, p.46). The built-up area in urban areas increased from 12 856 sq km in 1990 to 40 058 sq km in 2010 (National Bureau of Statistics 2011a, p.379). Large cities increased their population scale by merging with suburban counties. As a result, the administrative areas of large cities have been enlarged. Some new cities were created by merging two or more counties during this period (China Development Research Foundation 2010, p.64).

In 2010, about 35–40 percent of the population were officially recorded as urban residents under the *Hukou* system, plus 150 million rural–urban migrants living in urban areas but not recognized as urban residents (Chen 2012, p.4). Including migrants, the urbanization ratio was over 50 percent in 2011.

In summation, in the past 60 years, the urban population increased from 58 million in 1949 to 691 million in 2011. The urbanization ratio rose from 10.64 percent to 51.27 percent. This increase in urban population is a result of both the natural increase in population and rural-to-urban migration.

The number of cities increased from about 130 in 1949 to over 650 in 2010 (Hu 2005, p.46 and National Bureau of Statistics 2000–2012-a). This has been the result of government actions, but also reflected the society's demand for urbanization.

1.5 ASPECTS OF URBANIZATION

Urbanization in China is characterized by its scale and uneven distribution. This section will give a brief picture of the current status and distinguishing features of China's urbanization.

The Size Distribution of Chinese Cities

Henderson (2009) pointed out that most of the cities in China are under-sized. Half of China's increased urbanization simply involved the reclassification of 'rural' areas as cities. Most cities in China have populations too low to properly exploit the scale benefits of clustering local economic activity. Many prefecture-level cities are about half their efficient size. A doubling of the population in such cities would lead to a 20–35 percent increase in output per worker.

In 1952, the large and mid-sized cities were about 27 percent of the total, in terms of numbers, and 75 percent in terms of population. In the following years, the numbers of both large and mid-sized cities and small cities increased. In 2000, the share of the number of large and mid-sized cities increased to about 47 percent, but the share of population in large and mid-sized cities decreased to 63 percent. It seems that the large cities in China are not large enough: after 2000, the largest cities picked up their rate of expansion. This was because of the accumulation of the agglomeration economies of the largest cities, which attracted more and more resources and people, and the further relaxed regulation.

Types of Chinese Cities

Historically, Chinese cities were created for different reasons. First and most importantly, a city is an administrative division of the government. There are several types of administrative cities in China: municipalities directly under the central government (e.g. Beijing, Shanghai, Tianjin and Chongqing); provincial capital cities and deputy-province-level cities; prefecture-level cities which are governed by provinces or autonomous regions; and county-level cities which are sub-units of the prefecture-level administrative division. It is extremely important in China for a city to be raised to a higher level of administrative division, because government investments are distributed according to a city's administrative level. The higher the administrative level, the more resources go to the city. The government investments were the only source of investments during the planned period, and are still a very important source today. Two cities in Hebei province, Baoding and Shijiazhuang, were similar in the level of economic development in 1949. Twenty years later, Shijiazhuang became more advanced than Baoding, in terms of size and construction, because Shijiazhuang was chosen as the province capital by the central government.

Second, some of the smaller settlements have become cities due to the development of industries, for example Jixi, Daqing and Yichun in Heilongjiang province. Of 469 of the new cities established after 1949 which were investigated, 44 are coal-electricity cities, 24 are metals mining and processing cities, and 14 are petroleum extraction and processing cities (Gu et al. 2008, p.69). After 1978, a large group of export-oriented processing manufacturing and trade cities emerged in the eastern coastal area, for example Shenzhen, Zhuhai and Dongguan. As the special areas covered by the opening-up policy, large numbers of migrant workers and large amounts of foreign capital poured into these small settlements and made them develop rapidly. Shenzhen is a good example of this kind of new industrial city. Shenzhen was a simple rural hamlet which had a train station called Bao'an on the Mainland China–Hong Kong border in 1979, when the area was picked as the first of China's Special Economic Zones. Thirty years later, Shenzhen has become a major city in the country, with one of two major stock exchanges and the third-largest container port in China. The municipality covers an area of 2050 sq km (792 sq miles), with a total population of 26.8 million in 2011. Shenzhen is the economic powerhouse of China and the largest manufacturing base in the world. In 2010, Shenzhen's gross domestic product (GDP) reached RMB951 billion, ranked fourth among the 659 Chinese cities (only behind Beijing, Shanghai and Guangzhou) and its GDP per capita was RMB95000 ($14615). Shenzhen is a major manufacturing center in China with many domestic and foreign high-tech companies operating in the city. Shenzhen has 26 buildings at over 200 meters tall, including the Shun Hing Square, the eighth-tallest building in the world.

Third, trade cities developed as the government relaxed the control of market activities. Yiwu in Zhenjiang province grew as a national trading center for small commodities. It was upgraded from a county to a county-level city in May 1988. It had 700 000 people in 2001 and its overall economy ranked nineteenth of all counties (or county-level cities) of China in 2001. The customers of Yiwu's commodities come from all over the world.

Fourth, cities as hubs of transportation have developed as China accelerated the construction of railroads, highways, harbors and airports. Zhengzhou is the capital and the largest city of Henan province in north-central China. It serves as a major transportation hub for central China, as well as being the political, economic, technological and educational center of the province. The Longhai railway (east–west) meets the Jingguang railway (north–south) in Zhengzhou and nearly all trains on routes to Beijing, Shanghai and Xi'an pass through Zhengzhou. China's major north–south (Beijing–Hong Kong) and east–west (Lianyungang–Khorgas) expressways also meet near Zhengzhou.

Fifth, there are also a number of tourist cities emerging as personal income increases and travel becomes part of the life of middle-income families. Huangshan city is a prefecture-level city in southern Anhui province, east China. Huangshan means 'Yellow Mountain' in Chinese and the city is named after the famously scenic Yellow Mountains, which cover much of the city's vast geographic territory. The Yellow Mountains have at least 140 viewpoints open to visitors, and over 17.1 million tourists visited the mountains in 2005 (Huangshan Scenic Zone Administration n.d.).

The Geographical Distribution of the Chinese Cities

Approximately one-half of China's territory is not easily habitable. If you draw a line on the map of China from the north-east corner to the south-west corner, you will find that most of the population is located to the south-east of the line. The distribution of the cities followed the same pattern before 1949. The government tried to change this pattern after 1949, due to strategic and safety considerations. They thought another world war was inevitable, and therefore did not allocate the industries to the future battlefield. In the 1950s and early 1960s, the imagined enemies of China – the US, Japan, and the Nationalists in Taiwan – were to the east of Mainland China. Limited investment was put into the south-eastern cities, because the area was expected to be a future battlefield. This distribution pattern was inefficient, because the western cities were much smaller and had fewer agglomeration economies than the eastern cities. There were small relocations toward the eastern coast made in the late 1960s and the 1970s when the invasion of the Soviet Union from the north and west became a major threat. After 1978, economic development became the major consideration of the government and the focus moved back to the eastern coastal cities. These cities regained a high growth rate and had a large share of the national production (see Table 1.1).

Table 1.1   Shares of GDP, different geographical areas in China, 2011

Area	Share of GDP (%)
Eastern	58.5
Central	27.2
Western	14.2

Notes: Eastern area includes Beijing, Tianjin, Hebei, Liaoning, Shanghai, Jiangsu, Zhejiang, Fujian, Shandong, Guangdong, Guangxi, Hainan; Central area includes Shanxi, Inner Mongolia, Jilin, Heilongjiang, Anhui, Jiangxi, Henan, Hubei, Hunan; Western area includes Chongqing, Sichuan, Guizhou, Yunnan, Tibet, Shaanxi, Gansu, Qinghai, Ningxia, Xinjiang.

Source: Based on National Bureau of Statistics (2011a, table 2-14).

After the beginning of the economic reform and opening up to the world in the late 1970s, the cities in the eastern coastal areas experienced a second wave of rapid development. Based on their comparative advantage in obtaining technology and management knowledge, these cities attracted large numbers of migrant workers and large amounts of foreign capital, regaining their positions from before 1949.

1.6 CHALLENGES

The policymakers in China are facing many challenges in the process of urbanization. Firstly, urbanization has lagged behind industrialization in most of the past 60 years in China. If we use the share of non-agricultural production in GDP to measure industrialization, and use the share of urban population to measure urbanization, we will find that industrialization has progressed much faster than urbanization in China (see Chapter 3 for details).

Industrialization usually progresses with urbanization in countries with no government intervention. But in China, during the planned period from the early 1950s to the late 1970s, the government imposed a policy of industrialization without urbanization. Attempts were made to invest in urban industries, while keeping the separation between the urban and rural areas. After economic reform, policies on urban–rural separation were relaxed, but they still exist. The government was reluctant and slow to lift these regulations. Therefore, urbanization still lags behind industrialization. The lack of urbanization has a negative impact on the balance of economic and social development and has created many problems. Accelerating the progress of urbanization is a challenge facing the Chinese government.

Secondly, the government has been facing tough decisions on designing the scale structure of the system of the cities. In other words, should China concentrate on the development of small cities or large cities, or a mix of the two? Historically, policy has changed back and forth between focusing on large and small cities. Currently, hot discussion has been going on among scholars and policymakers. When the policymakers hesitate, the market force works to adjust the scale structure of the system of the cities.

Thirdly, the government has to deal with large negative effects of urbanization. Most of the problems correlate with the externalities due to human crowding in big cities. The most urgent problem is traffic congestion. Severe policies have been imposed in some cities, for example restraints on car purchasing, which hurt consumers' rights and business profits. Another problem is rising housing prices, which makes it difficult for middle-income households to buy a house. Government regulations have been imposed to raise the requirements for buying a house, which hurt consumers' basic rights and also slow the growth of the economy. Based on China's population, land scarcity, and the huge difference between cities and the countryside in terms of living standards which makes cities more attractive, it is expected that super-large cities will appear in China, which might be larger than many large cities in other countries. If this happens, China will face a much more severe problem of congestion and externalities and will need to find solutions.

China's urbanization is far from complete. The official numbers for urbanization are overestimated, in the sense that more than 100 million of 600 million urban residents have no full rights of citizenship. To give them full citizenship, governments – especially local governments – need to provide much more public services, which local governments have neither enough incentive nor the financial resources to provide. To address these problems, it is necessary to look first at the larger picture of China's economic reform since the late 1970s.

NOTES

1. Although Deng held power, he was never the Communist Party chairman officially. He was only a vice-premier of the government in late 1970s, while the Party chairman and the premier was Mr Hua Guofeng.
2. A county needs to apply to the State Council to promote itself to a higher rank, such as a county-level city. To do so, a county needs to meet certain standards.

2. The road map and logic of China's urbanization

In this chapter, I try to draw a larger picture of China's urbanization and discover the logic behind this great development. In particular, I try to find the relationship between economic development and urbanization in China, how the two stages of economic development connect to the urbanization, and how urbanization changes the nature of China's development and exports.

2.1 THE ROLE OF URBANIZATION IN CHINA'S DEVELOPMENT

China's first stage of development since late 1970s has been export-oriented. The target market of the Chinese producers was the world market, especially the market in North America and Europe. An export-oriented manufacturing and trade sector was set up, using foreign capital, domestic rural labor and entrepreneurship from Hong Kong, Taiwan and overseas Chinese communities. Most of this export-oriented sector is separated from the domestic market, importing raw materials, processing them, and re-exporting manufactured products to the world market. The system is simple and is operated by borrowing foreign transportation, insurance, distribution and marketing infrastructure. It turns out that selling goods abroad is cheaper than selling goods domestically, due to the high bureaucratic and transport cost within China. This take-off stage of the Chinese economy is also the logical starting point of the development of China since the late 1970s. This take-off stage was extended when China joined the World Trade Organization (WTO) in 2001, as many countries lowered their restrictions on Chinese products entering their markets. The first decade of the twenty-first century could be considered as the golden period for Chinese export-oriented industries.

This first stage of China's economic development is not sustainable. A large country, such as China or the United States, needs to root its industry in its own market in the long run. The question is how to transfer China from an export-oriented economy to a domestic market-oriented one. The answer is urbanization.

Urbanization is the process of moving people and capital from the countryside to the cities. It involves building a domestic market. The urbanization process in China includes two sub-stages: (1) city building (construction); (2) consumer market creation, to form a large middle class of consumers. The first sub-stage in China started in late 1990s, mainly led by government, and has made great progress. A large number of buildings have been built in the old and new urban areas. The urban areas have expanded rapidly. In large cities, such as Beijing, the whole urban area has been rebuilt. This sub-stage of development is relatively easy in China, because it is mostly due to government action. Under the current Constitution of China, all urban land is owned by the state, and all rural land is collectively owned by the villages. There is only one way to transfer rural land to urban land: government requisition, in which local government buys land from the villages at a low price, and resells it to the developers, usually at a higher price. The difference becomes a large portion of the local government's revenue. The local government is thus incentivized to move towards urban development because this is an important source of government income.

The second sub-stage of urbanization in China, the development of the consumer market, has been slow, partly due to unequal income distribution. Because the political mechanism of checks and balances is weak in China, the government holds much of the extra income created by the development in recent years. For example, the share of consumption by individual consumers dropped from 74.5 percent in total consumption in 2000 to 71.3 percent in 2010, while government consumption increased from 25.5 percent in 2000 to 28.7 percent in 2010 (National Bureau of Statistics 2011a, p.62). The government's budget revenue increased 20.0 percent per year from 2000 to 2010, while wages only increased 11.8 per cent per year in the same period (calculated using National Bureau of Statistics 2011a, pp.328, 276).

Another major source of uneven income distribution is the large income gap between urban and rural residents. This huge gap can be reduced only when a large number of peasants move from the countryside to the cities and become citizens. The local governments have incentives to use these migrants in the manufacturing and service industries in the cities, but hesitate to let them become full citizens to enjoy urban benefits, which would require reforming the *Hukou* system (residential identification). China needs large-scale institutional reform and creation, including the deregulation of restrictions on entering cities and the reform of the *Hukou* system.

The process of China's economic development since the late 1970s and the position of urbanization can be shown in Figure 2.1. In terms of growth, urbanization lags behind economic development.

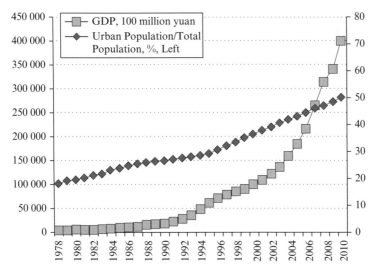

Source:　Based on National Bureau of Statistics (2011a, tables 2-1, 3-1).

Figure 2.1　China's development and urbanization

When China completes its urbanization process in 20–30 years, 60–80 percent of the people will live in crowded cities. If each family has an income close to that of the Japanese or Koreans today, China will be the world's largest market. All major countries will export products to China, and the performance of the Chinese economy will have a huge impact on the world. 'Made in China' will change to 'Made for China'. At the same time, China will still export to the world, maybe in a smaller proportion compared to imports. But the causes of export may be different. Before China reaches this turning point, exports will be based on cheap labor; after this point, exports will be based on the huge Chinese domestic market and efficiency created by the scale economy.

When China completes its urbanization, a group of super-cities will stand on the eastern coastal areas, with clusters of the tallest buildings in the world. The citizens will demand a large amount of consumer goods, including houses or apartments, and cars and public transportation services. More public transport will be necessary because the center of the cities will be so crowded that driving will be almost impossible, and private airplanes may be needed by the rich. The division of labor will much advanced to meet these diversified demands. Considering the size and population of the cities, the housing prices in the centers of future Chinese cities will be much higher than in Manhattan in the USA. The prices of other products in future Chinese cities will also be very high, despite the offset effects of the efficiency of services. Inflation in the future Chinese super-cities may affect world price levels.

2.2   THE ROLE OF GOVERNMENT IN URBANIZATION

Government plays a more important role in China than in most of the other countries in the world. Whether it is good or bad, this is the key to understanding China.

All cities and their mayors in China have an administrative degree on the bureaucratic system. Chung and Lam (2004) tells an interesting story about the Chinese mayors. An economic delegation from Shandong province was sent to South Korea, including mayors and deputy mayors from different cities. The hosts, who were not familiar with Shandong's administrative geography, did not know that Weifang was a prefecture-level city while Laixi was a county-level one, and treated the mayor of Laixi better than the deputy mayor of Weifang, resulting in the latter's anger.

China created a modern state in a very early stage of development, a centralized, uniform system of bureaucratic administration that was capable of governing a huge population and territory (Fukuyama 2011, p.21). There were multiple reasons for China's early state formation. With a dense population around rivers, Chinese created a system of agriculture and high-yielding crops, which generated more population. A leader was needed to rule the people and to make them work efficiently. War was a necessary condition of state formation. During the Eastern Zhou Dynasty (770–256 BC), using a group of modern political institutions, the kingdom of Qin defeated all the other states and unified China. These political institutions included: an army that directly conscripted large numbers of peasants; land reform giving land directly to peasant families; and social mobility undermining the power and prestige of the hereditary nobility (Fukuyama 2011, p.110). Qin built a two-level administrative structure, with 36 districts administered by commanders that were further divided into prefectures. The system was intended to directly displace the power of local elites. Qin standardized the written Chinese language, and established a family registration system, in which families were divided into groups that mutually supervised each other. The original purpose was to promote consistency in preparing government documents. Qin's harsh rule provoked a series of uprisings and led to the collapse of the dynasty in 210 BC. The Han Dynasty (206 BC to AD 220) finished the work of creating a uniform national state. Unlike Qin, Han made some concessions to the former rulers of localities, then gradually removed them from the bureaucratic system.

The national state system was something that subsequent dynasties attempted to continue throughout the rest of China's history. Feudalism, in which a family acquired a local power base independent of the central government, recurred periodically in subsequent history. The system of central government ruling was interrupted from time to time by a period of chaos. The mechanism for sanctioning a bad emperor was armed rebellion, which ended many dynasties. In the effort to build a national state system, Chinese individuals and society also sacrificed their freedoms.

It was the Chinese elite culture, which was so strong, that maintained the continuity of the state system in China. Before 1800, China was conquered several times by foreign countries, most of them from the north, but none of these foreigners could change the Chinese system. They found themselves absorbed into it. On the other hand, the periodic interruptions of this system show the difficulties facing a modern state when other institutions do not exist.

The Communists created a very strong state in 1949, partially due to the need to maintain political control of the population, and also due to the need to wage war against the outside world. The system changed private ownership to state and collective ownership, which was never done by any dynasties in China's history. From 1949 to 1977, the government tried to use the state to reform Chinese society. This top-down social engineering failed to meet its goals. From 1978 to the present, the government reduced the controls and let the market and individuals play some role in society. However, compared with other countries, Chinese government is still stronger, and plays a key role in many issues. China has a strong government and a weak society. Society is less developed, since historically the government has considered society as a potential source of violence. Society is not able to solve problems by itself. Problems will be solved only if the government acknowledges them and wants to solve them.

The state is very efficient in dealing with economic development. It used administrative measures to mobilize the masses to engage in economic movement in the planned period. Under this system, especially in the first 30 years of the People's Republic (1949–1977), cities were political and administrative (but mainly not economic) hubs. Not much independence or self-government existed for cities in this system during this period, and urbanization became a tool for developing the local economy. After 1977, the reformers relaxed government control and introduced market mechanisms. Another significant change was the competition among local governments, which dramatically increased local governments' incentive to change local economies. However, the traditional system of the state still played an important role, which was efficient in solving short-term economic problems. It also revealed many problems with the system. Without the coexistence of other conditions of a modern society, such as the rule of law and an accountable government, the state was weak in solving many problems in society. Society does not have enough mechanisms to solve these problems by itself. A problem can only be solved when the state notices the problem and pushes the lower-level governments to solve it. Local governments play an important role in urban development today, driven by a mixture of incentives, including officials' personal promotion, gross domestic product as an indicator of government performance, and officials' personal income.

It is extremely important to understand the role of the state in order to explain and understand China's urbanization. The state's more balanced role, and allowing other institutions in society to grow, will be fundamental for China's future development.

3.   Industrialization and urban development

Industrialization and urbanization progress together in modern world history. They are highly correlated in most countries. Three stages are usually included in the process. In the first stage, industrialization leads to urbanization, when the development of industries absorbs large amounts of labor into cities. In the second stage, industrialization and urbanization progress step by step, simultaneously. Finally, the growth of cities surpasses that of the manufacturing industries, when the service industries grow faster than the manufacturing industries in the cities. China roughly follows this pattern, but its urbanization lags far behind its industrialization, and its service industries lag far behind the development of manufacturing industries (see Table 3.1).

This process is also a market creation process. In the beginning, manufacturing produces for a market outside its own city. As population concentrates and personal income goes up, the city itself can become a market for its own manufacturing industries.

3.1   INDUSTRIALIZATION AND URBANIZATION

This section will briefly review the recent history of industrialization and its impact on urbanization in China.

Table 3.1   Industrialization and urbanization, China

	Urban population/Total population (%)	Industry/GDP (%)
1978	17.9	44.10
1990	26.4	36.70
2000	36.2	40.40
2010	49.9	40.10

Source: Based on National Bureau of Statistics (2011a, tables 2-2, 3-1).

Table 3.2   Estimates of shares of sector output value to GDP, China, 1900 and 1950

	Agriculture (%)	Industry (%)	Services (%)
1900	69	10	22
1950	59	21	20

Source: Zhou et al. (2008, p. 3).

Before 1949

The first wave of modern industrialization and urbanization in China can be traced back to the first half of the twentieth century. There was a combination of industrialization and urbanization in the eastern coastal area during the 1910s–1930s, which created large cities, for example Shanghai, Guangzhou and Tianjin. This process was stopped by the Second World War and the revolution.

The share of industrial output grew dramatically and urbanization progressed before the war. After the Second World War and the Civil War from 1946 to 1950, when the Communists seized power and the People's Republic of China was founded, the urbanization rate (share of urban population in total population) reduced to about 10 percent.

1949–1978

China was under a planned system from 1949 to 1978. All large companies were owned by the state, and all major economic decisions were made by the government. Large-scale industrialization came in the 1950s, when 156 large industrial projects were built with technical and financial support from the Soviet Union. The main part of this industrialization was heavy industries, and used capital-intensive technologies. While its direct impact on urbanization was limited, its indirect impact and the growth of small industries absorbed rural laborers into the cities. The urban population rose to 99 million, which was 15.4 percent of the total population in 1957. The Great Leap Forward, an economic and social campaign from 1958 to 1961, aimed to accelerate the process of industrialization, and raised the urbanization ratio further to 19.8 percent in 1960 (China Development Research Foundation 2010, p.9).

The Great Famine from 1958 to 1961 postponed the process of urbanization as well as that of industrialization. Thirty million urban residents were forced to move to the countryside, and the urbanization ratio reduced in 1963 and 1964. The *Hukou* system, a residential identification system that originated in 1958 and was tightened during the Great Famine, played an important role in separating cities from the countryside and reduced the population in the cities. More detailed discussion about the *Hukou* system can be found in Chapter 4. The urbanization ratio recovered to 17.9 percent in 1965. The Great Proletarian Cultural Revolution, a socio-political movement to enforce socialism by removing capitalist, traditional and cultural elements from Chinese society, started in 1966 and postponed industrialization and urbanization again, reducing the urbanization ratio for five years. Forty million high school and college students were moved from the city to the countryside. In 1978, the urbanization ratio was 17.9 percent, the same as that in 1965.

The slow growth in urbanization during the Soviet-type central planning period in China was due to the government's control of population movement between urban and rural areas. There was some progress in industrialization, but urbanization lagged far behind. This was consistent with Mao's ideal society: a large, equalized, rural society. As a result of this industrialization policy, China also relied on an unusually high proportion of heavy industry relative to its development stage.

Reform after 1978

Economic reforms began in 1978, which included two stages. In the late 1970s and early 1980s, the reform involved the de-collectivization of agriculture, the opening up of the country to foreign investment, and permission for private entrepreneurs to start up businesses. The reform in the late 1980s and early 1990s involved the lifting of price controls and the privatization of much state-owned industry. In the countryside, peasants were given the user-rights of the farmland and allowed to work separately on their own plots. This raised the productivity of farms.

The reform was successful in agriculture and foreign investment, but was not successful in state-owned enterprises (SOEs). The extra rural labor force moved first to small towns, and students who were moved to the countryside during the Cultural Revolution were allowed to move back to the cities. Urban residents increased by about 70 million from 1978 to 1984, and the urbanization ratio jumped to 23 percent in 1984.

The focus of reform turned from rural areas to the cities in 1984. Since 1980, Special Economic Zones have been established in Shenzhen, Zhuhai and Shantou in Guangdong province and Xiamen in Fujian province, as well as the entire province of Hainan. In 1984, 14 coastal cities – Dalian, Qinhuangdao, Tianjin, Yantai, Qingdao, Lianyungang, Nantong, Shanghai, Ningbo, Wenzhou, Fuzhou, Guangzhou, Zhanjiang and Beihai – were opened to overseas investment. Then, beginning in 1985, the state decided to expand the open coastal areas, extending the open economic zones to the Yangtze River Delta and Pearl River Delta.

Foreign capital flowed into the open coastal areas. A new manufacturing system began to be set up. This system was segregated from the domestic economy. Processing trade was developed, in which Chinese producers import all or most of the raw materials, parts and components of a product, and re-export the finished products after processing or assembly. This form of production combines foreign capital and cheap domestic labor from the countryside. It is almost totally foreign market-oriented. It has little impact on the domestic economy, except through the slow increase in domestic producers' profits and workers' wages.

This export-oriented industrialization accelerated the urbanization process in China's eastern coastal area. The urban population increased to 312 million in 1991, 80.9 percent higher than that in 1978. The urbanization ratio reached 26.9 percent in 1991 (National Bureau of Statistics 2011a, p.93; China Development Research Foundation 2010, p.10).

After China's joining of the World Trade Organization in 2001, the export-oriented manufacturing sector advanced further. The whole system includes production, distribution and marketing. Part of the process borrows financial and insurance systems from foreign countries. Transaction costs have since reduced dramatically. In the early twenty-first century, China became the second-largest country in the world to attract foreign direct investment (FDI), and attracted the second-largest amount of FDI in the world. According to Japanese researchers, one-third of China's industrial production was put in place by the $0.5 trillion of foreign money that has flowed into the country since 1978 (Japan's Research Institute of Economy, Trade and Industry 2004).

Although growth was slower compared to the export-oriented sector, the domestic industrial sector has made progress. A large number of non-state-owned businesses grew and are now active in the domestic market. There was a silent privatization of the small and mid-sized SOEs in the late twentieth and early twenty-first centuries. Despite privatization, however, the government continues to operate large state-owned companies.

China is now industrialized to some degree, producing a large variety of products, from shoes to parts for Boeing. The value of industrial products in gross domestic product (GDP) was RMB16.1 trillion in 2010, 40.1 percent of GDP (National Bureau of Statistics 2011a, p.44). Industrialization leads the process of urbanization. But in the past 30 years, China's urbanization has lagged behind industrialization until recent years. In 2010, China had 124 cities with a population of 1 million or more (National Bureau of Statistics 2011a, p.371), compared to nine in the United States.

3.2 MANUFACTURING VERSUS SERVICES

The worldwide experience is that the development of manufacturing in urban areas attracts people, which in turn creates demand for services. Industrialization, therefore, leads to the development of services. At some stage of urbanization, services replace manufacturing, becoming the key factor in promoting urbanization. However, the lag between industrialization and the development of services has been large in China.

In the planned period from the early 1950s to the late 1970s, the government put much more emphasis on the development of manufacturing rather than on services. Both sectors were provided by SOEs, and the government intentionally used much more resources on manufacturing. This was directly correlated to the Marxist economic theory, which argues that services do not create value to the society. Under this theory, services were not included in the calculation of national product, first in the Soviet Union and later in China. The direct result of this policy is the slow development of urbanization compared with industrialization. From 1953 to 1977, according to the recalculation by the National Bureau of Statistics of China, the urbanization ratio increased from 13.3 percent to 17.6 percent, while the share of services in terms of value-added declined from 30.8 percent to 23.4 percent. The greatest decline happened from 1961 to 1977, the period before and during the Cultural Revolution (Department of Comprehensive Statistics of National Bureau of Statistics 1999, p.3).

After the beginning of economic reform in 1978, the services sector increased steadily with urbanization. The urbanization ratio rose from 17.9 percent in 1978 to 50 percent in 2010, while the share of services in value-added increased from 23.9 percent in 1978 to 43.2 percent in 2010 (Table 3.3).

The structure inside the service sector has also changed after 1978. The shares in value-added increased for all sub-sectors, including trade and

Table 3.3   Structure of GDP (%)

	Current price		
	Primary industry	Secondary industry	Tertiary industry
1978	28.2	47.9	23.9
1990	27.1	41.3	31.5
2000	15.1	45.9	39.0
2010	10.1	46.7	43.2

Source: Based on National Bureau of Statistics (2012a, table 2-2).

catering services, transport, post and telecommunications, banking and insurance, real estate trading, and personal and social services. Personal and social services, banking and real estate trading had much larger shares in value-added.

Despite the growth in services in the past 20 years, many problems still need to be solved. The social security system covers only basic needs. Many urban public goods are provided to the households with *Hukou*, including priority in employment in certain fields, education and purchasing subsidized housing. Migrant workers are excluded from most of these services. The government monopolizes the provision of some social services, for example higher education, broadcasting and television, and hospitals. Changes have been made in recent years, such as the acceptance of migrant children in local schools in some cities, but advancement is still very slow. Foreign capital and domestic private capital are restricted from entering many service sectors, such as telecommunications, which is monopolized by a small number of large domestic companies.

While government, especially the local governments, played a leading role in China's urbanization in the past 30 years, the private firms also played an important role. Considering the harsh operating environment, these private companies did a wonderful job in helping cities develop. A large part of the cities have been developed by the efforts of these private businesses, with some support from local government. The following is an example of this.

Case: Ten Mile River, Beijing

Ten Mile River, a new wholesale–retail area concentrated on construction materials, is located in the southern part of Beijing (a relatively poor area). The area was originally developed by small, private construction firms in the 1990s. Now the area has more than ten large trading facilities providing 1 million sq meters of premises for small firms to rent and operate. Annual sales are over RMB10 billion. The area is crowded, with tens of thousands of businesspeople and consumers, causing serious traffic congestion.

The items sold in the area include construction materials and equipment, from cement and sand to screws and tools. Also for sale are furniture, carpets, lighting fixtures, doors and windows. A large number of vendors sell similar products, which keeps prices very low. It is also very easy to find transportation and construction services in the area. The sellers target different customers with very clear divisions of labor (*New Beijing Daily* 2013).

There are many examples of this kind of marketplace for selling construction materials in Beijing and China, with thousands of small businesses, a lot of them family-owned and -operated, selling construction materials, and providing transportation, construction and related services. These markets are highly specialized and very efficient. This has become one important aspect of city development.

To sum up, China's urbanization has lagged behind industrialization for various reasons. In the future, urbanization should catch up and develop alongside industrialization. Among the different obstacles to urbanization, most important one is the laws and regulations which have controlled population movement over the past 60 years.

4. Labor migration

Labor migration in China in the late twentieth century and early twenty-first century has been unprecedented in the entire course of human history. Rural–urban migration has been the main source of urban population growth and the main factor input of industrialization. The total number of migrant workers in the urban areas is estimated to be about 250 million, of which 150 million are permanently living in urban areas (National Bureau of Statistics 2011c).

The rural–urban income gap has been the driving force of the dramatic migration. The income of rural households was much lower than that of the urban residents during the planned period from the early 1950s to the late 1970s, mainly due to government policy. To promote the development of industries, the government manipulated the price system, with a very low price for agricultural products. It was a policy designed to lower the cost of industrial inputs. Because the prices were set by the government and the government monopolized the purchases of major agricultural products, the income of rural residents was extremely low. Moreover, rural households were not covered by the social security system and the public goods provided in urban areas.

The major force that kept peasants in the poor rural areas was the *Hukou* system. Under the planned system, no *Hukou* registration meant that you were excluded from the food rationing system and you could not survive in the urban areas. In terms of basic necessities, money was useless if not accompanied by food coupons. Under these conditions, peasants dreamed of changing their status to become urban residents. The limited ways to realize this dream included being a college student, joining the army, or running a government requisition of collectively owned land. All of these were extremely difficult to achieve. Therefore, any relaxation of the *Hukou* regulation would drive the bravest peasants to attempt to move to the cities.

4.1 A BRIEF HISTORY OF RURAL–URBAN MIGRATION

Government strictly controlled rural–urban migration from the late 1950s to the early 1980s. The most important institutional tool the government used was the *Hukou* system.

Hukou is a residence registration system used by the government to control migration of the population. Under the *Hukou* system, a household registration record officially identifies a person as a resident of an area, and includes other identifying information.

The *Hukou* system has been in existence in China since ancient times. According to the *Examination of Hukou* in Wenxian Tongkao published in 1317, there was a minister for population management during the Zhou Dynasty (1100–256 BC) named Simin (Chinese: 司民), who was responsible for recording births, deaths, emigration and immigration (Ma 1317). A real development was at the end of the Zhou Dynasty, when Yang Shang (390–338 BC), the chief adviser to Duke Xiao of the state of Qin during the late years of the Zhou Dynasty, established a family registration system, and divided families into groups of five and ten households, to mutually supervise each other (Fukuyama 2011, p.117). The *Hukou* system has been used to control residents since then. The system was further developed when the first Chancellor of the Han Dynasty (206 BC to AD 220), He Xiao added the chapter of Hu (Chinese: 户律) as one of the nine basic laws of Han (Chinese: 九章律), and established the *Hukou* system as the basis of tax revenue and conscription. A version of Yang Shang's system was resurrected during the Ming Dynasty (1368–1644) as the *bao-jia* system, in which a neighbor would be punished when a family committed a crime (Fukuyama 2011, p.117).

The modern *Hukou* system in China was set up in the 1950s after the founding of the People's Republic, and played an important role in controlling migration between the countryside and the cities. The *Hukou* system was used as an instrument of the command economy. It allocated resources among local authorities according to the number of residents under its administration. The system also exists in some other East Asian countries, but the Chinese *Hukou* system during the planned period was the most strictly implemented one. Figure 4.1 shows two books of *Hukou*.

Planned Period

1949–1957
This was a pre-government-control period, in which people had the right to choose their work and place of living. Industrialization absorbed a large

Figure 4.1   Books of Hukou

number of rural migrants. Employees in state-owned enterprises increased from 5.1 million in 1952 to 23.16 million in 1958 (Hui and Huo 2007, p.41). Most of the new employees came from the countryside.

1958–1963
In this period, political movements and government control caused large fluctuations in rural labor migration. The *Hukou* Registration Regulation was established in 1958, and included regulations on residency, temporary residency, birth, death, moves to and from an address, and changes. The regulation was strictly enforced. In 1958, 19 million new workers entered the industrial and construction sectors, and 10 million of them were from the countryside. Urban population jumped from 99 million in 1957 to 130 million in 1960.

Then came the Great Famine and large number of people were forced to return to the countryside due to the inability of the government to feed all urban residents. Long lines of rural migrants looking for food were physically kept out of the cities, where the minimum food supply was provided by the government. Since the peasants were forced to hand in all food to the government, they were in a much worse condition than the urban residents. The urban population reduced by 13 million and labor by 9.5 million in 1961. During the whole period of 1961 to 1963, the urban population reduced a total of 26 million and the urban labor reduced 20 million (China Development Research Foundation 2012, p.9).[1] Almost all of these re-migrations were involuntary and controlled by the government.

1964–1978

The Cultural Revolution started in 1966 and the chaos continued for ten years. The movement of labor from the countryside to the cities was severely controlled by the government during this period. Urban enterprises were banned from recruiting workers from the countryside. *Hukou* regulation was strictly implemented, and rural residents were completely excluded from industrialization. Urbanization was stagnant during this period. Natural growth in numbers of the urban residents accounted for 77.3 percent of the growth in the urban population.

After the Late 1970s

The planned period ended with a huge gap between the income and welfare of urban and rural residents, which could exist only because the doors of the cities were closed to the rural population. Economic reform starting in 1978 not only opened China's door to the world, but also the doors of the Chinese cities to rural residents. The great gap between urban and rural areas attracted rural labor to the cities, while the need for cheap labor in the urban manufacturing sector absorbed labor from the countryside.

The *Hukou* system still existed, but its implementation relaxed during this period. This relaxation has continued since the 1980s, which was consistent with the overall trend of relaxing the government's interference in economic activities after 1978. The government also considered it as a way to solve the problem of rural poverty. A provision was made to allow rural residents to purchase temporary urban residency permits for an affordable fee in order to work legally within cities. In 2003, protests over the death of Zhigang Sun, a migrant student beaten to death in a detention center by law enforcement officers for not having a temporary living permit, alarmed the government. The laws of custody and repatriation, an administrative procedure by which the police could detain people if they did not have a residence permit or temporary living permit, and return them to rural areas, were repealed.

About 150 million peasants have moved from the countryside to the cities in the last two decades and now live in the cities (National Bureau of Statistics 2011c). This migration has been the largest in human history. Estimates of the number of the people who have moved to the cities cannot be exactly accurate, but even using the most conservative estimates, the number matches the workforce of the United States.

The urbanization ratio increased to over 50 percent, if migrants who do not hold a resident ID are included. If only people with a permanent resident ID were counted, the urbanization ratio would be about 10 percent lower.

Table 4.1 Official statistics: number of migrants working in cities, 2011 (millions)

Total migrant workers	252.78
Outside hometown	158.63
In hometown	94.15

Note: No definition of 'inside hometown' is given by the National Bureau of Statistics, but from the text it seems to mean that the worker is within the county from which they originate.

Source: National Bureau of Statistics (2011c).

Two boom periods of labor migration existed in the late twentieth century: 1984–1988 and 1992–1996. A total of 55.7 million migrant labors moved from the countryside to the cities in 1984–1988. The average annual growth rate was 23.1 percent (Hui and Huo 2007, p.44). A total of 41.2 million rural laborers moved to the urban areas in 1992–1996, with an annual increase of 8.2 million.

The migration increased quickly in the first decade of the twenty-first century. In 2001, 80 million rural migrants lived in cities for more than half a year. This number rose to 150 million in 2009. From 2001 to 2007, the average annual increase was 11 million. Total number of migrant workers reached 252.8 million in 2011, including 158.6 million working outside of their hometown (Table 4.1).

Some migrants moved back to the countryside after staying in the cities for a while. Migrants who returned home were 2.5 percent of the total in 1998, according to the National Bureau of Statistics survey (2002d). This number should be deducted when calculating net migration.

How large is this rural–urban migration? It can only be seen during the *Chunyun*, or the Spring Festival travel season, a period of travel in China with an extremely high traffic load around the time of the Chinese New Year (Figure 4.2). It has been the largest human migration in the world so far. The largest proportion of passengers during *Chunyun* are migrant workers. The *Chunyun* usually begins 15 days before the Lunar New Year's Day and lasts for around 40 days. The number of passenger journeys during the *Chunyun* has exceeded the total population of China, hitting over 2 billion in 2008. Like Thanksgiving in the USA, Chinese New Year is a time for family reunions. Migrant workers return home from work to have a reunion dinner with their families on New Year's Eve. For many migrant workers, this is the only time for a family reunion during the year.

The most popular modes of transportation are the railway and road networks. About 340 million passengers were estimated to take trains during

Source: Baidu Photo. Retrieved August 29, 2013 at http://image.baidu.com/i?tn=baiduima ge&ct=201326592&lm=-1&cl=2&fr=ala0&word=%B4%BA%D4%CB.

Figure 4.2 Chunyun, the Spring Festival travel season

the 2009 *Chunyun* period, while the average daily capacity of the Chinese railway system is 3.4 million passengers. This shortage means many migrant workers wait in extremely long lines for hours or even days to get a ticket. Chuanming Li, a migrant worker working in Beijing, could not purchase a ticket even after waiting in line for three days in January 2011, according to *New Beijing News*. He was unable to purchase his ticket even though he was twentieth in line on the first day, and seventh on the second day. He was first from 10 a.m. on the third day and waited overnight without going to the men's room until he was interviewed by a reporter (*New Beijing News* 2011). Chaojun Lu and his wife rode a motorcycle 1300 km from Zhaoqing, Guangdong to his hometown, Tongren, Guizhou. The journey took three days and two nights. More than 100 000 migrant workers have chosen motorcycles as their means of transportation home in recent years. With so many motorcycles running together, the highways in Guangdong looked magnificent during the *Chunyun* period (*East Morning News* 2011).

'Scalpers' ('yellow bull' in Chinese) profit greatly during the Chunyun period. Organizations of scalpers pick up tickets in great numbers minutes after they go on sale, and then deal them out in and around the railway station at high prices. A 'real name and ID' requirement was implemented to deal with the problem, after QR (quick response) barcodes were included on tickets in 2010. An online ticket purchasing system was introduced in 2013, though it caused tremendous problems. The return tickets were sold separately, so one would have to use the system twice to purchase tickets if one needed to return after the holidays. Travelers can buy tickets no earlier than 19 days before their trips; for example, January 7 is the earliest day to buy a ticket for January 26. People wait to enter the website hours before tickets go on sale. As soon as the authority starts selling the tickets, the server jams immediately, and within a few minutes the tickets are sold out. To help people to buy the tickets online, some developers have created software which increases the probabilities of getting a ticket.

Who are these Migrants?

Firstly, they were very young in the 1990s and the early twenty-first century. The 0–15-year-old age group accounted for 14.3 percent of the total migrants and the 16–49-year-old group accounted for 79.8 percent in 2001. The migrants' demographic is getting older as the average age of the total population rises (Wan and Cai 2012, p.130). Secondly, these migrants possess low education. Of the migrants who moved into urban areas in 2001, 23.5 percent only finished primary school, 62.9 percent finished junior high school, 10.2 percent finished senior high school, and 0.7 percent finished college (Hui and Huo 2007, p.46). These numbers are lower than the average in urban areas, but higher than the author's expectations. Overall, the rural laborers who moved to the cities are the best of the rural laborers, in terms of their braveness, intelligence and work ethic.

The age structure in China has been getting older since the late twentieth century. The speed of aging is faster in rural area than that in the cities. Figure 4.3 shows that the share of population aged 15–24 years old was higher in the rural areas than in urban areas in 1989, but slightly lower in 2007. The relation of the population aged 50–59 between urban and rural areas was just the opposite. This shows a trend of faster ageing in rural than in urban areas.

In the long run, according to some estimates, the ageing level in China's rural areas will increase faster than that in the urban areas (Hu 2012, in Wan and Cai 2012, p. 133).

Where did these rural migrants move from, and where did they move to? According to an early government survey, cross-provincial migrants accounted for 3.9 percent of the total rural labor force in 1998. Among these migrants, 49.4 percent move to Guangdong, 6.9 percent to Zhejiang, 6.5 percent to Beijing, 6.0 percent to Shanghai, 5.2 percent to Fujian, and 4.6 percent to Jiangsu. The movement is mainly from the west to the east. Among the cross-provincial migrants, 83.1 percent moved into the eastern coastal area in 1998. Guangdong province absorbed half of the migrants. Of these migrants, 54.6 percent came from central China, 33.5 percent

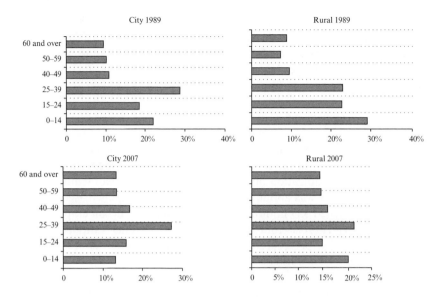

Note: 'City' does not include towns.

Source: Based on Hu (2012) in Wan and Cai (2012, p. 133).

Figure 4.3 *Age distribution of population, city and rural areas, 1989 and 2007*

came from the west, and 11.9 percent from the east (National Bureau of Statistics 2002d).

4.2 URBAN LABOR MARKETS

As mentioned in Part I, the official statistical category of 'urban employment' changed a lot in the past. The official statistics of urban population also missed a large number of migrant workers, since they live in factory dormitories. According to an official labor survey, those in cities of urban working age (16 and over), people with agricultural *Hukou*, who are not registered where they actually live, and have been living in the cities for more than half a year, account for 12.52 percent of total population (Wan and Cai 2012, p.151).

In the planned period from the early 1950s to the late 1970s, no job market existed in Mainland China. Students graduating from high schools or colleges were assigned a job in a 'unit' (a general name for offices and factories), at which most of them were going to stay for their whole lives.

No one had to worry about lay-offs, while changing to another job was almost impossible. Things have changed gradually since the late 1970s. A job market emerged first for temporary jobs, then for most positions. Some interesting changes happened in urban labor market, including the following.

Total Urban Employment

Even though there were large lay-offs from the state-owned enterprises in the late 1990s, the total employment in urban areas kept increasing during the process of urbanization and industrialization. In 1990, China's total urban employment was about 170 million. The number increased by 111 percent and reached 359 million in 2011. The share of urban employment in total employment rose from 26.4 percent to 50 percent (National Bureau of Statistics 2011a, pp. 93, 110). Of course, an important source of this increase was migrant workers.

Ownership Structure of Employment

In the early 1990s, the employment in state-owned and collective-owned enterprises accounted for more than 80 percent of the urban employment. This ratio reduced to 67 percent in 1997. After privatization in the late 1990s, the ratio decreased dramatically to 23.5 percent. Employment in privately owned enterprises and other unidentified ownership has increased significantly. The number of workers in the state-owned enterprises dropped to less than 100 million in 2010, while the total number employed increased to near 350 million (Figure 4.4).

Wage Difference and Job Segmentation

A large difference exists in compensation for regular urban workers and migrant workers. The average wage for regular urban workers was RMB3045 per month in 2010 (National Bureau of Statistics 2011a, p. 123), while the average wage for unskilled migrant workers in the eastern area was about RMB1000 in 2008 and RMB2000 in 2012.[2] This wage difference is not only due to the residence status of the workers, but also due to their education level, work experience and occupation. The job market is partially regulated by the government and open only to legal urban residents; for example to enter Beijing's taxi driver market, one has to have Beijing's residence ID. The other part of the job market is competitive. Because migrant workers have lower levels of education and limited working experience, they are concentrated in sectors such as construction

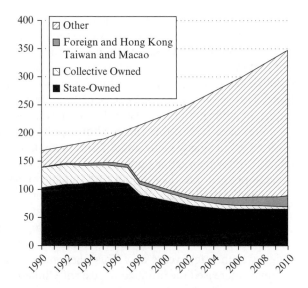

Note: 'Other' includes corporative units (owned by all members), joint ownership units, limited liability corporations, share-holding corporations with limited liability, private enterprises and self-employed individuals.

Source: Wan and Cai (2012, p.136), based on National Bureau of Statistics (2011a, table 4-2).

Figure 4.4   Ownership structure of urban employment, 1990–2010

for male workers, and retail and domestic services for female workers. In the 1980s, most of the housemaids in Beijing were from Wuwei county of Anhui province (Tieba n.d.). Although the wage migrants get is lower than that of a regular urban resident, it is still much higher than the income they get when doing farm work at home.

The low-wage labor market in Chinese cities has been based on a chain of interest. The firms get low-wage labor by hiring migrant workers (instead of urban residents), and lower the wages or delay payment. The poor residents or the residents living in the suburbs rent cheap houses to migrant workers and earn rent, though some of these houses are illegal buildings. The residents and migrant workers operate a large number of illegal retail stores, barber shops and small hotels, without licenses, and do not pay taxes. Finally, the lower-level government agencies welcome migrants joining the local economy, and ignore registration of small businesses to some degree, clearing the street vendors and collecting fines only occasionally.

A large hidden unemployment pool existed in China's countryside from the 1970s to the early twenty-first century, due to government control of movement from rural areas to the cities. It was estimated that China's rural unemployment amounted to several hundred million. The World Bank estimated that in 2000 the extra rural labor in China was 400 million (World Bank 2001). Other estimates vary a lot, from 100–150 million to 400–500 million. This rural unemployment pool kept providing young workers to the urban labor market and kept the urban wage level low for 30 years, until quite recently. But this cheap labor supply was not infinitive and the turning point finally came. Since 2010, many indicators have shown that this unemployment labor pool is close to dried up. Almost all employers have complained that they cannot find suitable migrant labors, even though they have raised wages significantly. The average wage rate increased at least 20 percent from 2009 to 2010, and kept at a similar rate in the following years. Everywhere, from Shenzhen to Beijing, you can see 'Help Needed' advertisements in stores and restaurants, with compensation much higher than a few years ago. This phenomenon of lack of migrant labor greatly increased the production costs of Chinese industries, especially the export-oriented processing manufacturing industries, and reduced the competitiveness of Chinese firms in the world market.

Official Unemployment Rate

The urban registered unemployment rate (number of registered unemployment workers divided by the sum of employed plus unemployed workers) published by the National Bureau of Statistics cannot correctly reflect the real unemployment situation. Because of the preconditions for registration, for example *Hukou* resident identification, a large portion of unemployed do not report their unemployment and are not included in the official statistics.

Case: The Rice-Cake Party

A large number of migrants from Xinjiang, a remote province in west China, have been selling Xinjiang glutinous rice-cake in large cities recently. Toolson (translated from the Chinese) has been selling rice-cake in Guangzhou, a major city in southern China, for six years and become a 'big brother' of a rice-cake group in Guangzhou, leading 100 young 'brothers'. He is 26 years old, of Uygur ethnicity, a high school graduate from Hetian county, Xinjiang province.

Every morning, Toolson and his brothers ride tricycles from rented housing in the suburbs to the entrance of the zoo, where large numbers of tourists visit. Every tricycle has a sign: '4.5 yuan per Liang (unit of weight, equal 50 grams), 45 yuan per Jin (Catty, weight equal to 0.5 kg). Cut whatever you want and no refund'. The raw materials were originally from Xinjiang, but now all raw materials are locally produced. Only three hours are needed to make a rice-cake of 400 kg that will sell for RMB18000, with a cost of RMB2000 to 5000. The cost for rebuilding each tricycle is RMB1600 and lunch costs RMB11. Groups of nine live in a room of 20 sq m without a window in a 'village in city' (an urbanizing village).

Toolson did not go to college after graduating from high school, as his family could not provide financial support. He went to a city 1000 km from his hometown when he was 17 in 2003, and earned RMB1300. In 2005 he was in Wuhan, a large city in middle China, where he learned Mandarin Chinese and entered the business of selling cantaloupe, earning RMB400 per month. Later, he was hurt by a gang of thieves and went home. In the same year, he went to Xinyang, Henan province, where he learned how to make rice-cake. He then visited Shenzhen and settled down in Guangzhou, selling mutton kebabs first and then selling rice-cake along the sidewalks. When interviewed by a reporter, Toolson said he has no plan to stay in Guanzhou forever and will return to his hometown to set up a small business after earning enough money in Guangzhou (Xi and He 2012).

This case gives us an example of a migrant worker, telling us who he is, where he came from, how much he earns, and many other details of his everyday life.

4.3   FUTURE REFORMS

The *Hukou* system played an important function in controlling the migration of population and allocated resources among local governments during the planned period in China. Economic reform starting in the late 1970s reduced the importance of *Hukou*, but this system has continued to have political and economic functions in the past 30 years of reform. *Hukou* is still the main institutional constraint on rural–urban migration, although the daily management of the *Hukou* system has been decentralized to local governments and is only partially implemented.

The local governments used cheap labor to develop industries by allowing migrant workers into the cities, but did not want to provide full public services to the migrants and their families. This partial urbanization policy led to many social contradictions, which made local governments realize that the policy would not be sustainable. However, without full financial support from the central government, local government incentives to reform the system are limited.

The *Hukou* system is one major obstacle to urbanization in China. The urban–rural segmented *Hukou* sytem must be removed. Equalizing the treatment of the Chinese people as a whole would be costly to the government. The provincial and municipal governments have begun some experiments in reforming the *Hukou* system. For example, Zhengzhou, Henan province and Shijiazhuang, Hebei province have reduced the requirements for a migrant to obtain an urban *Hukou* (Wan 2012, p.291). Overall, the progress has been slow and local governments do not have enough incentives to completely remove the *Hukou* system.

The mobile population in Shanghai, one of the largest cities in China, increased from 3.87 million in 2000 to 8.98 million in 2010. To retain the image of an 'open city' and to protect its own interests, the city government set up an access threshold for newcomers and gradually reduced it. At the beginning of the twenty-first century, only a small group who met the standard of the introduction of talent, who had higher degrees in certain fields, might get the Shanghai *Hukou*. In 2002, a temporary resident card system was introduced, for 'talents' (those with higher degrees or special skills), workers and family members, with a rating system (Dongfang Net 2009). In 2004, the temporary resident card was issued to all Chinese citizens who wanted to be residents in Shanghai but had no Shanghai *Hukou*. But further requirements included having a stable job and a stable residence, which meant having job contracts over six months and house rental contracts over six months (Chen 2012, p.54). The threshold has been further lowered in recent years.

The *Hukou* reform is still in debate in China today. The key issue is whether to give all residents full citizenship, not depending on where they live. I will discuss the policy issues in detail in Part III.

The migrants move to the cities and leave behind their land and lives in their hometowns. As the cities expand, more suburban land is included in the city limits. To produce more housing for increasing number of city residents, the developers need more land for construction. All these relate to land, a scarce resource with unclear ownership in China.

NOTES

1. This is slightly different from the official Statistical Yearbook.
2. Source: the author's field survey in eastern coastal cities.

5. Land and local government finance

Land is a scarce resource in China, in comparison to the abundant labor supply. Rapid urban spatial expansion demands large amount of land. The urban built-up areas increased from 12 856 sq km in 1990 to 40 058 sq km in 2010, with a 5.8 percent increase annually (Table 5.1). The per capita floor space of residential building in urban areas reached 32.7 sq m in 2011 (National Bureau of Statistics 2011a, pp.378, 379). There had been no specific terms about the ownership of land in China's Constitution until 1982.

Land ownership is not clearly defined, nor is it fully protected by law in China today. According to the 1982 version of China's Constitution (1982 version, Chapter I, Article 10):

> Land in the cities is owned by the state. Land in the rural and suburban areas is owned by collectives except for those portions which belong to the state in accordance with the law; house sites and privately farmed plots of cropland and hilly land are also owned by collectives. The state may, in the public interest, requisition land for its use in accordance with the law. No organization or individual may appropriate, buy, sell or lease land or otherwise engage in the transfer of land by unlawful means. (National People's Congress 1982)

Until very recently, only the government could transfer rural land into urban land by requisition. From the planned period to the present time, land requisition by the government has been the main legal source of urban land supply. How to provide land to accommodate urbanization is therefore a policy issue.

Table 5.1   Urban spatial expansion (built-up area, sq km)

1981	7438
1990	12 856
2000	22 439
2010	40 058

Sources: Based on National Bureau of Statistics (2011a, table 10-37) and China Development Research Foundation (2010, p. 210).

5.1   A BRIEF HISTORY OF LAND REGULATION IN CHINA

Land regulations are crucial to the expansion of urban areas and the public finance of the local government. Urbanization needs large amounts of land, which is monopolized and regulated by the government. There have been some changes in land regulation since the economic reform, but far from enough to meet the needs of urbanization.

Land Regulations Before the Reform

Under the planned system, the ownership of rural land was not clearly defined in China. This did not have much impact on the government's operations on rural land. The municipal governments increased their land supply through requisition, which converted land ownership from the collectives to the state. Here the word 'collectives' means communes or villages under the planned system. The package of compensation to the peasants included: (1) job offers in which the peasant could work in the factory established on the acquired land; (2) housing compensation as resettlement fees; (3) compensation for the loss of crops and belongings connected to the land; and (4) urban resident status (*Hukou*) (Ding 2007).

This package did not give peasants compensation measured by market value, but the peasants were willing to accept it during the planned period, because a non-agricultural job and especially a city *Hukou* were worth much more than the land. It means that the peasant could change his status, obtain access to social benefits, and enjoy the local public goods for his remaining life. Under the planned system, peasants had been excluded from the subsidized social benefits and public goods provided in the urban area. This gave the peasants more incentives to accept the land deal with the government.

Since there is a scarcity of farmland, the government set up a policy to keep the total farmland above the threshold of 1.8 billion mu (15 mu equals 1 hectare). Any activity transferring farmland to land for urban development should fulfill the precondition that the total amount of farmland does not change.

Land Regulation After the Reform

The urbanization process speeded up after the late 1970s and land problems became more and more urgent. Thirty years after the reform, the way to transfer rural land to urban land is still through government requisition. Most of the reforms in land regulation so far are concerned with the amount of compensation and the requirement for all leasehold rights to be sold at public auction.

To deal with the problems, the Land Administration Law (LAL) was passed in 1986. LAL followed the old model of government requisition used in the planned period, with four compensation components: land compensation, resettlement subsidies, compensation for crops and attachments, and labor resettlement. The law stipulated that land compensation be three to six times the three-year average annual output value, and that resettlement subsidies be two to three times the average annual output value. LAL further required that compensation for crops and attachments should be given to the peasants, while land compensation and resettlement subsidies should be retained in collectives (the villages) and used for resettlement.

The 1986 version of LAL was revised in 1998 to meet the needs created by the rapid urbanization of the 1990s (National People's Congress 1998). The amendment to LAL in 1998 was distinctive from the 1986 version in several respects. The revised law raised compensation levels. The land compensation was required to be six to ten times the average annual output value, and resettlement was required to be four to six times the output value of the acquired land. Under these requirements, the average land compensation and resettlement subsidies were RMB20000–30000 per mu (1/15 hectare) in Zhejiang province in the eastern coastal area in 2002 (Ding 2007). A new version of LAL was passed in 2012, which regulated that the land and resettlement compensation be no more than 30 times the average output value of the previous three years (National People's Congress 2012).

Two levels of land markets exist in China today. On the first level, the government leases the government-owned land to the users for a certain number of years. This market is monopolized by the local governments. On the second level of the market, the users sell, rent, mortgage or sub-lease the land to third parties. Because the land belongs to the state, the government leases the land to users for a certain number of years instead of selling it.

On the first level of the land market, the local governments perform price differentiation strategically. To attract large companies, the local government sets the land price low in competition with other cities. These large companies have many options countrywide. To raise revenues, the local government sets the price of land high for residential housing. The housing developers are usually local and compete with each other. The revenue from the land market is extremely important for local governments, accounting for a large portion of the local government revenue.

A lot of information on land leasing is published online. There are websites, for example ChinaLands.com, showing plots for sale on the market.

Case: Land Sale in Beijing

Wan and Cai (2012) provides a case of the land market in Beijing, the capital and the second-largest city in China. All developers must obtain a user's right of land from Beijing's Bureau of Land Resource. Before 2004, this transfer was achieved by making contracts. After 2004, to avoid corruption in the process of land transfer, the central government required that all land transfers should be made through public auction. The Beijing municipal government set up a Land Resource Center to deal with land auctions. The center gets land from rural or urban land owners through requisition, finishes demolition, and puts it on the auction market. The highest bidder gets the land.

The Beijing Land Database includes all pieces of land which were transferred by the government via public auction from 2004 to June 2006. The total number of pieces of land was 145. The summary statistics are as shown in Table 5.2.

Table 5.2   Summary statistics of Beijing Land Database, 2004 to June 2006, mean (standard deviation)

	All areas	Areas for residential housing
Price (yuan/sq meter)	7344 (9846)	4312 (6198)
Area (1000 sq meter)	56 (83)	67 (90)
Allowed 'volume rate' (construction area/land area)	2.36 (1.76)	1.93 (1.08)
Distance from city center (km)	30 (23)	32 (21)

Source: Based on Wan and Cai (2012, p. 168).

The land-leasing fee in Beijing increased dramatically after 2006.

5.2   PROBLEMS OF LAND REQUISITION

Under the current law, land in rural areas owned by collectives can be transferred to urban land only through government requisition. One problem of LAL is just and fair compensation for the peasants who lose land. Fair compensation depends on the definition of comparable living standards. LAL failed to give a measurable standard. This resulted in a

Table 5.3　Land requisition compensation

Item	Compensation standard
Compensation for land	6–10 times of the average output value in previous 3 years
Resettlement subsidies for persons	Number of persons need to be resettled = area of land/land per person; subsidies per person are less than 3–6 times average output of the land in previous 3 years
Resettlement subsidies for land	Total subsidies are less than 15 times the average output of previous 3 years
Compensation for attachments and young crops on the land	Determined by local government

Source:　National People's Congress (2012, Article 46).

wide range of compensation in different localities, much of which was much lower than the market price.

Fairness

The 2012 version of the Land Administration Law (draft) announced the new standard of land requisition compensation. Compensation is issued according to the original revenue of the land (Table 5.3).

Under the guidance of LAL, most of the municipal governments exercised their political power to undercompensate the peasants. For instance, the annual farming output was RMB1014 per mu when Highway 318 was constructed in Sichuan province in 2001, while the land compensation and resettlement subsidies were only RMB650 per mu (Song and Ding 2007, p.90).

Even using the highest compensation standard of 30 times the average output in the previous three years (2012 version of Land Administration Law), if the output per mu is RMB2000, the compensation fee of RMB60000 is still much lower than the government's selling price. For example, in a southern city, the government paid RMB24 million for 200 mu of land from farmers and resold the land for RMB200 million (Xiaoxiang Chenbao 2013).

Furthermore, under the planned system, agricultural prices were artificially suppressed compared to industrial prices in order to promote industrialization. Therefore, since the product itself is undervalued, the peasants are not satisfied with the compensation, despite it being several times the product value.

In a way, the requisition cost of China's urbanization has been much lower than that in other countries in the world, due to the government-monopolized requisition. Cheap land is one explanation of the rapid geographical expansion of Chinese cities in the past 20 years. A survey shows that land cost accounts for only 3–5 percent of the total investment, and the land compensation and resettlement subsidy accounts for 40 percent of the land cost (Ding 2007, p.93).

Compared with land compensation, job resettlement is more problematic. The pressure of the labor market makes job resettlement increasingly difficult. The life of peasants might not be adversely affected by land requisition, but it is affected by the failure of job resettlement.

Urbanization under the *Hukou* system is an incomplete urbanization or a half-way urbanization. Many migrations to the cities are temporary and short term, including single person migration rather than the relocation of the whole family. These partial migrants are still connected to the land in rural areas and do not have the welfare benefits that urban residents receive, for example social security for low-income families, health insurance and housing subsidies.

The injustice in rural land requisition has increased the social tensions between the government and the peasants. In a rapidly growing economy, a fixed standard of compensation cannot catch up to the increase in prices. At Tsinghua University in Beijing, one can always see a group of peasants protesting. They sold their land to the government-supported university several years ago. The price of land increased dramatically and now the peasants want a higher compensation. It is difficult for the lawmakers to give a fair compensation standard in a period of rapid economic growth and structural change. A possible solution is by using the market price. To do this, it is first necessary to create a land market. To create a land market, it is necessary to clarify the ownership of the land.

At the beginning of 2013, during the process of transition of China's leadership, an amendment to the Land Administration Law, which removes the limit on rural property compensation during land expropriation, was drafted but not included in the discussion in the first session of the new National People's Congress Standing Committee. The draft proposed making the improvement of farmers' living standards a premise before land seizure is carried out, and scrapping the cap on land compensation, which the standing law said was not to exceed 30 times the land's average annual output in the previous three years (Zhao 2013).

Land Ownership and Land Markets

According to China's Constitution, 'rural land ownerships' belong to the collectives or communes, which refer to townships or villages. In 1949, the People's Political Consultative Committee, a temporary legislative organ, declared the 'land to the tiller' principle in the 'Joint Guidelines', the interim Constitution. Under this principle, peasants were assigned plots of land and dwellings, and some of the land came from the old landlords. The peasants enjoyed full property rights of their land and houses, including the rights of transferring the property. The government issued an official certificate of land to the peasants. Then, starting from 1953, collectivization began, followed by industrialization. One purpose of collectivization was to control the agricultural surplus in order to provide resources for industrialization. The People's Congress officially reclaimed all land rights from the peasants and turned them over to the collectives in 1956. The collectives (villages) were transformed in 1958 into People's Communes, which had political and economic functions. The People's Communes led to the Great Famine, and soon were divided into production brigades (large villages) and production teams (small villages, or parts of large villages). The collectivized peasants worked together, like factory workers, every day. They had no incentive to work hard. Agricultural production declined and the peasants lived in poverty.

Some peasants, supported by some local officials, created a 'household-contracted responsibility system' in their cooperatives to increase working efficiency. Yongjia County, Zhejiang province, decided to subcontract collective land to individual households in 1956. The peasants were responsible for giving a portion of their gains to the state and the collectives. The land ownership did not change, while the peasants got the user rights of the land. The system spread to most rural areas in China in a short time. Mao denounced the system and criticized it as a 'capitalist principle'. Even though it was banned by the government, the system continued in some areas.

After the passing of Mao, 17 peasants of Xiaogang village, Anhui province applied their fingerprints to a household-contracting document, which was considered as the beginning of China's new wave of land reform. Supported by Xiaoping Deng, the system spread quickly to most rural areas in China in the early 1980s. The system increased agricultural productivity dramatically, and solved the problem of food supply in a few years. The land lease system was further extended to 15 years and 30 years by the Party's Central Committee, to reduce the uncertainties of the contract (Zhang, Jialin n.d.).

The user rights of farmland have been given to individual families since the early 1980s. As more peasants migrated to the cities, large amounts of idle land were left in the countryside. The current rural land user rights are equally divided and distributed to all members of a village, and the distribution of land between village members is adjusted periodically. According to a survey, the average adjustment since the economic reform is 1.7 times for a sample of 215 villages in six provinces (Brandt et al. 2002). However, this land could not be transferred or traded or used as collateral under the existing law. Farmers created new ways to transfer their land within the limit of the law. The migrant farmers subcontracted or leased their land-use rights to other farmers.

A Law of Land Contract was passed by the People's Congress in 2002, which announced that the entire rights of use, revenue and transfer of farmland were contracted to the farmers' households for the 'long term'. To make this true, much work needs to be done.

To make the land tradeable, ownership needs to be clarified at the family level. It is difficult because of the frequent changes in land ownership since the 1950s, such as the distribution of the landlords' land to peasants in early 1950s, collectivity in the late 1950s, and partial privatization in the early 1980s. Some provinces, for example Sichuan province and Chongqing province, have been performing experiments on clarifying the ownership of rural land.

The next step after ownership is clarified is to create land exchange markets, which have also been experimented with in several provinces. The markets should allow users and sellers enter freely and trade land as a commodity. These markets are supposed to eventually eliminate the monopoly of land requisition by the government and solve the problem of social and economic injustice.

The City of Chengdu was chosen by the central government as an urban and rural comprehensive reform pilot area in 2007. The reform includes industrial development, income distribution and the *Hukou* system. The most successful so far are the land rights clarifications in the suburbs of Chengdu. The first Land Rights Certificate was issued at Heming Village in 2008. It was considered by some researchers as the second land reform, following the household-contracted responsibility system reform in the late 1970s. To clarify the changes in land rights since the early 1950s, the government set up 'Villagers' Meetings', consisting of elderly villagers. The reformers first used tax information to measure the size of the plots, which were less than the actual size because the villagers under-reported their plot size in order to pay less taxes. To correct this problem, the reformers measured the plots in the fields (Zhou, Qiren 2012; Huang et al. 2012).

Many new forms of user rights trading have been created in China today. In many areas, farmers have established their shareholding businesses with their land as the equity stake, and let a professional manager run the business. Annual distribution of profits to each shareholder is much higher than the income from agricultural work. Three hundred farmers at Qiling village, Chongqing province, pooled their land to produce a new type of orange. Songzhuang village, in a suburb of Beijing, became an area for artists. The author visited the village in late 2012. The villagers had established several shareholding companies to manage the economic activities in the village, such as road construction, commercial area design, and land leasing to developers. Members of these companies received a distributed profit of RMB40000 per person. They also received income from renting their house to artists and/or working in the museums, stores and restaurants.

The ownership of land makes the farmers who live in the suburbs of cities rich. As soon as the expanded city limits reach the village, the residents in the village become millionaires when the price of land soars.

Land ownership trading has created large modern farms that are more efficient and raise productivity. These large farms are developing in some areas, especially in north China.

The central government has not officially endorsed the widespread practice of land rights transfer and trading. They are worried about several things. First, the transfer of the rights of management may mean transfer of ownership, which means the actual owners of the land are the farmers, not the 'collectives'. Second, the transfer of land rights may lead to concentration of land in the hands of a small group of farmers, and increase the number of landless farmers. This has happened many times in China's history, and led to social instability. Third, large-scale transfer of land may lead to a reduction of farmland and the grain supply. This may lead to dependence on foreign trade and will cause food shortage in cases of conflict with other countries.

5.3 LOCAL PUBLIC FINANCE AND LAND

Land requisition is highly correlated with local public finance, because land requisition and public land leasing has created an important revenue source for local government in recent years. In 1993, the central government implemented a tax reform to readjust the financial relationship between the central government and local government. The reform set up a system of tax division between the central and local governments.

From 1970s to 1993, a system of *Baogan* (contract or franchise) was followed to deal with the financial relationship between the central government and local government. Under this system, the central and local

Table 5.4   Taxes shared by central and local government

	Central government	Local government
Value-added tax	75%	25%
Resource tax	All collections from land resources	All collections from ocean resources
Security tax	50%	50%

Source: State Council (1993).

governments signed a contract that set up a quota of financial transitions during a certain period. A province with a surplus had to turn over the amount of revenue defined by the contract to the central government, while a province with a deficit could receive a subsidy defined by the contract from the central government. The quotas for different local governments varied according to their fiscal performance. The contract was negotiated and signed for several years, sometimes renewed every year. The system stimulated the local governments' incentives to create more revenue.

As the economic reform went on and the local fiscal conditions improved, the central government found that its share in total revenue decreased. A new system of tax division was introduced in 1994 to readjust the financial relationship between the central and local governments (Table 5.4). The new system included two components. Firstly, dividing the responsibilities of public good provision between central and local governments: for example, national defense, foreign relations and macroeconomic adjustments to the central government; and local economic development, security and education to local governments. Secondly, dividing the rights of tax collection between the central and local governments: for example, tariffs, consumption tax collected by customs, corporation tax from central-government-owned state-owned enterprises (SOEs) and banks to the central government; and business tax, corporate income tax from local-government-owned SOEs, personal income tax, and small taxes related to real estate to local governments. The value-added tax, resource tax and security trade tax were shared by central and local government. The value-added tax was the most important tax at the time (State Council 1993).

The 1994 tax reform was successful in improving the fiscal condition of the central government. It stabilized the central government's revenue. But the revenue share of the local governments was not commensurate with the increase in their responsibilities. Since the central government received a large share of the value-added tax, the local governments' incentives to develop local industrialization were reduced. The local governments shared about 60 percent of budgetary expenditure, but had much less budgetary revenue (Zhang 2008). For a couple of years after the reform, a large number of local governments were facing budget problems.

After some years of searching, the local governments found that land requisition and public land leasing could be an important source of revenue. The local government buys the land from the peasants paying a low requisition fee, and leases the land to developers for a fee higher than the market price. The higher price is due to the local governments' monopoly power in the land transition process. The local government often leases the land to large national or international industrial companies for a low rent, when they want to attract these companies to the localities. But they usually lease the land to residential developers for a higher rent, since these developers do not have many options in choosing their location. For example, one village in Fujian province paid RMB10000 per mu to peasants and resold the land to developers for RMB200000 per mu where industrial zoned, and for more than RMB0.75 million where residential zoned (Joint Investigating Group of Ministry of Land and Resources 2003, in Song 2007, p.85).

Currently, the local government revenue from land leasing, which is non-budgetary revenue, accounts for a large portion of their total revenue. It is called the 'secondary revenue' of the local governments. It includes taxes related to land, and rent, land leasing fees and user fees. In 2012, the area of assignment of state-owned land was 322800 hectares (ha), and the value of the assignment contract was RMB2.69 trillion (Ministry of Land and Resources n.d.).

Local governments in China are not allowed to issue debt, by law, and can only issue a small amount of debt through the central government. As an illegal alternative, recently local governments have set up investment platforms to issue debt for local government. A large amount of local government debt repayment depends on land leasing revenue. It is estimated, by different government agencies or officials, that the total local government debt is RMB10–20 trillion (People's Net 2013). The local governments leased a large amount of land in the first half of 2013 to repay their debt (*China Economy Weekly* 2013).

Local governments also collect various taxes related to land (Table 5.5), including five collected only from the housing sector (and housing property tax for foreign firms) – housing property tax (not implemented nationwide), urban land use tax, land appreciation tax, farmland occupation tax and deed tax; five related to housing – business tax, firm income tax, personal income tax, urban maintenance and construction tax, and stamp tax; and many fees, such as land management fees, vegetation development funds, public service project development fees and land use rights fees. It is estimated that the five taxes collected only from the housing sector

Table 5.5 Land-related taxes

Tax	Rates	Tax base	Administration
Housing property tax	1.2% of the remaining value of the house or 12% of the rent (4% preferential rate)	Remaining house value or rent	Except some experimental cities, not implemented
Urban housing property tax	1.2% of the remaining value of the house or 12% of the rent		Only for foreign-invested firms and foreign citizens
Urban land use tax	RMB0.6–30 per sq m	Area of land	
Land appreciation tax	30–60%, progressive rate	Value added	As one kind of resource tax
Farmland occupation tax	RMB5–50 per sq m	Area of farmland occupied	Varies by locality
Deed tax	3–5%	Contract value	Local tax
Business tax	3–5%, 5% for real property transfer	Value of services provided or sales of real property	
Firm income tax	18%, 27%, 33%, for different sizes of firms	Income	
Personal income tax	3–45%, progressive	Income	
Urban maintenance & construction tax	1%, 5%, 7%, depending on the size of city	Value-added tax, consumption tax or business tax	Additional tax
Stamp tax	0.005%–0.1%	Contract value	

Source: State Administration of Taxation (n.d.).

increased more than ten times from 2003 to 2012 (Huaxishibao 2013). Currently in China, most of the land-related taxes are collected in the transaction stage. An actual property tax is not collected nationwide.

In 2001, the share of land leasing revenue in total local financial revenue was only 16.6 percent. In 2009, the leasing revenue increased to RMB1.6 trillion, 48.8 percent of the total local government financial revenue (including both budgetary revenue and non-budgetary revenue). According to a report from the Research and Development Center of the State Council, land-related taxes account for 40 percent of the local governments' budgetary revenue, and land leasing net revenue accounts for 60 percent of the local governments' revenue not included in the budget (*Baike Mingpian* 2013). It is estimated that 60 percent of the housing sales revenue went into the pockets of the government, in terms of assignment revenue, taxes and fees (Liu 2013).

Land leasing revenue is crucial for the local governments to repay their debt. According to a report by the government's auditing administration, at the end of 2012, four provinces and 17 provincial capital cities had RMB775 billion of debt, or 55 percent of total debt, based on promises to be paid from land leasing revenue. The total debt to be repaid using land leasing revenue in these provinces and cities in 2012 was RMB232 billion, 1.25 times the total land leasing revenue. These cities, therefore, are considered insolvent. Guangzhou is the only super-large city in this group. The dependence of Guangzhou on land leasing revenue has increased since 2008, though the land leasing revenue reduced in 2012, partially due to central government's control of land supply, which shows the effect of the reduction in land leasing revenue on local public finance (Table 5.6). The land leasing revenue came back in the first five months of 2013, reaching RMB35 billion, reflecting local governments' efforts to keep a high level of land leasing against the control of central government (Zhang, Xiaoling 2013b; *China Economy Weekly* 2013).

Qiufeng, an independent scholar, pointed out two types of land financing: (1) the primary type: the government gets direct revenues via the margin between the requisition cost and reselling price; and (2) the advanced type: financing other investments based on land resources. Two conditions are needed: (1) increasing housing prices; and (2) increasing the scale of land resources in hand in order to make the banks believe the risks are under control (Tong 2011, p.46). Therefore, land financing will push government to keep enlarging its land reserve.

The stream of land leasing income gives local governments big incentives to keep the current public finance pattern, and the local governments and the developers have become an interest group connected by the land rents. The high prices that local governments charge in the land leasing

Table 5.6 Debts and land leasing revenue, Guangzhou city (RMB billion)

Year	Financial revenue	Land leasing revenue	Land leasing revenue/ Financial revenue (%)
2008	84.3	17.3	20.5
2009	110.8	32.3	29.2
2010	139.9	45.6	32.6
2011	160.7	47.5	29.5
2012		41.2	Approximately 20+

Note: Financial revenue includes general budget revenue and government funds revenue.

Source: Zhang, Xiaoling (2013b).

market have been one reason for high prices and rents in the urban housing market.

5.4 LOCAL PUBLIC FINANCE: SOCIAL BENEFITS

To the local governments, the main benefit of urbanization is the labor inputs provided by the migrant workers; and the main cost of urbanization is the social benefits they have to provide to the migrant workers and their families. The latter is the major resistance to China's urbanization. The local governments have incentives to accept the migrants for local development, but do not have enough incentives to provide social benefits to these migrants.

A large number of migrant workers currently work in cities, but do not enjoy the benefits a citizen should have. These migrant workers are living and working in cities, but they do not have health and retirement benefits. They do not live in ordinary urban housing facilities and their children cannot attend regular urban schools.

Tu Zhang, the son of a migrant worker who sells strawberries in Beijing, cannot attend the National College entrance examination in Beijing, because his father has no Beijing *Hukou*. Tu, an eleventh grader, has been for more than ten years among the top 30 percent of students at a very good senior high school. Rumors have been widely spread on the Internet that his mother, divorced from his father after he was born and now in the United States, can help him apply for US citizenship, which would allow him to sit China's college entrance examination. People believe that the law allows a foreign national to sit the entrance exam without requiring a *Hukou*, but this story turned out to be an urban myth (*China Weekly* 2013).

The government, mostly local governments, must provide these public services. To do this, governments need to commit to huge financial inputs, which are the costs of urbanization. Until recently, the Chinese government pushed the urbanization in the least costly way, by minimizing the public services to the migrant workers while using their labor as the inputs of development. But they cannot do that forever. It is time for the government to pay the debt owed to the migrant workers from the past 30 years.

There have been various estimates of the public costs for each migrant worker who enters cities, from RMB150000 to RMB100000 per person. A recent study by the China Development Foundation (2010) estimates the costs to be RMB100000 per person (Yanzhao Dushibao 2013). Urbanization requires governments, private firms and migrant workers to input their labor, services and money. The government expenditures are the key input in China's urbanization. The Development Research Center of the State Council (2013) calculates the government costs for urbanization, by including six cost items: education for migrants' children, health insurance, retirement insurance, other social security expenditure, expenditure for social administration, and indemnificatory housing. The cost estimates are based on field surveys in four cities: Chongqing, Wuhan in Hubei province, Zhengzhou in Henan province, and Jiaxing in Zhejiang province. The long-term retirement insurance subsidy per capita is estimated to be around RMB35000. The housing and education costs are about RMB24000, while the social security and public administration costs are RMB560.

Central and local governments need to pay the costs of urbanization. Some of these costs are actually the debt the governments owed to the migrant workers in the earlier stage of urbanization.

Land ownership and local public finance have been two extremely important problems in China's urbanization, which have not been completely solved. A closely correlated problem is the construction of infrastructure and housing on the land.

6. Infrastructure and housing construction

> To get rich, build a road first; to get rich first, build a fast road. (Chinese saying)

Urbanization is both a process of concentration of population and a process of geographical expansion. The infrastructure and housing construction played a great role in Chinese cities' geographical expansion. Cities of all sizes in China have been rebuilt during the past 30 years. Someone who left the country five years ago might not find their way around in their today hometown because every block has been rebuilt.

Infrastructure is here defined as: (1) public utilities, for example electricity and water supply, telecommunications and waste collection; (2) roads and irrigation; and (3) railroads, urban transportation, harbors and airports (World Bank 1993).

Urbanization increased the demand for investment in infrastructure. In the past decade, economic growth in China became infrastructure-led growth. Some research shows that the marginal contribution rate of infrastructure investment to gross domestic product (GDP) is higher than that of the whole fixed assets investment (Yu et al. 2008).

China has followed an infrastructure model of building ahead of demand, 'building impressive infrastructure at lightning speed' (Kim and Nangia 2008). China has had an extremely high savings rate in the past decade and allocated a large amount of resources for investments in general (Table 6.1). China's savings and investments were much higher than those of many countries in the world.

There have been two institutional factors involved in China's infrastructural investment process. First, the investment decision-making has been and remains mainly with the central planning authority, the State Development and Reform Committee (SDRC), the former State Planning Committee. A lot of large investment projects have to be approved by the SDRC. The local government has to lobby the SDRC, using connections. This is similar to the behavior of local government before the economic reform. The centralized state controls make it possible to take risks that would have been difficult for local government. Second, competition among local governments gives local governments incentives to make

Table 6.1   Savings and capital formation (% of GDP)

	1980	1990	2005
Gross domestic savings	35.0	39.9	49.0
Gross fixed capital formation	29.3	26.0	42.3
Gross capital formation	35.4	36.4	43.5
Foreign direct investment	0.03	1.0	3.54

Sources: *World Development Indicators* (2007) and ADB (2005), in Kim and Nangia (2008).

large-scale infrastructural investments. This is a new phenomenon after the economic reform.

A much higher speed was achieved in housing construction in China, compared with other countries. For example, I was teaching in a building at a university in Beijing in June 2011. The building contained more than 20 large classrooms. Shortly before the end of the semester, some construction work began. Then it turned out that the building, built about ten years before, would be totally demolished and rebuilt over the course of the summer break. I returned to the building and taught in a new classroom during the second week of September 2011 (the builders failed to meet their promise to finish in the first week of the new semester). In just three months the workers, most of them migrant workers, tore the building down and rebuilt it. They worked shifts, day and night. Some professors refused to teach in the new building, because the interior construction continued when classes were in session. This is an example of the speed of construction in China today, with both merits and demerits. Though the migrant workers worked ten hours or more every day and earned very low wages, they reduced the cost of construction and increased the speed of construction significantly.

Most of the structures in China today are short-lived. The average building life is about 30 years, which is much shorter than that in many other countries. The short building life is directly correlated to the poor quality of the construction. In 2009, a 13-floor building under construction collapsed due to an error in the design of its foundations (Tong 2011, p. 38). The poor quality is due to the frequency of change in local government leaders, and government leaders' incentive to pursue a high level of GDP.

6.1   A HISTORY OF INFRASTRUCTURE AND HOUSING CONSTRUCTION

Infrastructure and housing construction experienced different levels of investment before and after the reform started in the late 1970s.

Before the Reform (1952–1980)

The infrastructural investment level was very low during this period. The share of infrastructure investment in total capital construction was trivial. During 1963–1965, the level of infrastructure investment was lower than that in 1953–1962, while the share of infrastructure investment in total capital investment in 1966–1975 was lower than that in 1952–1962. This was directly due to the famine of 1959–1961 and the political turmoil during the Cultural Revolution from 1966 to 1976.

Overall, the low level of infrastructure investment was the result of: (1) the planning principle of giving higher priority to production than to the improvement of living conditions; (2) the scarcity of natural resources and capital goods, all of which come from the government; (3) the inefficiency of governmental infrastructure management.

1980s and 1990s

More emphasis was placed on infrastructure investment by the government. The lags in infrastructure under the planned period created large demand at the beginning of the reform. Infrastructure investment in the 1980s reached more than five times the total infrastructure investment in the previous 25 years. The share of infrastructure investment in total capital also increased (Jiang 2010, p.26). However, due to the low level of investment in the planned period, infrastructure shortages could still be found in many fields, such as water and gas supply, road construction and waste collection.

More improvements were made in infrastructure investment and construction in the 1990s. Infrastructure investment increased from RMB95 billion in 1990 to RMB1128 billion in 1999. The share of infrastructure investment in total capital investment increased from 21 percent in 1990 to 38 percent in 1999 (Jiang 2010, p.75). The sources of investment diversified during this period, and private capital began to enter this field.

Table 6.2   China's investment in fixed assets (RMB trillion)

	Total	Urban	Urban/Total (%)
1995	2	1.56	78
2000	3.29	2.62	80
2005	8.88	7.51	85
2010	27.81	24.14	87
Annual growth	19%	20%	

Source: National Bureau of Statistics (2011a, table 5-2).

The First Decade of the Twenty-first Century

Infrastructure investment and construction accelerated further during this period. The growth rate in infrastructure construction was much higher than the growth rate of GDP during this period. Table 6.2 shows the investment in fixed assets, which is a more general term for investment, including capital construction, investment in innovation and real estate development. According to the National Bureau of Statistics, investment in fixed assets reached RMB31.1 trillion in 2011, including RMB30.2 trillion in urban areas (National Bureau of Statistics 2012a, p.158). There were some changes in the statistical definition of 'investment in fixed assets' by the National Bureau of Statistics in 2011. Compared with India, China's growth rates of annual GDP, telephone subscribers, electricity and the railway network length were higher than India's from 1990 to 2005, but growth of the road network length was not (Figure 6.1).

The city building movement

Local officials have the incentive to present a good record when their term of office is over, which reveals the limits of their terms of office. Changes in the chief officials of local government, controlled by the central government, usually also bring about changes in ideas and policies. Thus each new local chief official will begin a new wave of urban construction.

The *Telegraph* reported in January 2011:

> City planners in south China have laid out an ambitious plan to merge together the nine cities that lie around the Pearl River Delta. The 'Turn the Pearl River Delta Into One' scheme will create a 16 000 sq mile urban area that is 26 times larger geographically than Greater London, or twice the size of Wales. The new mega-city will cover a large part of China's manufacturing heartland, stretching from Guangzhou to Shenzhen and including Foshan, Dongguan, Zhongshan, Zhuhai, Jiangmen, Huizhou and Zhaoqing [see Figure 6.2]. Together, they account for nearly a tenth of the Chinese economy. Over the next six years,

around 150 major infrastructure projects will mesh the transport, energy, water and telecommunications networks of the nine cities together, at a cost of some 2 trillion yuan (£190 billion). An express rail line will also connect the hub with nearby Hong Kong. (Moore 2011)

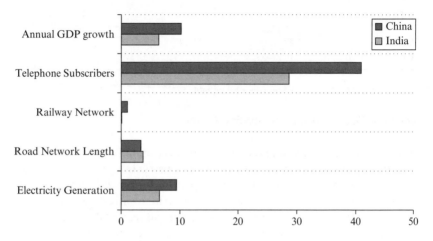

Source: Based on data in Kim and Nangia (2008, Table 2).

Figure 6.1   China's infrastructure, compared with India, average annual growth rate, 1990–2005 (%)

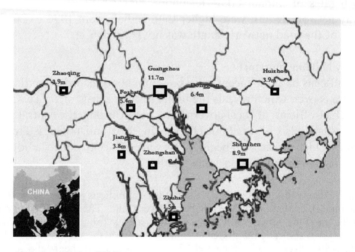

Source: Based on Moore (2011).

Figure 6.2   A map of 'Turn the Pearl River Delta Into One' plan

Table 6.3 Length of roads, China ('000 km)

Classification	1980	1990	2000	2005	2011
Expressway	0	0.5	16.3	41.0	84.9
Class I	0.2	2.6	25.2	38.4	68.1
Class II	12.6	43.4	177.8	246.4	32.1
Class III	108.3	169.8	305.4	344.7	
Class IV	400.1	524.8	791.2	921.3	
Substandard	367.1	287.2	363.9	338.8	652.8
Total	888.25	1028.4	1679.8	1930.5	4106.4

Note: Data not available for class III and class IV in 2011, but the total of expressways and class I–IV highways is 3453.6 9, in '000 km.

Sources: 1980, 1990, 2000, and 2005 data from Kim and Nangia (2008). 2011 data from National Bureau of Statistics (2012a, p. 619).

Structure of the infrastructure

Over 40 percent of infrastructure investment in China was in transportation, including railroad and highway construction. The development of road infrastructure was relatively unimportant in China's development strategy during the planned period. The road infrastructure was poorly developed and maintained at the beginning of the reform. The investment in road infrastructure remained low during early years of the reform. Since the mid-1980s, the Chinese government has increased the investment in roads. In the 1990s, the government started to invest massively in road construction. Table 6.3 shows a continuous increase in both the length and the quality of the road system in China. China had no expressways before 1988, when the first expressway was built. From 1988 to the end of 2012, 98 364 kilometres (61 121 miles) of expressway were built in China. Currently, China's expressway system[1] is longer than that of the European Union and the US. China's expressway construction plan has been revised several times. The original plan of 35 000 km of national trunk highway started in 1988 and was scheduled to finish in 2020. Seventy percent of the trunk highways are expressways. The plan was completed at the end of 2007, 13 years ahead of schedule. A second plan was announced in 2005 to build a network of 85 000 km of expressways over the next three decades, connecting all provincial capitals and cities with a population over 200 000 (Wikipedia n.d.-e). This plan will be completed by the end of 2013, and the government is working on a more ambitious plan. Some research shows that the greatest effect on poverty reduction comes from investment in the rural transportation system. An efficient road network in rural areas increases access to economic opportunities. These investments cover infrastructure that is not within city boundaries. The second-largest portion of infrastructure investment was utility production, which is more or less under the control of local government.

Geographically, most of the infrastructure investment has been located in the eastern coastal areas. The investment in the eastern area was greater than the sum of that in the 20 provinces in the central and western areas in 2010. Due to the investment by the central government to balance investments nationwide, the share of investment in central and western areas increased in the first decade of the twenty-first century.

6.2   HOUSING CONSTRUCTION AND PRICE

In the past 20 years in Chinese cities, housing has been transferred from being state-provisioned to being market-provisioned. Since the housing reform in the late 1990s, investment in residential housing has increased dramatically (Table 6.4).

Urban residential housing was provided and distributed by the government and state-owned enterprises (SOEs), or *Danwei* (state-owned working units; for example factories, government offices, schools and stores). From 1949 to 1990, 1.73 billion sq m (87 percent) of residential housing was built in Chinese cities and towns by the public and collective sectors, and 0.25 billion sq m (13 percent) was built by individual families, mostly in the countryside (Wang and Murie 1999, in Li n.d., p.5). In the cities, housing leases were for life and would never expire, but not everyone was guaranteed to get a unit. This system was referred to as the Welfare Housing System. The rents were extremely low and the housing was under-maintained. Due to the low rent, no state-owned construction company had an incentive to build apartments, and no working units (government offices, factories, schools and so on) had the incentive to maintain them. Living space got smaller and smaller because of the small amount of

Table 6.4   Investment in residential buildings (RMB trillion)

	Total	Urban
1995	0.47	0.33
2000	0.76	0.54
2005	1.54	1.28
2010	4.59	3.95
Annual growth	16%	18%

Source: Based on National Bureau of Statistics (2011b, table 5-6).

housing that was built, and some young people had to share their parents' or grandparents' apartments with their parents.

The housing reform started in 1980s. Rents were increased but houses were still owned by the working units. This system of government distributed housing ended in late 1990s. The State Council issued a document, the 'State Council's Decision on the Deepening of City and Township Housing Reform', in 1994 (Li n.d., p.8), which provided a framework for housing reform. The new system aimed at raising rents to the market equilibrium level and allowing home ownership by individuals. The government and SOEs were allowed to sell the existing housing units to sitting tenants at a discount rate. The buyers obtained a limited ownership of the house (the owner has to sell the house to their *Danwei* if they want to sell it). The *Danwei* will not provide housing for new employees. They have to go to the residential housing market to buy their houses.

Before the reform, the Chinese families spent 1–2 percent of average family income on rent (Fong 1989, in Li n.d., p.9). In the 1990s, rents were gradually raised, with a housing subsidy included in salaries. The housing subsidy comes from the funds that (state-owned) *Danwei* used to build or buy housing for their employees; part of it comes from the state. The *Danwei* issues the subsidy to its employees who have not enjoyed welfare housing, monthly or as a one-off payment. The amount of subsidy depends on the rank of the employee (Baidu Baike n.d.-a). In Beijing, rents were raised to RMB1.8 per sq m in 1998, representing 15 percent of a household's income (Lee 2000, in Li n.d., p.9).

Housing Bubble

The residential housing market in China has developed in the first decade of the twenty-first century. The huge demand caused housing prices to soar. Housing prices in Suzhou, a mid-sized city near Shanghai, averaged about RMB500/sq m around 2001. By 2007, the average seemed to be hovering around RMB7–8000. At the low point in the late 1990s, much of the prime real estate in Pudong, a new central business district (CBD) in Shanghai, was selling for RMB1000–2000/sq m. In 2007, decent real estate in Pudong started at RMB13000 per square meter. Residential apartments near the famed Oriental Pearl Tower in Pudong go for over RMB100000/ sq m (China Expat n.d.). Many residents in China cannot afford to buy a house of their own if they are forced to on the open market today. The rental price of housing is also increasing. In the first quarter of 2013, the average rental price of a unit rose to RMB3660 per month, 82 percent higher than 2008 (Wang 2013).

Housing prices are closely correlated with land prices, based on floor area.

The land price per floor area in Beijing increased from about RMB6000/sq m in 2009 to RMB 10000 in 2012. Excluding low-income housing, the land price per floor area was more than RMB14000/sq m in 2012, estimated by Ren, Zhiqiang, a famous housing developer (Jin 2013). In China, all urban land is owned by the state. The only way to transfer rural land to urban land is through government requisition, in which the local government rents the land to developers. The supply of land thus affects the developers' cost of production and the housing price. Since the land leasing revenue is an important part of local government revenue, it creates incentives to raise the land price. On the other hand, local governments have to follow the central government's instructions to control the housing price. Based on the consideration of social stability, the central government wants to control the housing price. The housing price control has not been successful, partly due to the local governments' reliance on land revenue. Rising land and housing prices causes developers and consumers to expect future price rises.

The housing bubble was partly driven by the government policy in early years of the first decade of the twenty-first century. During this period, housing was set up as the pillar industry to accelerate economic growth, which was extremely important for the local governments. Other possible contributors leading to rising housing prices include rising income, cheap credit, and developers' promotions. The state-owned banks were allowed to provide cheap credit for both the construction and the purchase of residential property. Local governments had the incentive to sell land when they relied more and more on land sales for income. Young people are also faced with cultural pressures encouraging home ownership, particularly for a young man seeking a wife.[2] Investment in residential property became an easy and quick way to accumulate wealth, compared with manufacturing. Companies of all kinds opened real estate divisions, expecting higher profits than in their core businesses.

Case: Nanjing Xiaguan Imperial Land

Xiaguan is an area on the Yangtze river shore in Nanjing, the capital city of Jiangsu province, which is a central area of future Nanjing city. The area was covered by old factories, port facilities and residential buildings. The city government started a reform of the area in 2005, which involved an area of 157000 sq m, 200 factories and 12000 households. By 2013, 90 percent of the factories and households have been relocated. To relocate the residents, the government used various measures, including cutting the supply of water and electricity and raising the relocation compensation. One resident told the *21st Century Economic Report* that the compensation the government gave to him was RMB7200/sq m, which is not enough to buy an apartment elsewhere. One new apartment built in the area was sold for RMB35000–40000/sq m in 2013.

On September 19, 2010, two key pieces of land in the area, #1 and #3, were sold to Nanjing Linjiang Old Town Rebuilding Construction Investment Co. Ltd in an auction with no competition. The total price of RMB20 billion is the second-highest total price in China up to early 2013. Then on November 30, 2012, another piece of land, #2, was sold to the same buyer for RMB5.6 billion, the highest price nationwide in 2012. The total area of the three pieces was 1.03 sq km, 3.63 percent of the Xiaguan River shore area. The total price was RMB25.6 billion.

The Ministry of Land and Resources (MLR) of the central government became aware of the deal, and conducted an investigation on the deal of land piece #2 on December 18, 2012, concerning the amount of land and the background of the buyer. It was reported that large SOEs were involved in this deal of market-priced land (Wang, Haiping 2012).

Housing Price Control

As the housing bubble enlarged, the central government imposed housing price controls as early as 2006. During the inflation in 2010–2011, the government realized that housing prices were an important contributor to overall inflation and began to enact laws to stop the housing bubble. The government imposed new curbs on housing prices in 2010; most of them were administrative measures (Table 6.5). The policy of *Xiangou* (purchasing restrictions) was imposed in many big cities. Local governments, under pressure from the central government, put restrictions on second-home purchasing or required second-home buyers to make a higher percentage of down payment. The Beijing municipal government banned, for five years in 2011, the sale of homes to people who did not have a Beijing residence ID. The number of homes a Beijing resident could own was limited to two, while non-resident ID holders could only buy one home. A mortgage discount for first-time home buyers was also eliminated. Higher minimum down payments for second homes and a residential property tax were introduced in Shanghai and Chongqing (Bloomberg News 2011b).

The most recent regulation, the Details of National 5 Regulations, includes the following regulations:

- Purchasing restrictions: the area of purchase restriction is expended to the whole administrative area of cities. The type of housing under purchase restrictions should include all new commercialized residential buildings and secondary hand housing. The regulation unified the rules of purchasing restrictions in different cities. Before

Table 6.5   Control measures imposed by central government since 2006

Date	Name of policy	Major measures imposed
June 1, 2006	National 6 Regulations	Down payment no less than 30 percent, 20 percent for the first unit which is less than 90 sq m.
September 27, 2007	Central Bank New Deal	Second unit down payment no less than 50 percent, and interest rate increases.
October 24, 2009	National 4 Regulations	Strengthening the implementation of loan differentiation and carrying out economy housing project.
January 10, 2010	National 11 Regulations	Second unit down payment no less than 40 percent.
April 17, 2010	New National 10 Regulations	Temporarily stop issuing loans for the third unit.
January 26, 2011	New National 8 Regulations	Second unit down payment 60 percent and tax for secondary housing less than 5 years.
February 20, 2013	National 5 Regulations	Restraining investment housing purchases, strictly implementing purchasing restrictions, and enlarging experiments for property tax.
March 1, 2013	Details of National 5 Regulations	Uniforming standards for purchasing restrictions, raising second unit down payments and interest rates, and 20 percent income tax for secondary housing deals.

Source: Zhang, Xiaoling (2013a).

this regulation, cities had different rules. For example, Changsha city's purchasing restriction only covered units under 90 sq m, while Guiyang city's purchasing restriction only covered housing within the inner ring road.

● Second unit: the new regulation further increased the down payment requirement and the loan interest rate for the second unit.
● Tax for secondary house selling: income tax of 20 percent of revenue will be collected for secondary house selling. Before the new regulation, 1–2 percent of the transaction value was collected as a tax. The new regulation caused hot debate and increased the number of transactions before the deadline of the old regulation. This regulation increased the expectation of implementing property tax in the near future. (Zhang Xiaoling 2013a).

These policies have had some effect, at least in the short run. Housing prices have been stable or have fallen slightly since 2011. A new housing bubble is expected to come in 2013, because the local governments still have incentives to promote housing booms, and a new Cabinet is taking over. The price index for new residenial housing in 70 large- and middle-sized cities increased 5.5 percent and 6.3 percent in May and June 2013, compared with the same period in the previous year (Wen 2013). If the pressure of housing price increases continues to exist, the central government will keep implementing the price control policies in the mid-term, which will reduce producers' profit further. Since land is a scarce resource in China, land and house prices will keep increasing in the long run, at least in the large cities.

Dwelling Narrowness

A 2009 TV series, based on a novel of the same name by Liu Liu (2007), tells a story of two sisters struggling with life in Jiangzhou, a fictional city that resembles Shanghai, the largest city in China. Haiping, the elder sister, born in a small city, attended college in Jiangzhou and remained in the city after graduation with her husband. They live in a shabby room and save money in order to buy an apartment. Haiping convinces her mother to let her younger sister, Haizao, come to Jiangzhou to attend college, too. Four years pass after Haizao's graduation, and Haiping still cannot afford an apartment due to rising prices. Haizao finds a job working for a housing developer. She meets Song, a middle-aged, influential government official, during a business dinner. Song is attracted to Haizao's beauty and attempts to win her heart, despite his being married. Song gives money to Haizao so that she can help her sister pay for her apartment. In return, Haizao begins an affair with Song. Song and his superior have been involved in brokering housing deals and are under investigation. He gives a large amounts of money to Haizao, who is pregnant. Song's wife finds out about the missing money and finds out where Haizao lives. Haizao is beaten and has a miscarriage. Song hears of Haizao's condition before being arrested, and drives to the hospital. He is chased by the police and dies in an accident. Haizao is depressed for months and finally leaves for the US, when Haiping and her family move into their new apartments.

The series shows how difficult it is to buy a house in the city, and has become a symbol of the housing bubble in the first decade of the twenty-first century in China. The series was cut short by the censorship board and was criticized as one that 'focuses on sex, dirty jokes, and corruption stories'.

Forced Demolitions

Forced demolitions without due process and fair compensation have been seen in the process of housing construction. A large number of deadly property disputes occur due to conflicts of interest among property owners, developers and the government. In many cases, when a property owner does not agree with the compensation given by the developer and refuses to move, the developer uses force to drive them out and demolishes the house. In October 2010, demolition workers broke into a house slated for demolition that belonged to a 54-year-old man, Fugui Meng, in Shanxi province. The owner was pulled from the house and beaten to death. The case was widely reported and sparked public outrage. Jianwei Meng, a college student and Fugui Meng's son, posted news of his father's murder online and attracted nationwide attention. This case reflects the widespread violation of landowners' rights by forced demolition in China today.

In some cases, the compensation is too low for the house owner to accept. In March 2010, two farmers in Jiangsu province set themselves on fire, killing one and injuring the other, to protest the low compensation plan. Less than six months later, a similar case took place in Jiangxi province, ending with one homeowner being killed and two badly burned (Xinhua n.d). These forced demolitions were carried out by either private or state-linked companies, with the support of the local government.

Some of other cases include: Fuzhen Tang, a woman entrepreneur who lived in Chengdu, the capital city in Sichuan Province, set herself on fire and died in November 2009; Xia Zhang, a woman who owned a small business in Qingdao, a large city in Shandong province, set herself on fire in October 2009 when the police came to enforce demolition; Na Wang, living in Chifeng, a middle-sized city in Inner Mongolia, set the house on fire and seriously hurt herself when the court enforced the demolition of her parents' house.

The case illustrates the widespread violation of landowners' rights by demolitions in China today. Media and online social networks play important roles in attracting public attention to these cases. Such violence and mistreatment of property owners has fueled social unrest. On December 9, 2009, five law professors of Peking University wrote a letter to the Standing Committee of the National People's Congress (NPC) pointing out that the existing demolition regulations are unconstitutional, and urged revisions of the existing laws and regulations. Then the NPC made draft regulations and the State Council called for public input, which was unprecedented in the country's regulation history (WSJ 2011). It was estimated that over 100000 opinions were received, and 45 seminars were held for the public, legislators and government (Horsley 2009).

The first demolition regulation was published by the State Council in 1991, when the housing market was dominated by SOEs. The regulation was revised in 2001. Under this version of the regulation, the demolishers were allowed to demolish the house before finishing the requisition process. A company could be both a developer and a demolisher, and the developer should pay the compensation to the homeowner.

In January 2011, the State Council issued a new regulation that promised to end the forced demolitions without legal approval, and ensure fair prices to homeowners who lost their property. According to the regulation, the power of local governments to order demolition was ended and the disputed cases were required to be decided by the courts. The changes of the law reflects government's responsiveness to the public, although some people doubt that the effectiveness of the implementation of the regulation.

Housing with Limited Property Rights

Housing with limited property rights is housing built with licenses issued by the township government (not the city government). These houses are built on suburban land owned by farmers' collectives and sold to the urban residents, mostly migrant workers. According to current laws, it is illegal to build commercial houses on the collective-owned land. The owner could be deprived of their rights at any time in the future. However, these houses have helped governments to provide a large number of cheap residences for migrant workers, while governments did little in providing affordable housing for them in the first decade of the twenty-first century.

Case: Housing with Limited Property Rights in Shenzhen

Shenzhen is a new city in south China near Hong Kong, created by Deng's 'open to the outside world' policy and developed in the past 30 years. A Special Economic Zone was set up within the Shenzhen area, which had a special favorite treatment for foreign investors. The Shenzhen municipal government imposed a uniform requisition which transferred all land within the special zones from collective-owned to state-owned in 1992. Another uniform requisition was imposed in 2004, which transferred all land out of the special zone in the Longgang and Baoan districts of Shenzhen city to the state. A large number of buildings in these areas were built on former collectively owned lands and the property rights over these buildings were not recognised by the government. The negotiations on compensation took years, without result. To strengthen their negotiating powers, the former collectives built more and more illegal buildings on the land, in order to negotiate for more future compensation. This has recently become a serious social problem. Professor Qiren Zhou of Peking University and his students undertook a lot of field surveys in Shenzhen, which were recorded in Cui (2013) and many other documents.

Infrastructure and housing construction are important for the expansion of the cities, and the conflicts among interest groups during city construction need institutional reform. The government needs to develop more functions to accommodate the conflicting interests of different groups in the society.

NOTES

1. Not including the expressways administered by the provincial-level governments.
2. The male to female ratio has been dramatically higher in China than in most of other countries due to the 'one child policy'.

7. Social aspects of urbanization

It was Mao's dream to create an equal society to minimize the difference between ordinary people and government officials. He was partially successful. The urban society was relatively equal, but the inequality between urban and rural residents was maximized. The economic reform since 1978 has enlarged inequality in Chinese society, a side effect from raising efficiency in the system. One of the guidelines of the reform was 'to let a small group of people get richer first', which has been realized 30 years later. The recent development of urbanization relocated wealth among individuals on an extremely large scale, through the redistribution of wealth and the changes in property values.

Inequality is currently a serious problem in China. Under the planning system, the differences in income within urban and rural areas were trivial. But the difference between city and countryside was dramatic. To promote industrialization, the government manipulated the relative price between industrial products and agricultural products in the planned period before 1978. This price system and the agricultural product tax created a poor rural population. During the planned period, residents in the countryside were also excluded from the pension and healthcare insurance system in the cities. They did not have resident IDs (*Hukou*), and therefore had no right to live and work in the cities. Most importantly, they did not have food rations. Under the food rationing system, anyone who needed to buy basic food in the cities needed to use both money and food ration coupons. Those without rations were unable to make extended stays in cities. The production activities in rural areas were also restricted, as the government ordered that the farmers should use most of their land to produce grain, since grain is important for survival. Non-grain production (e.g. vegetables, fish, and livestock) was limited, since the grain demand was not yet fulfilled. Under this system, a peasant did not have most basic rights of a citizen, such as food ration, residency and work permit in cities, pension and healthcare, and would keep their status for their whole life. The only chance to change a person's status was, unfortunately, by government requisition of their land, besides the limited chances of becoming a college student or joining the army. The fundamental source of inequality during the planning system was the division between urban and rural residents.

Inequalities can be considered from two dimensions: regional and urban–rural relations. It is estimated that the difference of per capita GDP between the eastern area and the western area was roughly RMB7000. Now it has enlarged to RMB21 000 (Tong 2011, p.4). The ratio of urban per capita disposable income and rural per capita net income increased from 2.6 to 3.1 in 2011. Wan and Cai (2012) and Zhang and Wan (2006) point out that urban–rural inequality has been a large source of overall inequality in China and its role has become larger and larger. They also find that almost all fluctuations in inequalities were due to changes in urban–rural inequality.

At the beginning of the economic reform in the late 1970s, the leadership faced a trade-off between economic development and equality. Economic development was chosen as the priority. To encourage hard-working residents, the government allowed a portion of the people to become richer than others within cities and the countryside. This caused inequalities to increase. At the same time, peasants were allowed to move and work outside of their home villages; first in small towns, then in big cities. The second step may have reduced inequality, or at least offset some of the increase in the overall inequality in the 1980s and 1990s. The urban–rural inequality was reduced at the early stage of reform, but increased in the past ten or so years, mainly due to strong growth in urban areas.

The factors causing the urban–rural inequality include education, working experience, family size, health, financial transfer and location. Regional inequalities in China have two major sources: rural–urban inequalities, and inequalities between eastern and western areas. The rural–urban inequality has become the most important source of overall inequalities in recent years, according to Wan and Cai (2012, p.101). Trade and foreign direct investment have been important factors causing regional inequality, while education, experience and family burden rate (the ratio between number of persons who do not work and number of persons who work in a family) play important roles. Domestic private investment plays an increasing role in reducing regional inequality. Residents in urban areas and cities receive higher-quality education than rural residents, because most high-quality education is concentrated in urban areas. Rural students have fewer chances to go to college, because universities discriminate against them, and a higher grade is required for them to enter college. The rural residents have less working experience in modern industries. The impact of education on urban–rural income differences has been the greatest and has increased in recent years, according to some recent research. On the household level, the welfare benefits received by residents living in central and western regions were much less than those received by residents in the eastern area. Financial transfer payments play a trivial role in reducing regional inequality. Middle and western Chinese families receive fewer social benefits. Important social benefits, such as food and health, are positively correlated with income before tax and transfer payments. The lowest-income working group is not covered by the social benefit system (Wan and Cai 2012, p.103).

7.1 THE NEW POVERTY IN THE CITIES

In the past 30 years, 150 million peasants moved into the cities. This great migration tremendously increased the income level of these people and their families. On the other hand, they brought poverty into the cities. These migrant workers do not have a family life before they are 35 years old, according to a joke, because their wives or husbands or children stay in the countryside; they do not have social security after 35, because they do not have *Hukou* registration.

Several factors contributed to the continuing poverty conditions of the migrants in the cities. First and most importantly, municipal governments did not provide full services to the migrants due to the lag in local public service reform. It is still extremely difficult for rural migrants to get urban residency ID, *Hukou*, and other benefits in the cities. As a result, rural migrants do not have access to many urban amenities, including subsidized housing, education for their children and health care. Second, the urban labor market is segmented and the migrant workers can only work in low-wage jobs, which require low levels of education and experience. Third, policy loopholes allow farmers in the urbanized villages where they grew up to build cheap housing units and rent them out to the migrants.

The main difficulty for migrants living in the cities is access to urban housing. Many married migrant couples have been living separately for years, because they could not afford regular urban housing. Many migrant workers travel to the cities, leaving their wives and children at home. Some married migrant workers have organized 'temporary' second families in cities, which causes the tragedy of family breakdown. The existing affordable housing system in China is targeted towards urban residents who have city residence permits or *Hukou*. Migrant workers and floating populations without *Hukou* are not covered by the affordable housing system. These people have to find shelter in the informal housing market with substandard living conditions, in crowded urbanizing villages.

The Villages within the Cities

The villages within the cities, or urbanizing villages (*ChengZhongCun* in Chinese), refer to the ghettos in urban areas in which rural migrants live in inexpensive housing. These villages were recently included in city territories due to the expansion of the cities, but this does not prevent their poor conditions. In the city of Guangzhou, 277 urbanizing villages existed with about 1 million inhabitants in 2000 (Zhang et al. 2003, in Song and Ding 2007, p.145).

The design and construction of buildings in these urbanized villages are not constrained by the application, inspection and approval procedures for other urban areas. The zoning regulations of building height, floor-area ratio, width of corridors, and many others, do not cover the new urban areas just transferred from the countryside. Without regulations, the farmers living in these villages are thus able to build substandard housing units and rent them out to the migrants. These farmers have become a new generation of landlords in urban areas, and earn a significant amount of rents. In the urban villages, the housing density is very high and each tenant only uses a small space. In a village near my apartment in a big city in China, a car cannot be driven through the village because the streets are too narrow. The villages in the cities are open spaces not covered by the administration of the municipal government. They help the government in providing cheap shelter for low-income migrant workers and have freed the government from providing expensive housing programs during the beginning stage of urbanization.

The crowded living conditions have created many problems, such as safety, health, environmental and social problems. First, the housing constructed in the villages cannot meet the requirements of fire-control standards, and the streets are too narrow for fire trucks to enter the villages in case of an accident. This creates a safety problem. Second, garbage is scattered everywhere in the villages and no standard waste disposal systems have been constructed. Pollution is a serious problem for both the village and the neighboring areas. Third, the limited living space creates social problems in these villages, including burglary, robbery, violence and prostitution. The crime rate is high in these urbanized villages and is a public concern.

Saoziying village (Figure 7.1) is located in Qinglongqiao Jiedao, Haidian district, Beijing, west of Yuanmingyuan (former emperors' garden) and Yanbeiyuan (teachers' dorm of Peking University), south of the Summer Palace, north-east of the National School of the Communist Party. The area totals 270 000 sq m. There are 2868 residents (1282 households) in the area, with residential ID (Baidu Baike n.d.-b). A large number of tenants

Figure 7.1   Saoziying, a village within the city

live in the village, probably more than the original residents; a lot of them are migrant workers.

Because of the social problems, and the temporary nature of the buildings, the villages within the cities are also facing forced demolition. To reduce the social and safety problems, the municipal governments have the incentive to demolish the villages and redevelop these areas. Many cases of the violation of landowners' rights by demolitions have happened when villages were demolished.

Before demolishing the villages within the cities, the government has to consider the problem of housing new residents. It is a tough job, considering the number and the income of the migrant workers. Low-income housing is a policy issue which has been hotly debated by researchers and the public.

Education of Migrant and Leftover Children

With the development of urbanization, thousands of young people are flocking into cities in China, leaving their small children at home. Usually, the children's grandparents or their parents' friends or relatives look after these children. Guardians seldom care about the children's study, their psychological needs or mental demands. Another group of children migrates with their parents to the cities. Since they do not have *Hukou*, they could not enter the regular public schools in these cities until very recently. Sometimes, they enter the schools for migrant workers, which usually have a lower quality of education.

A national survey of 1 percent of the population by the National Women's Federation in 2005 shows that there were 58 million migrant workers' children left in the countryside nationwide, which account for 28 percent of all children under 17 years old in rural areas. Different sources show that some leftover and migrant children have psychological problems. The leftover children score lower than the average at school. The migrant children worry more about relationships with other people than the average. Data from courts in Beijing show that the crime rate of migrant children was three times higher than the average (Tong 2011, p. 130).

The government recently began to address the education problem of migrant children.

7.2   LOW-INCOME HOUSING

The rising prices in the housing market and the lack of affordable housing for low-income households have posed risks and challenges for the stability of the Chinese society. Whether owning a house should be a basic human right and a government target is heavily debated by the public.

In China, subsidized housing for low-income households is defined as indemnificatory housing, consisting of low-rent housing, affordable housing and policy-regulated rental housing. Affordable housing is subsidized housing for low-income owners to purchase and own. The low-rent housing and policy-regulated housing are subsidized housing for rent. In the early years of the first decade of the twenty-first century, the Chinese government focused on affordable housing, while recently the focus has changed to low-rent housing.

Under the planned system, and in the early years of economic reform, most urban resident housing was provided by the government and state-owned-enterprises. These houses were rented to the residents at a subsidized rental rate, accounting for a small share of income. Urban housing was reformed in the 1990s. The new policy encourages urban residents to buy the house they were living in, at a subsidized price. After the reform no subsidized housing is provided by the government to any above-middle-income resident; they have to buy houses in the housing market at market prices. At the same time, in 1998 the government announced a low-income housing policy. Under the policy, government will provide subsidized housing for low-income households.

In the first decade of the twenty-first century, low-income housing was provided on a small scale, which was not enough to meet the demand. The developers had no incentive because of the low profitability, and the local government had no incentive because it does not create revenue. The focus of the policy was affordable housing, instead of low-rent housing. From 2006 to 2010, 11 million indemnificatory housing units were constructed. The public criticized the policy. Many people pointed out that it is not acceptable to use taxpayers' money to subsidize low-income households to own houses, and that low-rent housing is a better solution. The government made a major change in 2007 and 2008. More resources were put into low-income housing and the focus changed to low-rent housing.

The Chinese government accelerated the construction of the indemnificatory housing after property prices climbed in 2009 and 2010, partly because it was thought that the low-income housing supply would reduce the market price of housing; low-income housing could be used as a potential tool for controlling housing prices. In 2011, the government announced a plan to build 36 million indemnificatory homes over five years from 2011 to 2015 (which is the period of the 12th National Economic Plan). Twelve million units were due to start construction in 2011, which was more than the low-income housing built in the previous ten years. This is an extremely large number meaning to comprise 20 percent of China's housing market. The plan includes the construction of: (1) low-rent housing, for low-income households; (2) public rental housing, for lower-middle-income households; (3) affordable housing, owner-occupied, and other types of indemnificatory housing, and the rebuilding of shanty areas in cities. According to another source, in 2011, 38 percent of the indemnificatory housing for which construction had started was low-rent housing and policy-regulated rental housing, 20 percent were affordable (owner-occupied) housing, and 42 percent were the rebuilding of shanty areas in cities (Ren 2011).

Taohuayuan Qifu town is an example of a design of an affordable housing project in Nanning, Guangxi province. The total area is 289 831 sq m and the construction area is 570 000 sq m. There are 5000 housing units, and 21 000 residents will live in the project. Most buildings have six stories. There are shopping facilities, schools and parks near the residential buildings. The requirement for residency includes: (1) middle-low income households currently without housing; the income requirement was defined as household income between six times the last year's average wage in the city and 50 percent of this average income; (2) households with current living space less than 15 sq m per person; (3) households whose house will be demolished for public purposes (Lai 2010).

This plan of indemnificatory housing is huge in terms of its size and funding. If each household has three members, over 100 million Chinese will live in these houses when their construction is finished. Excluding land costs, the plan needs RMB1.3 trillion or $198 billion, estimated by Housing and Urban–Rural Development Vice Minister Ji Qi. According to Mr Qi, the central and local governments will only provide RMB500 billion (Bloomberg News 2011b), which means a 60 percent gap in funding. In the short run, loans from local banks may fill the gap partially. But in the long run, these debts need to be repaid with interest in the future by the local governments.

There are plenty of problems other than the funding gap:

1. Since the local governments are required by the central government to lower the land leasing price for public housing, which is the main source of local government revenue, the plan will also damage the financial position of local governments. Considering the large share of land leasing in total revenue, there is no doubt that the local governments are reluctant to construct affordable housing.
2. There are not enough regulations for residency requirements and the administration of the finished low-rent housing; for example the income limit above which the current residents have to move out of the subsidized housing. It is quite possible that a large number of middle- or high-income households which have connections with government officials will occupy the units and live there forever.
3. Considering the limited land supply in a city, the large increase in land demand for low-income housing will reduce the land supply to the regular housing market. This market is more important for overall economic development and the revenues of local government. In the long run, the capacity of low-income housing construction depends on the development of the regular housing market. An extraordinarily large share of low-income housing is not sustainable in the long run.
4. Developers have no incentive to participate in this program due to the low returns of building public housing.

Some researchers questioned the base of China's indemnification housing plan of 2011. How did the planner get the target number of 36 million units in five years? What factors did they consider when making the plan? In the long run, what is the target of China's decisions concerning housing from the point of view of the whole society? All these questions should be answered before the publication of the low-income housing plan.

Professor Xinqiao Ping of Peking University argues that low-income housing is segregated from the ordinary housing market and therefore the low-income housing policy cannot be used as a tool to reduce soaring prices in the regular housing market. The regressions he did show that there is no negative relationship between the construction of low-income housing and the housing price increases in the regular housing market, therefore it is not a suitable tool for controlling bubbles in the regular housing market (Ping 2011).

No detailed report about the latest developments in the construction of low-income housing has been published, but it seems the local governments were slow to implement the plan. At the end of 2011, there was evidence that local and provincial officials falsified statistics to overstate the level of affordable housing construction.

In this chapter, I discussed social problems directly correlated to urbanization, most of them correlated to income distribution and housing. The next chapter will deal with more social problems in the process of urbanization, including traffic congestion, environmental pollution and social unrest.

8. Other problems with urbanization

Large cities create tremendous problems as urbanization advances in China. Traffic congestion and environmental pollution are examples of these problems. These problems contribute to the negative utilities of large cities and eventually will determine the limit of the Chinese super-cities.

8.1 TRAFFIC CONGESTION

China's traffic congestion is growing faster than economic growth.

Cars

In the near future, China is going to face serious traffic congestions in all cities. This country is just entering a period of exploding numbers of motor vehicles.

In 2010, a traffic jam stretched more than 100 km for 11 days of total grid-lock, caused by a combination of roadworks and thousands of coal trucks travelling from Inner Mongolia's coalfields to Beijing. The *New York Times* called this event the 'Great Chinese Gridlock of 2010' (Wines 2010). Here gridlock is defined as 'A state of severe road congestion arising when continuous queues of vehicles block an entire network of intersecting streets, bringing traffic in all directions to a complete standstill' (Wikipedia n.d.-c).

Traffic jams are more serious within the cities. It is estimated that 15 Chinese cities lost RMB1 billion each day due to traffic congestion (Huaxia Jingweiwang 2010). The average transit time is more than 40 minutes in Shanghai, Beijing and Guangzhou (China.com 2012). A report asked a researcher, 'Is it really so serious?' The researcher answered, 'Bring a pack of playing cards when you are driving somewhere.' (It will be useful when waiting in the traffic.)

Taxis

Taxis are an alternative to private cars and public transportation. In large Chinese cities, taxi rates are controlled by the municipal governments. The governments set the rate based on political considerations, and have held the rates at a fixed level for many years. The governments consider taxi rates should be sensitive to people's perceptions of their quality of life, and that therefore the rates cannot be raised too often or by too much.

Taxi drivers in big cities, therefore, face low rates, high costs, government regulation, traffic jams and customer complaints. Because they may lose money while waiting in traffic, some of them refuse to drive certain customers to certain places during the rush hour. In fact, given the low rates and bad traffic, the drivers select the customers, not the opposite as is usual. They do not want to pick up old people, suspicious-looking men, or foreigners. A foreign student said that during his first week in Beijing, no taxis stopped for him when he tried to hail one. A young lady approached eight taxis parked at the side of a road during a Friday afternoon in Beijing. The questions and answers were the same: 'Going to downtown?' 'No.' 'Uptown?' 'No.' 'Which direction do you go?' 'Just the east.' There is an expressway in that direction. When the price is fixed too low by the government, the taxi drivers want to go on the expressway, because there are no traffic jams and their operating cost is low.

After waiting for several years, the Beijing municipal government announced on June 5, 2013 that the taxi rates would be raised to RMB2.3 per extra kilometer with a fixed payment of RMB13 for the first 3 km, from RMB2 plus RMB10 for the first 3 km. The government also allowed a small telephone reservation fee. The reservation fees were raised by customers above the threshold set by the government, when demand for reservations was high. The entry regulations to the taxi driver market were not lifted, under which only people holding a Beijing *Hukou* can be hired as taxi drivers by the taxi companies (Xinhua Net 2013).

Safety

'Being a pedestrian in China is extremely dangerous,' said Eileen Finn. 'It seems that most drivers don't care whether the lights are green or red'. According to the World Health Organization, an average of 250 000 people die each year in fatal traffic accidents in China (Finn 2010). This is partially because of the substantial number of new drivers; partially because drivers and pedestrians are not used to following traffic rules; and partially because of the lack of enforcement of the rules.

Policy

The municipal government of Beijing tried to reduce traffic by allowing cars with even and odd numbered license plates to drive only on alternate days during the 2008 Summer Olympics. Afterwards, they relaxed the rule, but cars with two specific last digits on the license plate are not allowed to drive on a given day. In December 2010, the municipal government of Beijing announced a new regulation on car buying. The city would only license 240 000 new vehicles, allocated through a lottery system. This was only about one-third of the new licenses issued in 2010. Ironically, but predictably, the regulation provoked the biggest car-buying spike in the city's history: the number of new cars registered skyrocketed to 30 000 a week before the New Year of 2011 (McCarthy 2010).

The city of Shanghai adopted a different approach: to issue new licenses by auction. The lowest winning bid for a regular set of plates reached RMB75 000 ($12 067) at the first auction of 2013, up RMB6100 from the previous month, according to a report in the *Shanghai Morning Post* (Guo 2013). Beijing did not follow Shanghai because of considerations of equality, since if they used auctions to issue licenses, only rich people would get them.

Urban transportation policy is a hotly debated area within China. According to economic theory, a person will use the road if her willingness to pay for the trip (marginal benefit) exceeds the private cost. Since a car entering traffic creates external costs for other people, a trip's social costs are higher than its private cost. The difference between social cost and private cost is the externality created by the driver. The socially efficient number of vehicles is reached when the marginal social benefit equals the marginal social cost. The simple solution to the congestion problem is to enforce a congestion tax to internalize the externality.

I designed a congestion tax system for Beijing. The system includes all expressways in Beijing. Each car is forced to be equipped with a transponder, which allows sensors along the road to identify a car when it passes. Each road (or each lane) at a certain time has a price, which is determined by its congestion level and the neighboring roads' congestion levels. Different roads have different prices or tax rates. Over time, the relative rates between roads change. The rates are calculated by a system like that used in calculating airplane ticket prices. The prices are publically announced through a radio broadcast and internet system. Faced with the changing congestion taxes, the drivers make their decision concerning whether to drive and on which road they should drive. To reduce the political pressure, the tax could be in a range from negative to positive values so that the government makes zero profit. The driver who drives at midnight on an empty road could get a credit (Zhang 2011). The idea was published in a paper and also sent to the municipal government, but no response has been received so far.

Economists Xiong and Gu (2011) designed a system of tradeable driving permits. Each permit allows a car to drive on the road at a certain time.

The municipal government sets a limit for the total number of cars driving per day and distributes the permits equally to all citizens, driving or not driving. The government set up a market for driving permits and the citizens can trade the permits online. This will let the citizens decide whether to drive or to sell their permits. The total amount of traffic is controlled.

The municipal governments of big cities are hesitant to set a congestion tax, for it may cause dissatisfaction among the masses. They have implemented some alternative measures to reduce the traffic, such as raising central business district parking fees. As congestion becomes more serious, the local government is considering more policy options, including congestion taxes.

8.2 ENVIRONMENTAL POLLUTION

Chinese cities are facing serious environmental problems as urbanization progresses. According to the World Bank, 16 of the world's 20 most polluted cities are in China (Lim 2007). Rapid industrialization has been the number one reason for these problems.

Air and Water Pollution

Air pollution is the most urgent environmental problem in Chinese cities. One-quarter of country's total land area and 600 million people are affected by pollutant haze, according to the National Development and Reform Committee (China News Net 2013).

One important contributor of air pollution is industrialization. Linfen city, Shanxi province, has been the most polluted city in China for several years. A reporter wrote, 'At 7:30 a.m. on Linfen's street, it feels more like the middle of the night because it is still dark and drivers need their headlights on in order to navigate the haze of pollutants.' 'The hospital is one of the busiest places in the city, and the respiratory diseases department is the busiest of all.' 'The air is acrid and sulfurous, making residents' eyes sting and their throats dry and scratchy' (Lim 2007). The source of this air pollution is the low-quality coal that is the mainstay of the local economy. Polluting factories, such as coal-processing factories, coke ovens and power stations, play an important role in Linfen's economic development.

Air pollution is getting more serious recently, even in the capital city Beijing. On January 13, 2013, on a scale of 0 to 500, Beijing's air quality (measured in terms of tiny hazardous pollutant particles in the air, or PM 2.5) hit 'Crazy Bad' at 755. At the same time, choking smog blanketed a large area in north China for most days in January. The smog levels were literally off the charts, threatening the health of city residents (Van Sant 2013). This was the worst air quality recorded since the US Embassy in Beijing began to recording levels in 2008. The US Embassy set up a monitor to measure PM 2.5 particulates as an indication of the air quality in the Embassy compound located in Chaoyang district, Beijing. Anybody can go to the Embassy's website to see the monitor. The monitor was originally intended provide a resource for the US community in Beijing. The monitor was criticized by the Chinese government as being an extra-legal authority monitoring China's environment, and one that is not accurate since it only covers one geographical point (Jiang and Lai 2012). The air quality reported by this monitor was widely talked about among residents in Beijing (US Embassy in Beijing 2013). Recently, the Chinese Ministry of Environmental Protection began to provide its own report of PM 2.5 levels for cities throughout China (Ministry of Environmental Protection 2013). The air quality problem is causing growing anger among Chinese people, especially Internet users. This may make the Chinese leadership consider the future size of the cities.

There are many contributors to the recent choking smog in Beijing. One of them is emissions from coal-fired plants around Beijing. The other is emissions from the 5 million vehicles in Beijing. The government's immediate reaction has been: (1) to close the large factories around Beijing by issuing administration orders; and (2) to reduce car driving in the capital city. One possible approach to realize the second is by allowing cars with even- and odd-numbered license plates to drive on alternate days, which was implemented temporarily during the 2008 Summer Olympics. Now it might become a policy for every working day except the holidays.

Besides air pollution, 90 percent of urban water bodies are severely polluted. Beijing has also become one of the cities in the world with the greatest water shortage. Beijing has a tap water resource of 3.7 billion sq m, and annual per capita water used is less than 200 sq m, one-tenth of China's average and 1/40th of the world average (Tong 2011, p.95). Most of the rivers in China have been polluted. Most large cities in China are facing water shortage and water pollution problems. The water shortage problem is partially due to water use in agriculture in the suburbs of cities, water use in restaurants and hotels, and water used in watering trees along the streets and washing the sidewalks. Provinces and localities fight over taking water from the same river. Thousands of water reservoirs have been built along the Yellow River. The capacity of these reservoirs is just a little bit less than the volume of water in the river; therefore, the river has no water for a large number of days in a year (Tong 2011, p. 111).

Environmental Policy

The Chinese central government has acknowledged the environmental problems and reacted to them. But these policies have not been enough to stop the trend of environmental damage.

China's environmental problem is a problem of the priority of economic growth. All levels of government, central and local, consider growth as more important than the environment. The central government recently realized the urgency of the environmental problem to some degree, and raised the priority of the environment, but still keeps growth in first place. Competition among the local governments is still mostly based on economic growth. All levels of government in China have some incentives to protect the environment under a precondition of satisfactory economic growth. Regulations are issued by the central government, but are actually monitored and enforced by the local governments, which are more interested in economic growth. Heavy industry, one source of pollution and dominated by state-owned enterprises, has many privileges such as access to cheap loans, energy, land and other resources. The implementation of environmental regulations is not strong enough, and the regulation agencies do not have enough power to implement the policies against other much stronger government agencies and state-owned enterprises (SOEs). Non-governmental organizations have trivial influence, but are putting more and more pressure on the government.

In recent years, the Chinese government has tightened environmental regulations, shut down some polluting factories, cancelled some subsidies to polluting industries and promoted clean energy technology. However, many environmental targets were missed and the overall environmental condition has deteriorated. For example, the state-controlled gasoline price is lower than equilibrium and encourages increasing car ownership.

To improve the environment, it is necessary to change the incentives of both central and local governments. It is a process which includes the following steps. First, the environmental problem should be serious enough to push the central (and local) government to raise the priority of environmental protection. Second, the central government needs to change the evaluation measure for the local officials to that based more on the local environment. Third, the local governments must change their incentives, either due to the changes in evaluation measures or because of the competition with other local governments. The non-governmental organizations will play a more influential role in this process.

8.3   SOCIAL UNREST

Social unrest has been increasingly frequent in China in recent years. According to Guangnai Shan, a researcher at the Chinese Academy of Social Sciences, illegal land seizures and relocation, labor disputes, and environmental pollution are the three factors driving popular protests (ChinaFile 2013).

Some of this unrest is related to urbanization. In 2011, the villagers of Wukan, Guangdong province, held mass protests, accusing officials of the village of selling off their land to developers without giving them proper compensation. The land belongs to the collective of the villagers. The villagers suspected that the deal involved corruption. They ousted the existing village committee and elected new leaders. During the event, the provincial leaders exercised restraint and did not use police force. The troubles of Wukan may be repeated in other villages if the farmers' rights to land are not clearly defined and protected (BBC 2013).

In recent years, the slowdown in orders from the developed countries, the tight domestic credit environment, and increasing wage pressures have led to a series of strikes in the factories. In January 2012, steelworkers of Pangang Group Chengdu Steel and Vanadium held a peaceful street march, demanding higher wages. Strikes have been increasingly frequent at privately owned factories, often involving workers demanding higher wages and better working conditions (*The Economist* 2012).

The number of mass protests caused by environmental issues has grown since the beginning of the twenty-first century. In the past few years, popular protests in Ningbo, Shifang and Qingdao were caused by environmental issues. In October 2012, protesters marched to protest the construction of a chemical plant in Ningbo, Zhejiang province. Demonstrations were also seen in Dalian and Xiamen, against paraxylene (PX) plants; the latter was in the form of a mass 'stroll' and prompted the local government to move the project out of the city. In August 2011, a protective dike around the Fujia factory in the Jinzhou industrial complex in Dalian was breached by rain and high waves caused by Typoon Muifa. Tens of thousands of protesters marched on the streets of Dalian to demand a relocation of the plant. The city's party secretary and the mayor promised to move the project out of the city (Watts 2011).

The Internet has played an important role in conveying information about the protests to huge audiences. The official media usually stays silent, to prevent the spreading of unrest. But the growth of the Internet has made it impossible to keep information within a small group of people.

Dealing with the protesters has become an important skill for local government officials. They are restrained by the central government in that they are not allowed to use police force unless the situation is urgent. If a protest cannot be stopped within a short period, local government officials may have trouble in their future political careers. When city officials are faced with environmental protesters, they usually announce a halt to whichever project is being protested about. But the local government may soon resume the project, which causes more protest.

Overall, China's urbanization and its related economic development involve housing bubbles and potential risks. The expansion of built-up areas is driven by government investments, which have grown much more quickly than consumers' income and demand. The political and social problems in the process of urbanization, such as forced demolitions, also have potential risks. All these may slow down China's urbanization process.

To solve the social unrest problem fundamentally, China needs to: (1) change the local government's priority, from emphasizing economic development to achieving balanced growth, making the local government more responsible for the benefits of the local population; (2) develop a local society (such as residents' organizations, unions, and consumer organizations) and rely more on the local society to solve its own problems.

9. The system of the cities

Historically, most of the population and cities in China were geographically concentrated in the eastern area of China. Mr Huanyong Hu drew a line on the maps from Heihe (currently Aihui) of Heilongjiang province in the north-east to Tengchong of Yunnan province in the south-west, and pointed out that most of the Chinese population live to the east of the line. This line is called the 'Hu, Huanyong line' following its creator's name (Figure 9.1). About 36 percent of the land east of the line has fed 96 percent of the population since the Song Dynasty (more than 800 years) (Tong 2011, p.5). Most Chinese cities are also to the east of this line.

9.1 SPATIAL STRUCTURE OF THE CHINESE CITIES

The development of spatial structure has been an important aspect of urbanization in China. The Chinese cities have seen rapid spatial outward growth in the past 20 years. At the same time, these cities undertook internal spatial reorganization.

Hub-and-Spoke System

Using the number of connection points and their potential energy, Gu, Yu, and Li (2008) develop a gravity model method to classify Chinese cities into hub-and-spoke systems.[1] They classify Chinese cities into two systems, the southern and northern systems. The hub of the southern system of the cities is Shanghai, under which are three second-class hubs, Wuhan, Chongqing and Guangzhou. The hub of the northern system is Beijing. The northern system is less developed, with all third-class hubs directly connected to Beijing, except one second-class system of Shenyang–Harbin–Changchun under Beijing.

Based on gravity models, Gu et al. (2008) estimates the special structure of the Chinese city system. Three class township hinterland areas, which indicate the geographical relationship of central cities and their surrounding areas, are calculated. According to this research, in 2003, China had two first-class township hinterland areas, southern and northern systems,

Note: Part of the line was drawn outside China, because China included Mongolia when Hu drew the line in 1935.

Source: Based on Baidu pictures (http://xiangce.baidu.com/).

Figure 9.1   'Hu, Huanyong line'

centered on Shanghai and Beijing, respectively. The southern system included four second-class township hinterland areas: Shanghai, Wuhan, Chongqing and Guangzhou. The northern system had three second-class township hinterland areas: Beijing, Shenyang–Harbin, and Lanzhou–Urumqi. In 2003, 64 third-class township hinterland systems existed in China, 30 of them in the south, and 34 of them in the north (see Table 9.1).

Overall, hinterland areas of the eastern cities are smaller than those

Table 9.1   Chinese city system, 2003

Class I	Class II	Class III
Northern	Beijing	Beijing, Shijiazhuang, Handan, Qingdao, Yantai, Jinan, Jining, Zhengzhou, Luoyang, Sanmenxia, Xian, Taiyuan, Baotou, Hailar.
	Shenyang–Harbin	Shenyang, Jinzhou, Dalian, Dandong, Changchun, Tonghua, Baicheng, Yanji, Harbin, Jixi, Jiamusi, Tsitsihar.
	Lanzhou–Urumqi	Lanzhou, Jiayuguan, Yinchuan, Xining, Urumqi, Aksu.
Southern	Shanghai	Shanghai, Nanjing, Xuzhou, Huainan, Taizhou, Wenzhou, Fuzhou, Xiamen.
	Wuhan	Wuhan, Xiangfan, Changsha, Hengyang, Nanchang, Jingdezhen, Ganzhou.
	Chongqing	Chongqing, Chengdu, Guiyang, Kunming, Lhasa.
	Guangzhou	Guangzhou, Shantou, Zhanjiang, Haikou, Nanning, Liuzhou.

Source: Gu et al. (2008, pp. 36–37).

of the western cities. The relationship of administrative subordination is clearer in the eastern cities than in the western cities. The central cities in the west have not yet formed a complete system including different-sized cities. There are competition relations among many city groups, such as Shijiazhuang–Taiyuan or Changsha–Nanchang.

China's system of cities has been affected heavily by the political system of the cities. A city ranked higher in the administrative system usually has more economic resources and has a higher growth rate. Economic factors have played a more important role in the development of the cities during the economic reform in the past 30 years.

Metropolitan Regions

As single cities grow, the open space between cities shrinks and metropolitan regions appear. These regions usually consist of several interconnected cities and large number of residents.

According to a World Bank report (Leman 2006), there are currently 53 metropolitan regions in China. Twenty-nine percent of the population are living in these metropolitan regions. Fifty-three percent of gross domestic product (GDP) is produced in these regions.[2] The three largest metropolitan regions, those in the Yangtze River delta, the Pearl River delta and the Beijing–Tianjin–Tangshan area, have taken shape. China's population has been moving into the three largest metropolitan regions since the late 1990s. The density of population in these Chinese metropolitan regions is still less than that in Japan's largest metropolitan regions. There is space for further development of these Chinese metropolitan regions.

Three Largest Metropolitan Regions in China

Currently, the Yangtze River delta, Pearl River delta, and Beijing–Tianjin–Tangshan area are the three largest metropolitan regions in China (Table 9.2).

Yangtze River Delta

The Yangtze River delta is a 100 500 sq km area, located at the mouth of the Yangtze River, consisting of Shanghai, eight large cities in Jiangsu

Table 9.2   The three largest metropolitan regions in China, 2010

	Population (year end)		Urban area		Population density	Gross regional product	
	mil	%	sq km	%	per sq km	RMB billion	%
Yangtze River delta	79.09	5.9	100 504	1.0	787	6825	16.9
Pearl River delta	37.85	2.8	56 704	0.6	668	5476	13.6
Beijing–Tianjin–Tangshan area	64.15	4.8	166 653	1.7	385	3619	9.0
China	1340.91	100.0	9 600 000	100.0	140	40 326	100.0

Notes:
Calculated following China Development Research Foundation (2010 p. 89).
Yangtze River delta includes Shanghai, Nanjing, Zhenjiang, Wuxi, Changzhou, Suzhou, Nantong, Yangzhou, Taizhou, Hangzhou, Ningbo, Jiaxing, Huzhou, Shaoxing and Zhoushan.
Pearl River delta includes Hong Kong, Macao, Guangzhou, Shenzhen, Dongguan, Foshan, Zhongshan, Zhuhai, Jiangmen, Huizhou and Zhaoqing.
Beijing–Tianjin–Tangshan area includes Beijing, Tianjin, Tangshan, Langfang, Baoding, Qinhuangdao, Zhangjiakou, Chengde and Cangzhou.
The population in the Pearl River area is less than some other estimates.
China's total population and GDP do not include Hong Kong and Macao.

Sources: National Bureau of Statistics (2011b, pp. 33, 44, 93, 103, 949, 1005).

province, seven large cities in Zhejiang province, and many county-level cities. The area has 5.9 percent of China's population and produces 16.9 percent of China's GDP. The area has developed a system of cities, centered on Shanghai. The cities in the region are expected to develop toward a system with large and small cities in the near future, instead of one with a large number of middle-sized cities.

The Yangtze River delta is one of the most developed areas in China. It produces about one-sixth of the country's GDP. Manufacturing industries have been developed in many cities in this area. The region has attracted a large amount of foreign direct investment, and it is well connected with the outside world via its sea ports. Cities to the west of Shanghai in southern Jiangsu province, such as Suzhou, Wuxi and Changzhou, and cities to the south of Shanghai in Zhejiang province, such as Ningbo, Jiaxing, Taizhou and Wenzhou, and many more small cities and towns, have become international manufacturing centers, selling their products to many countries. Cities around Nanjing, such as Zhenjiang and Yangzhou, have become centers of petrochemical industries.

The cities in the area are connected by high-speed railroads, expressways and river networks. The high-speed railroads have enlarged the city limits of Shanghai to Suzhou and Jiaxing, less than two hours' driving from the center of Shanghai. More than ten cities are developing on both sides of the Yangtze River.

It is estimated that the area will have an urban population of 91 million, and the urbanization ratio will become 72 percent in 2020, with per capita GDP of RMB110000 (China.com 2010). Seventy-four cities will have a population of more than 0.2 million in 2020, including five over 3 million, 34 between 0.5 and 3 million, and 34 between 0.2 and 0.5 million (Gu et al. 2008, p.114).

Pearl River Delta

The Pearl River delta is another developed metropolitan region in China, located at the southern end of Chinese mainland, including Hong Kong, Macao, Guangzhou and many other cities. It has 2.8 percent of population and 13.6 percent of GDP.[3] The population in Pearl River delta is larger than that of the metropolitan area of Tokyo, or of New York. The urbanization ratio reached 70 percent in 2000.

A large number of cities exist in the Pearl River delta, most of them created in the past 30 years. The number of cities increased from four in 1978 to 23 in 2000. The number of designated townships increased from 32 in 1978 to 403 in 2000, and 368 of these townships have a population of more than 10000 (Xu 2000).

The Pearl River delta has seen two kinds of urbanization in the past 30 years: one of them has been led by the government, the other initiated by ordinary people. This was mainly due to local government relaxing control of urban resident registration. The creation of two new cities, Shenzhen and Zhuhai, represents the urbanization led by the government. Shenzhen was a small village near the border between Mainland China and Hong Kong, while Zhuhai was a village near Macao. The government set up the two cities in 1980, with special policy support. The two cities grew quickly, to become large cities today. A large number of people poured into the two cities, partly because it is easy to get urban *Hukou* from the governments.

The second source of urbanization in the Pearl River delta is from the grassroots. A large number of migrant workers moved into the area. The number of temporary residents has increased dramatically since 1985. Currently, 28.7 million temporary residents are in Guangdong province, 96 percent of them living and working in the Pearl River delta and 86 percent in Shenzhen, Guangzhou, Dongguan and Foshan. In Shenzhen, a city with 15 million population, only 2.7 million residents are permanent residents with *Hukou* and the majority are temporary residents. The migrant workers in the area have made great contributions to the economic development in the area (Zhan 2012).

Beijing–Tianjin–Tangshan Area

The region has two super-large cities: Beijing, the capital city of China, and Tianjin. The major cities are concentrated on the Beijing–Langfan–Tianjin corridor, the Qinhuangdao–Tangshan–Tianjin–Canzhou corridor, and the Qinhuangdao–Tangshan–Beijing–Baoding–Shijiazhuang–Xingtai–Handan corridor. The center of the area, the Beijing–Langfang–Tianjin corridor, has experienced rapid growth, which has had an impact on the neighboring regions.

Different from the Yangtze River delta and the Pearl River delta, the Beijing–Tianjin–Tangshan area has large iron, coal and oil reserves. It is well connected with Japan and Korea through ports in Tianjin and Tangshan. Many resource processing and manufacturing industries have concentrated in the area. The area also has a strong human capital base, with large numbers of universities and research institutes in Beijing and Tianjin. Since the area surrounds the capital city, Chinese central government provided large amounts of financial support directly to the area, which is one unique advantage of the area.

The Beijing–Tianjin–Tangshan area is facing serious environmental problems and the scarcity of some natural resources. This includes the scarcity of underground water, which is considered as the bottleneck to further development of the region. Beijing is experiencing severe air pollution; the city is often blanketed in a thick smog or pollutant haze. In January 2013, particulate matter in the air was ten times above the accepted standard. Half of the pollution comes from the industries surrounding Beijing in Hebei province, and half comes from auto traffic in Beijing. Beijing is also facing a serious traffic congestion problem, which is expected to grow as Beijing and Tianjin become a super-city in the near future.

Another problem the area experiences is the administrative coordination between the governments of Beijing and its surrounding areas, most of them in Hebei province. As the capital city of China, Beijing is in a superior position when negotiating with its neighbors.

Some kinds of specialization between Beijing and its surrounding areas have developed in the past decades (Table 9.3). Beijing is more specialized in financing, housing development and services, while the surrounding areas are more specialized in manufacturing. Large numbers of factories have been moved from Beijing to surrounding areas, for example, Shoudu Steel and Iron Company, a large steel and iron complex, has been moved to Tangshan in Hebei province.

The data show that the manufacturing industry is moving out of the region to surrounding areas. Within the region, information and computers, finance, business services, research and technology, education and health sectors are highly concentrated in Beijing.

Table 9.3   Employees in selected sectors, Beijing, Tianjin and Langfang ('000s)

	Beijing		Tianjin		Langfang	
	2005	2010	2005	2010	2005	2010
Manufacturing	1545	1005	777.2	753	46.7	108
Construction	685.2	394	91.2	102	11.3	29
Information and computers	250.1	417	24.3	22	2.4	4
Finance	158	272	51.2	70	9.2	12
Research and technology	316.4	457	53.1	65	4.6	11

Sources: 2005 data are from National Bureau of Statistics (2004–2011b). 2010 data are from National Bureau of Statistics Division of Urban Social Economic Survey (2011, pp. 61–97).

9.2 SCALE STRUCTURE OF THE CHINESE CITIES

Like in other countries, cities of different sizes can be seen in China today. Whether to support the development of large cities, or that of small cities or towns, has been a hot policy debate since the 1950s.

Scale Structure of Chinese Cities

At the end of 2007, China had 140 cities with a population of more than 0.5 million, 232 cities with a population of 0.2–0.5 million, 283 cities with a population of less than 0.2 million, and 19 234 administrative townships (China Development Research Foundation 2010, p.11).

The population pattern of the Chinese cities shows that a large number of people live in the super-big cities, while the population in the middle-sized and small cities is relatively small (Table 9.4). In 2007, 316 million people were living in 655 cities, while 268 million people lived in county-level cities and townships.[4] The share of population living in small cities has reduced dramatically in the past decade (Dingjun 2013b).

The data show that: (1) the middle-sized and small cities are less developed and have more space for further development; (2) the urbanization ratios in different regions have large variations, reducing from the east to the west. Shanghai, Beijing and Tianjin have the highest urbanization ratios, while the western area has a much lower average urbanization ratio. The top ten provinces had an average urbanization ratio of 65 percent, while the bottom ten provinces had an average of 35 percent (China Development Research Foundation 2010, p.12).

Table 9.4   Distribution of cities and their population, China, 2007

Population/City	Cities		Non-agricultural population		
	Number	%	Million	%	Average population per city (million)
> 1 million	58	8.9	148.3	46.9	2.6
0.5–1 million	82	12.5	56.0	17.7	0.7
0.2–0.5 million	232	35.4	74.1	23.5	0.3
< 0.2 million	283	43.2	37.6	11.9	0.1
Total	655	100	316.0	100	0.5

Sources: Ministry of Housing and Construction, Bureau of Planning (2007); China Development Research Foundation (2010, p.120).

Big towns

Almost all cities in China have been developed as an administrative unit in the government bureaucratic structure. Their sizes are constrained by their levels in the bureaucratic structure. Some cities or towns, however, were created mainly by market forces and grew quickly since the start of economic reform in the 1980s. Some of them have become large cities, such as Shenzhen in Guangdong province near Hong Kong (a detailed description of Shenzhen is included in Chapter 6 in this book). Some towns expanded quickly and have a large concentration of people, although they cannot be called 'cities' according to the government's definition.

'The Richest Village in the World' (Baidu Wenku n.d.)

Huaxi village is located in Jiangyin, Jiangsu province. The village had 380 households, 1520 villagers and covered 0.96 sq km. In 2001, Huaxi village merged with other 15 villages, and organized the great Huaxi village, which covers 30 sq km and over 30000 villagers. In 2004, the average salary in the village was RMB122600 per person, compared with the average net income of Chinese farmers of RMB2936, and average disposable income of urban residents of RMB9422. The village is organized like a company. Sales in 2010 were more than RMB50 billion. A 74-floor hotel in the village has just been completed.

Policy debates

There have been hot debates among policymakers and researchers about the future development of the size structure of Chinese cities. The dominant points in the 1980s and early 1990s were regarding developing small cities and towns. It was argued that China should have its own route of urbanization, which should focus on the development of small cities and towns. Some researchers pointed out that the development of large cities should be the target of China's urbanization, because of their scale efficiency (China Development Research Foundation 2010, p. 77).

The Chinese government emphasized the importance of controlling the size of large cities, and set the development of middle-sized and small cities as the target of urbanization in the 1980s and early 1990s. To support this target, the central government adjusted the administrative levels of cities and towns. Many prefectures were changed into prefecture-level cities (*Di Gai Shi*) and many counties were changed into county-level cities (*Xian Gai Shi*). The number of administratively defined cities increased dramatically in the 1980s.

The policy of controlling the size of large cities was not successful in practice. The area and population of large cities have both been increasing since the 1980s, at a speed much faster than that of the middle-sized and

Table 9.5 *Growth of population and area of built-up districts, by the size of cities, 1981–2008*

City population	Total population growth (%)	Growth in area of built-up districts (%)
> 2 million	309	415
1–2 million	268	317
0.5–1 million	276	317
0.2–0.5 million	282	311
< 0.2 million	231	192

Note: China had 225 cities in 1981, 207 of them were comparable in 2008. Other cities were not comparable, because of changes in their administrative district, or data errors.

Source: China Development Research Foundation (2010, p. 78).

small cities. Table 9.5 shows that the population of 32 cities with a population over 2 million in 2008 was three times that of 1981, with a higher growth rate than the other 175 smaller cities.

The top ten super-large cities in the country grew much faster than the average of the Chinese cities, even though they have been under much severe growth control. The population of Shanghai, Beijing, Guangzhou, Chongqing and Tianjin increased by 12 million, 9.7 million, 6.5 million, 6.9 million and 2.9 million, respectively, from 1981 to 2008. The built areas of these super-cities increased by 606 sq km, 376 sq km, 553 sq km, 970 sq km and 289 sq km, respectively, in the same period (China Development Research Foundation 2010, p. 79). This shows the great aggregation economy of the super-cities in China, as when a lot of producers concentrate in an area the efficiency of production increases dramatically.

Small cities and towns have seen some development since 1980s, but not as much as the big cities. The development of small cities and towns was accompanied by the growth in the village and township enterprises and the farmers' markets in rural areas in the late 1970s and the 1980s.

From the economic point of view, the policy focus on small cities and towns is more costly. The development of large and mid-sized cities occupies less space, which is important in China, considering its large population and relatively small land area. The small cities and towns are not able to provide enough jobs.

From the point of view of social development, to develop small cities and towns may be good for development of the society. The small cities and towns may provide a better foundation for the development of a democratic society. The competition among large number of small cities may be good for the stability of China.

Table 9.6   Area of built-up districts, China (sq km)

	Cities	County-level cities	Townships
1881	7438		
1990	12856		8220
2000	22439	13135	18200
2008	36295	14776	30160
2011	43603		

Sources: National Bureau of Statistics (2012a, table 11-5) and China Development Research Foundation (2010, p. 57).

Urban Construction

Since the early 1980s, there has been rapid growth in construction in Chinese cities (Table 9.6). The growth accelerated in the first decade of the twenty-first century. As a result, a large number of low-density cities were created, with decreasing population density. For example, in Beijing–Tianjin New Town, a villa district located between Beijing and Tianjin, it was planned to build 8000 villas in an area equal to 33 Tiananmen Squares. Five years after starting construction, only 1000 villas were built and 90 percent of them were still empty (Tong 2011, p.50). More 'empty cities' and 'sleeping cities' have emerged in China in the past decade.

This increase in built-up districts was largely the result of a city construction campaign led by local governments. In the Chinese political system, a city is a lower administrative level of government. The mayors are appointed by and report to the higher level of administration, and compete with other cities. To demonstrate his achievements, a mayor has the incentive to increase the speed of city construction, and has fewer incentives to provide public goods (education, social security and health care) to the migrants working in the city. Construction is supported by the land sale income of the municipal governments and cheap debt from the state-owned commercial banks.

This city construction campaign led to a decrease in urban population density. From 1981 to 2008, the population density of all sizes of Chinese cities decreased. The built-up area population density decreased from 19000/ sq km in 1981 to 10000/ sq km in 2008. This is mainly because of official statistics underestimating the migrant population (China Development Research Foundation 2010, p.73). A reason for density decrease is low volume rate: the ratio between area of construction and the area actually used. This results in waste of land.

The construction campaign is due to the behavior of local governments.

Under the current public finance system, local governments have no stable financial resources. A large part of local government revenue comes from land-related income, mainly land-selling (leasing) income and land-related tax. This financial system gives local governments the incentive to collect and sell more and more land. Due to their monopolized position in land requisition and the large margin between purchase and selling prices, local governments do not pay much attention to the efficient use of land. Compared with many cities in the world, especially in developing countries, the density of Chinese cities is not very high.

According to a report, the 'National Plan for Healthy Development of Urbanization (2011–2030)' (unpublished as of June 2013; see Li 2013) will define 21 urbanization regions (Dingjun 2013a). There is competition for government permits to create national-level metropolitan regions, which are strictly limited in number by the government. Currently, only the Yangtze River delta, the Pearl River delta and the Beijing–Tianjin–Tangshan region are national-level metropolitan regions. The northeast, Sichuan–Chongqing and Hubei–Jiangxi–Hunan–Anhui regions are making plans for upgrading to national metropolitan regions.

CONCLUSION OF PART I

The first part of this book deals with the domestic aspect of China's urbanization. I have discussed the major elements of the urbanization in China, the *Hukou* system, rural–urban migration, the land and housing market, and local public finance. In the past 30 years, China's urbanization was driven by joint efforts of the central and local governments, who pursued high-speed economic growth; the migrant workers, who want to achieve a better life, like that of urban residents, by working hard; and private and public businesses, who want to earn profits by paying low wages to migrant workers. The expansion of this urbanization triggered tremendous problems and social conflicts, which calls for further progress of economic reform and the completion of the urbanization. Considering all these forces, I believe that this process will continue in the near future. As a result, urbanization in China has had and will have dramatic impacts on the rest of the world, which will be discussed in Part II of this book.

NOTES

1. When distance friction coefficient b = 1, for class one hub cities, the connection number $N^{max} > 25$ or perennial energy $G_i > M + 3S$ and $N^{max} > 10$, where M and S are mean and

standard error, respectively. For class two hub cities, $N^{max} > 15$ or $G_i > M + 2S$ and $N^{max} > 10$. When $b = 2$, all cities with $N^{max} > 2$ are hub cities.

2. The standard of a metropolitan region usually includes the following. The number of large cities in the region is not less than three but not more than 20, with one central city of more than 1 million population. Population in the region is more than 20 million, with no less than 10 million urban population. Per capita GDP in the region is more than $3000. The extent of railroads is more than 250 km/10 000 sq km and road density is more than 2000 km/sq km. Non-agricultural production is more than 70 percent of total production, and non-agricultural workers are more than 60 percent of total workers. There are also many other criteria. (China Development Research Foundation 2010, p.91.)

3. The China Development Research Foundation (2010, p. 89) estimated a higher regional population for 2006.

4. According to the China Development Research Foundation (2010), the two numbers cannot add up to 600 million population in cities. The detailed number comes from a different source (Ministry of Housing and Urban and Rural Construction 2007). The total is from the National Bureau of Statistics. The difference between the two numbers is possibly because the China Urban and Construction Yearbook did not include the new residents living in the cities for more than six months.

PART II

China's impact on the world market

Hundreds of millions of people are moving into the huge urban area in China's eastern coastal area, which raises the price of land, labor, housing and all consumer goods. In turn, in response to the high price of land, sky-scrapers are being built in the city centers. What does this mean for the rest of the world? How will China's urbanization affect the rest of the world? To analyze China's impacts on the world economy, I am going to provide a rough estimate of the Chinese economy up to 2030.

10. Overall estimates and assumptions

China's impact on the world economy depends on the development within China. Further progress in China's urbanization depends on fundamental political, economic and social reforms. Given the current openness of the Chinese economy, China's urbanization is also affected by the situation of the world economy.

10.1 BASIC ASSUMPTIONS

To evaluate China's advance in urbanization, it is necessary to make some basic assumptions. In my baseline forecast, I assume: (1) the Chinese leadership will make some fundamental social-economic reforms, such as the reform of the *Hukou* system, the reform of the central, provincial and local government revenue and taxation system, and the opening-up of the capital market in the next decade; (2) after the global financial crisis and the European debt crisis, the world economy will return to its long-term growth path. Even though I expect that China will make some fundamental reforms, I believe that after reform China will still be a society with unequal distribution of political power and economic wealth. This will have some impact on the size and structure of the future Chinese market.

Economic development has been a main and fundamental task of every generation of the Chinese leadership since Xiaoping Deng, secondary to the stability of the current political system. In the past decade, China's reform has stagnated, mainly due to the task of maintaining political and social stability. To maintain economic growth, the new generation of the leadership, who took power at the end of 2012, needs to carry out some reforms. It is quite possible that they will choose a controllable social-economic reform instead of a radical political reform.

There is another possibility that China's economic and political reform will continue to be stagnant in the next decade due to the resistance of the influential vested-interest groups. An economic crisis is possible in the short and medium term due to the bubble created during the period of rapid growth. Under this situation, China's urbanization will stay at its present level. This situation is possible, but not as possible as my baseline assumptions. Therefore, in the long run I still expect steady economic growth in China, with a lower growth rate than in the past 30 years.

Under these baseline assumptions, the future changes will be concentrated in the following fields. Firstly, China's urbanization will affect the world commodity market. China's long-term appetite for commodities of all kinds will be sustained by its massive transportation, housing and infrastructure projects during the process of government-led urbanization. This demand can be divided into two parts, the demand for raw materials and capital goods, and the demand for consumer goods. For the raw materials and capital goods, the effects have been seen in the past ten years. For consumer goods, the effects have not been significant so far and it will be crucial for China to create a consumer market in the near future, which depends on the progress of urbanization. China's urbanization will change the direction of the world commodity flow through its huge exports and imports. As President Xi Jinping said, China will import 10 trillion goods and services from the rest of the world in the next five years (Xi 2013).

Secondly, China's urbanization will alter the production factor allocation in the world economy. Foreign capital will flow into China to invest in domestic market-oriented firms. This is quite different from the pattern of foreign investment in China in the past 30 years, which has been focused on China's export-oriented sector, especially the processing manufacturing and trade sectors, targeting the world market. More foreign labor may flow into China due to the attraction of the domestic market and increasing wages, and more foreign labor will work for the Chinese market from abroad.

Thirdly, China's macroeconomic situation will affect the world economy. China's macroeconomic fluctuations will affect the booms and recessions of other countries in the world. China may export inflation to the world when China's super-cities raise domestic price levels. This is also significantly opposite to the deflation effect exported by China during the past 30 years.

When all these happen in China, the world may look different. Although the following chapters will discuss China's exports and imports, I will focus on the impacts of China's domestic demand on the world economy in Part II of the book.

10.2 AN OVERALL FORECAST OF THE CHINESE ECONOMY

An overall growth model of the Chinese economy with urbanization will be presented in this section. I use annual data of gross domestic product

(GDP), labor input and capital formation to estimate migration, urban production and rural production, respectively.

The theoretical framework includes three equations: (1) a rural–urban migration equation; (2) an urban production function; and (3) a rural production growth forecast function. In the rural–urban migration equation, the dependent variable is the logarithm of the urbanization ratio divided by one minus the urbanization ratio, which is estimated by the difference between urban disposable income and rural net income, urban unemployment rate and dummy variables for migration policy changes. The urban production function models urban real GDP as a function of urban labor input, urban real capital stock and dummies for economic reform in the urban area in different periods. The rural production function uses a simple growth rate to estimate rural GDP. In this model, urban GDP growth is partially determined by labor inputs growth, which is affected by the scale of migration. The scale of migration is determined by the difference between urban disposable income and rural net income, the urban unemployment rate and the reform of the policy.

One crucial parameter of the model for explaining rural–urban migration is the rural–urban income differences. The gap has been large for the past three decades; the average growth rate of income was 7.6 percent in urban areas and 7 percent in rural areas from 1978 to 2011, and 9.3 percent and 7.8 percent 2000 to 2011. The gap slightly narrowed in 2010 and 2011, when the rural income growth rate reached over 10 percent and exceeded the urban growth rate. Based on recent evidence, I assume that rural real net income will grow 10 percent annually from 2013 to 2015 and then reduce gradually to 7.5 percent by 2030, while the urban real disposable income will grow 7 percent from 2013 to 2015 and then gradually reduce to 5 percent by 2030. This leads to an estimated migration of over 10 million annually before 2019, reducing to below 8 million in 2030, in my baseline estimate. This estimated migrant labor is added to the urban labor force, after considering the natural growth of the urban labor force. Total labor input, real capital stock and total factor productivity (TFP) determine the urban real output. I assume that capital stock increases 18 percent before 2020 and 15 percent in 2021–2030, and TFP increases 0.8 percent before 2020 and 0.5 percent in 2021–2030 in urban areas in my baseline analysis. The resulting real urban GDP is estimated to grow to near or more than 7 percent before 2020, and will gradually reduce to 5.1 percent in 2030 (Table 10.1).

Using GDP and its components data, I calculated the size of the Chinese domestic market (Table 10.2).

Table 10.2 shows a large increase of China's share in the world market from 3.9 percent in 2005 to 10.1 percent in 2011. Many structural changes

Table 10.1 Estimated migration, urbanization rate and urban real GDP growth, China, 2013–2030 (baseline estimate)

Year	Migration (million)	Urbanization rate (%)	Urban real GDP growth (%)
2013	11.9	53	7.6
2014	11.9	54	7.6
2015	11.8	55	7.5
2016	11.4	56	7.3
2017	10.9	57	7.2
2018	10.4	58	7.1
2019	9.9	58	6.9
2020	9.4	59	6.8
2021	9.1	60	5.4
2022	8.8	60	5.4
2023	8.5	61	5.3
2024	8.3	61	5.2
2025	8.0	62	5.2
2026	7.9	63	5.1
2027	7.9	63	5.1
2028	7.9	64	5.1
2029	7.9	64	5.1
2030	7.8	65	5.1

Table 10.2 The size and composition of the Chinese domestic market

	1978	2005	2011
GDP (RMB trillion)	0.36	18.74	46.57
Consumption	62.1%	53.0%	49.1%
Household consumption	78.6%	73.4%	72.2%
Rural	62.1%	27.4%	22.7%
Urban	37.9%	72.6%	77.3%
Government consumption	21.4%	26.6%	27.8%
Gross capital formation	38.2%	41.5%	48.3%
Net export	–0.3%	5.4%	2.6%
GDP ($ trillion)		2.29	7.21
Market ($ trillion)		2.16	7.02
% of the world market		3.9%	10.1%

Note: The market size equals expenditure approach GDP subtracts net exports.

Source: Based on National Bureau of Statistics (2012a, 2009a).

can be seen in the table. The share of consumption reduced from 62.1 percent in 1978 to 49.1 percent in 2011, while capital formation increased from 38.2 percent in 1978 to 48.3 percent in 2011. Within consumption, the share of households went down while that of government rose. Within household consumption, the share of urban consumption increased from 37.9 percent in 1978 to 77.3 percent in 2011, while the rural share reduced from 62.1 percent to only 22.7 percent. All these reflect the dramatic changes in demand structure in the past three decades in China.

China's domestic market is large, in terms of its size, and has space for future development. To some extent, the consumer part of China's domestic market is less developed and provides more opportunities for the future.

APPENDIX 10: A MODEL OF CHINA'S URBANIZATION AND GROWTH

Three equations are included in the theoretical framework: (1) a rural–urban migration equation; (2) an urban production function; and (3) a rural production growth function. The coefficients are estimated using annual data from 1978 to 2011.

In the rural–urban migration equation, the dependent variable is the logarithm of the urbanization ratio minus the natural growth of urban population, divided by one minus the difference of urbanization ratio and natural growth rate, which is estimated by the difference between urban disposable income and rural net income, urban unemployment rate, and dummies for migration policies in different periods:

$$\log\left(\frac{u-n}{1-(n-n)}\right) = -4.99 + 0.53(I_u - I_r) - 0.18E - 0.06D_1 + 0.17D_2$$

where u = urbanization ratio, n = natural growth of urban population, I_u = urban real disposable income (2011 price), I_r = rural real net income (2011 price), E = urban unemployment rate, D = dummies for resident registration reforms. When calculating the urbanization ratio, the urban population includes migrants to cities staying for more than six months, with or without *Hukou*. This equation inherently restricts u – n to a zero–one interval.[1]

The urban production function models urban real GDP as a function of urban labor input, urban real capital stock, and dummies for economic reform in different periods:

$$\log(Y) = 2.11 + 0.14K + 0.79L + 0.19D_3 + 0.42D_4$$

where Y = urban real GDP at 2011 prices, K = urban real capital stock in 2011 price, L = urban labor input (equals previous year's labor input times natural growth plus migrants), D_3 and D_4 are dummies for urban reform in different periods.

The rural production function model is a simple model using the growth rate to estimate rural real GDP at 2011 prices.

In this framework, urban GDP growth is determined by labor inputs growth, which is affected by the scale of migrations. The scale of migration is determined by the difference between urban disposable income and rural net income, urban unemployment rate, and residential registration policy changes.

Table 10A.1   Assumptions of key parameters, growth rate (%)

Year	Urban real disposable income (%)	Rural real income (%)	Urban real capital (%)	Urban TFP (%)	Urban labor natural growth (%)	Rural GDP (%)
2013	7.0	10.0	18.0	0.8	0.5	6.0
2014	7.0	10.0	18.0	0. 8	0.5	6.0
2015	7.0	10.0	18.0	0.8	0.5	6.0
2016	6.8	9.8	18.0	0.8	0.5	6.0
2017	6.5	9.6	18.0	0.8	0.5	6.0
2018	6.3	9.4	18.0	0.8	0.5	6.0
2019	6.0	9.2	18.0	0.8	0.5	6.0
2020	5.8	9.0	18.0	0.8	0.5	6.0
2021	5.6	8.8	15.0	0.5	0.5	5.0
2022	5.5	8.5	15.0	0.5	0.5	5.0
2023	5.3	8.3	15.0	0.5	0.5	5.0
2024	5.2	8.0	15.0	0.5	0.5	5.0
2025	5.0	7.8	15.0	0.5	0.5	5.0
2026	5.0	7.5	15.0	0.5	0.5	5.0
2027	5.0	7.3	15.0	0.5	0.5	5.0
2028	5.0	7.0	15.0	0.5	0.5	5.0
2029	5.0	6.8	15.0	0.5	0.5	5.0
2030	5.0	6.5	15.0	0.5	0.5	5.0

Table 10A.1 shows some assumptions of the key parameters. I assume that rural real net income grows faster than urban real disposable income, which is consistent with the actual data in 2010 and 2011. The real capital growth rates are assumed to be 18 percent before 2020, and 15 percent in 2020–2030. The actual real capital growth rates have been more than 18 percent from 2006 to 2011. I also assume an urban TFP (total factor productivity) grow at 0.8 percent before 2020 and 0.5 percent 2021–2030. I assume that urban labor grows at 0.5 percent annually without including migrants, based on the natural growth rate of urban population.[2] Considering the actual rural GDP growth rate (growth of the primary industry) of 7.4 percent 1978–2011, I assume rural GDP grow 6 percent before 2020 and 5 percent from 2021 to 2030.

Table 10A.2 presents my lower-bound and upper-bound forecasts of number of migrants, urbanization rate, and urban real GDP growth from 2013 to 2030. The lower-bound estimates assumes that urban real income grows at 5 percent 2013–2015 and gradually reduces to 3 percent 2015–2030. The upper-bound estimate assumes that urban real income grows at 10 percent 2013–2020 and gradually reduces to 8.5 percent 2023–2030; rural real income grows at 8 percent 2013–2020 and gradually reduces

Table 10A.2   Comparison of baseline, lower-bound and upper-bound estimates

Year	Migration (millions)			Urbanization rate (%)			Urban real GDP growth (%)		
	Low	Baseline	High	Low	Baseline	High	Low	Baseline	High
2013	8.37	11.9	17.17	53	53	54	6.8	7.6	8.7
2014	8.35	11.9	17.12	54	54	55	6.7	7.6	8.5
2015	8.33	11.8	17.02	54	55	56	6.7	7.5	8.4
2016	8.13	11.4	16.89	55	56	58	6.7	7.3	8.2
2017	7.92	10.9	16.73	56	57	59	6.6	7.2	8.1
2018	7.36	10.4	16.54	56	58	60	6.5	7.1	8.0
2019	6.79	9.9	16.34	57	58	61	6.4	6.9	7.8
2020	6.23	9.4	16.13	57	59	62	6.2	6.8	7.7
2021	5.67	9.1	15.15	57	60	63	4.5	5.4	7.4
2022	5.30	8.8	14.19	58	60	64	4.5	5.4	7.2
2023	4.92	8.5	13.24	58	61	65	4.4	5.3	7.0
2024	4.72	8.3	13.05	59	61	66	4.3	5.2	6.9
2025	4.53	8.0	12.85	59	62	67	4.3	5.2	6.9
2026	4.53	7.9	12.65	59	63	68	4.3	5.1	6.8
2027	4.50	7.9	12.45	60	63	69	4.3	5.1	6.8
2028	4.46	7.9	12.24	60	64	70	4.3	5.1	6.7
2029	4.42	7.9	12.02	60	64	71	4.3	5.1	6.7
2030	4.38	7.8	11.80	60	65	72	4.3	5.1	6.7

to 6.5 percent 2023–2030; urban capital increases 14 percent 2021–2030; urban TFP grows at 0.9 percent 2021–2030. All other assumptions are the same as the baseline estimates.

NOTES

1. A single linear model with urbanization rate on the left of the equation may result in a negative urbanization rate, which is not a satisfied result.
2. According to the Sixth Population Survey in 2010, China's population was 1.34 billion, while the natural growth rate of the population was 0.479 percent (National Bureau of Statistics 2012a, table 3-2). According to some estimates, China's population growth will be negative in 2018 (Yi, F. 2012).

11. Raw materials and capital goods

China's urbanization has created a huge demand for raw materials and capital goods. This demand has been largely due to government-led urbanization, in which the local governments played an important role. The campaign of city construction needs steel, cement, glass and much more. China's imports of base metals have been increasing dramatically since 2000 and China has become the world's largest raw material consumer. China's demand for raw materials is reshaping world commodity markets. Roughly estimated, China consumes 25 percent of the world's steel, 40 percent of the world's cement, and 35 percent of the world's coal (Tong 2011, p.109). The total value of imports increased dramatically from 1990 to 2011, for both primary goods and manufactured goods, as shown in Figure 11.1.

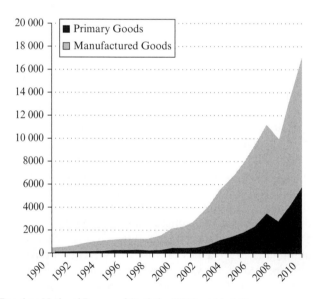

Source: Based on National Bureau of Statistics (2012a, table 6-5).

Figure 11.1 Import value by category of commodities, China (USD 100 million)

China's urbanization and the world economy

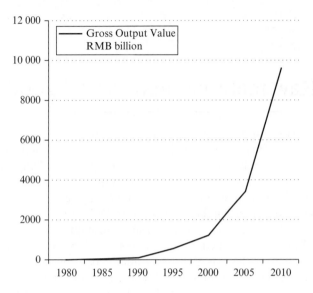

Source: Based on National Bureau of Statistics (2012a, table 15-1).

Figure 11.2   Output value of construction enterprises, China (RMB billion)

Andy Home of Reuters told a story of a seagoing traffic jam in 2004 in Newcastle, Australia. Thirty-four freight ships sat anchored, waiting their turn to load coal for power plants in China. They waited for at least two weeks. At its worst in March that year, the queue stretched to 56 ships. Local people drove to a lookout point for amusement, counting the ships marooned off their shores (Home 2012).

The extremely large scale of construction in Chinese cities has been going on for almost 20 years. The gross output value of construction enterprises increased significantly since 2000, in terms of renminbi (see Figure 11.2). The construction of housing and infrastructure – for example, highways – has created a great demand for concrete and steel tubing. Aluminum, steel, wood and glass are needed for tens of millions of new windows and doors. Copper, aluminum and plastics are used in air conditioners, which are installed in every unit of a new apartment building.

The construction of Chinese cities in the past 20 or so years has been led by the central and local governments, especially by the latter. After the economic reform, the governments kept most of the power that they had during the planned period. At the same time, huge revenues came into the pockets of the governments as a result of economic reform and development. This has been through an unequal distribution system, over which ordinary people have little influence. The local governments have played a major role in the process of rebuilding cities. Their incentives partially come from the promotion-based evaluation system of the centralized bureaucratic system. The rebuilding of cities in China during the first ten years of the twenty-first century has been carried out at a scale never before seen in the modern world's history, which has created a huge demand for energy and raw materials from all over the world. This demand will continue to exist in the near future, though probably at reduced growth rates.

11.1 ENERGY

To keep its fast economic growth and urbanization, China needs a large amount of energy. China has become the largest energy consumer in the world (EIA 2012). China's energy consumption and imports have been increasing dramatically since its first wave of urbanization a decade ago. After a short spell of reduction in growth around 2012 and 2013, China's energy demand will continue to increase in the second decade of the twenty-first century, by my baseline estimate. In the long run, the growth rate will slow down, and reach its maximum level in certain fields.

Although China as a whole has abundant energy resources, China's energy resources per capita are small, and there is a geographical mismatch between the location of the energy fields in the north and west and the industrial centers in the east.

Currently, China is the second-largest oil consumer in the world, behind the US. China's total energy consumption increased from 571.4 million tons of SCE[1] in 1978 to 3.249 billion tons of SCE in 2010, while domestic production increased from 627.7 million tons of SCE in 1978 to 2.97 billion tons of SCE in 2011. A major change is that the consumption has surpassed domestic production during this period (Figure 11.3).

China's energy consumption and production include three major types: coal, crude oil and natural gas, and electric power. Coal is still the main energy source in China, but consumption of crude oil has increased much faster, due to the popular use of automobiles in the past ten years in China. Electricity, a secondary product of coal or crude oil, is widely used in China for industrial production and household consumption. Electricity consumption in China has been considered by some economists and officials, including Premier Li Keqiang, as a more reliable indicator of the national economy than gross domestic product (GDP).

Table 11.1 shows some important trends in energy production and consumption in China. Firstly, the total energy production and consumption

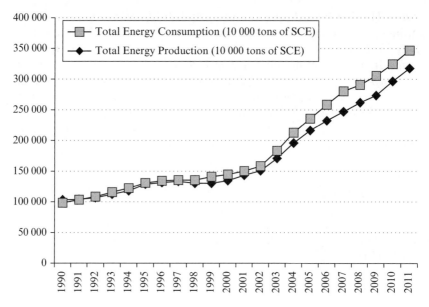

Source: National Bureau of Statistics (2012a, tables 7-1, 7-2).

Figure 11.3   Energy consumption and domestic production, China

increased dramatically from 1978 to 2010, although it was slower than the
growth of GDP during this period. Secondly, the composition of energy
consumption did not change very much during the same period, while
the share of coal production rose and the share of crude oil production
dropped from over 20 percent to less than 10 percent. This gap has been
filled by imports.

China's energy industry has been experiencing a series of economic
reforms since the 1980s. The core area of the reform is that of the pricing
system, which has made great progress but is still far from complete.
Currently, the prices of coal are basically market-determined, but the
prices of electricity and oil are still under the control of the government.
The reform contributed greatly to the development of China's energy
industry, while the unfinished reform has become a major obstacle for the
further development of the industry.

In the planned period, energy prices were completely controlled by the
government. At the early stage of the economic reform, a dual-pricing
system was adopted, under which both the planning price and the market
price co-existed for each energy product. Firms which had met the planned
production quotas could sell any extra products they produced, on the

Table 11.1   Production and consumption of energy and its composition, China

Total consumption of energy and its composition

Year	Total energy consumption (10 000 tons of SCE)	As % of total			
		Coal	Crude oil	Natural gas	Hydro-power, nuclear power, and wind power
1978	57 144	70.7	22.7	3.2	3.4
1990	98 703	76.2	16.6	2.1	5.1
2000	145 531	69.2	22.2	2.2	6.4
2010	324 939	68	19	4.4	8.6
Annual growth	5.6%				

Total production of energy and its composition

Year	Total energy production (10 000 tons of SCE)	As % of total			
		Coal	Crude oil	Natural gas	Hydro-power, nuclear power, and wind power
1978	62 770	70.3	23.7	2.9	3.1
1990	103 922	74.2	19	2	4.8
2000	135 048	73.2	17.2	2.7	6.9
2010	296 916	76.5	9.8	4.3	9.4
Annual growth	5.0%				

Source: National Bureau of Statistics (2011a, tables 7-1, 7-2).

open market. The system gave firms the incentive to improve their management, but also caused speculation. The government relaxed the price controls for large coal mines in 1993 and relaxed all of the coal price controls in 1994, except that of the coal for electricity power production. Coal mines were allowed to set their own prices. The State Council ended the dual-pricing system for oil in 1994 and linked domestic oil price setting to international oil prices. The crude oil prices were set every month by nominated large oil companies, while retail gas prices were controlled by the government. The wholesale price for electricity was also deregulated, while the retail price of electricity was still controlled by the government. Overall, the upstream part of the energy sector has been deregulated, while downstream prices are still controlled by the government, for consumer protection. The marketization of the energy industry is lagging behind the average level of marketization in the entire economy.

The downstream part of the oil production industry has been open to foreign investors since the 1990s. A number of oil refineries have been built by multinational companies in the eastern coastal area. A significant proportion of investments in oil processing sectors have been foreign investments. However, the opening-up of the oil and electricity sectors is still only partial; some key areas are not open to foreign investment. For example, electricity transportation is not open to foreign investment. Foreign investments in oil exploration and finished oil, wholesale and retail, are still restricted by scale restrictions. The scale of domestic private investment is very low in oil exploration and electricity, mainly due to the scale limitation of the domestic private investors (Table 11.2).

Table 11.2   Foreign and domestic private economy in energy industry (2005, %)

	Foreign investment		Domestic private investment	
	Value of industrial output	Value of assets	Value of industrial output	Value of assets
Coal, mining and washing	1	1	10	5
Extraction of petroleum and natural gas	9	3	0	0
Processing of petroleum	12	12	14	11
Production and supply of electric power and heat power	14	11	1	1
Production and supply of gas (for heating)	23	21	3	1
Industry total	28	26	28	16

Source: Research Institute for Industrial Economy (2008, p. 213).

Crude Oil

According to Xinan Zhang, a deputy director of the Global Resources Research and Development Experimental Center of the Ministry of Land and Resources, China's proven geological reserves of oil were 24.8 billion tons, and its proven recoverable oil reserves were 6.8 billion tons in 2004, of which 4.3 billion tons have been recovered, leaving 2.5 billion tons avail-

Table 11.3   Petroleum balance sheet, China (10 000 tons)

	1990	2000	2010	2010/1990 (%)	Annual increase (%)
Total energy available for consumption	11 435	22 631.8	44 178.4	286	7.0
Output	13 830.6	16 300	20 301.4	47	1.9
Imports	755.6	9748.5	29 437.2	3796	20.1
Exports (-)	3110.4	2172.1	4079	31	1.4
Stock changes in the year	−40.8	−1244.6	−1481.2	3530	19.7
Total energy consumption	11 485.6	22 495.9	43 245.2	277	6.9
Consumption by usage					
End-use Consumption	9305	19 950	40 394	334	7.6
Industry	5180	8860	14 758	185	5.4
Intermediate consumption (consumed in conversion)	1630	2353	2657	63	2.5
Power generation	1234	1178	459	−63	−4.8
Heating	356	427	593	66	2.6
Gas production	40	26	0	−100	−100.0
Losses in petroleum refining	296	722	1605	443	8.8
Other losses	255	193	194	−24	−1.3
Balance	−51	136	933	−1944	

Source: Based on National Bureau of Statistics (2012a, table 7-4).

able for extraction (Xinhua Net 2005). In 2010, China's proven reserves available for extraction were 2 billion tons (China Industry Map Editing Committee 2012, p.9). The Statistical Yearbook, edited by the National Bureau of Statistics, shows that the confirmed reserves of petroleum were 3.2 billion tons in 2011 (National Bureau of Statistics 2012a, table 12-4).

Currently, China is the world's second-largest consumer of oil only behind the United States (EIA 2012). According to the official data, petroleum consumption in China increased from 114.9 million tons in 1990 to 441.8 million tons in 2010; that is, by 286 percent during this period, and growing 7 percent annually (Table 11.3). The domestic output grew from 138.3 million tons in 1990 to 203.0 million tons in 2010, with an annual growth rate of 1.9 percent, much lower than that of the annual GDP. To fill the gap, imports of crude oil increased from 7.6 million tons in 1990 to 294 million tons in 2010. Imports of crude oil increased by 38 times during the period with an annual growth rate of 20.1 percent, much higher than the growth rate of GDP (National Bureau of Statistics 2012a, table 7-4). In

2010, China was the second-largest net importer of oil in the world (EIA 2012).

The industrial sector's share of petroleum consumption decreased from 63.7 percent in 1990 to 40.3 percent in 2010, but still ranked first in 2010. The share of transport, storage and post increased from 14.7 percent to 34.4 percent, and ranked second in 2010. Non-production consumption of petroleum, including petroleum used by private automobiles, grew from 2.5 percent to 8 percent and ranked third in 2010. The changes in the last two sectors reflect the fact that the growth in Chinese crude oil consumption was mainly because of a large-scale transition away from bicycles and mass transit toward private automobiles. Before 1978, no consumers had private cars in China; almost all demand for cars came from the government or state-owned enterprises (SOEs). Private cars have become more affordable for ordinary urban residents since China's admission to the World Trade Organization in 2001.

China's petroleum production and imports are controlled by the central government. The regulatory agency and policy-making framework are highly centralized. Priority is placed on industrial demand. Crude oil production and wholesale trading are dominated by two giant SOEs, Chinese National Petroleum Corp. (CNPC) and Sino Petroleum Corp. (Sinopec), which control 80 percent or more of the domestic petroleum market. The government delegates import rights to five large SOEs; other companies have to compete for the small portion of import rights remaining. The National Development and Reform Commission (NDRC) sets the petroleum price for the domestic retail market. The slow price adjustment by the NDRC results in lags in domestic prices compared to the world price.

China's rapid increase in demand for crude oil enlarged its share in world crude oil demand significantly, from 2.9 percent in 1980, 3.6 percent in 1990, and 6.2 percent in 2000, to 10.8 percent in 2010 (Figure 11.4). During the same period, the share of the US decreased from 28.5 percent to 22.1 percent (calculated using data retrieved from Index Mundi).

Saudi Arabia provided 20.5 percent of China's imported crude oil in 2010, and ranked first among China's top oil providers. Other top providers include Angola (15.8 percent), Iran (11.4 percent), Russia (7.5 percent) and Sudan (6 percent) (International Trade @ Suite 101 n.d.).

According to the CNPC Petroleum Economics and Technology Research Center, China's petroleum demand and consumption are estimated to be 483 million tons and 455 million tons in 2011, respectively. The demand is estimated to increase by 6.4 percent in 2011. The actual crude oil imports were 252 million tons in 2011. The petroleum demand is estimated to grow at an annual rate of 4 percent 2011–2015. The crude oil

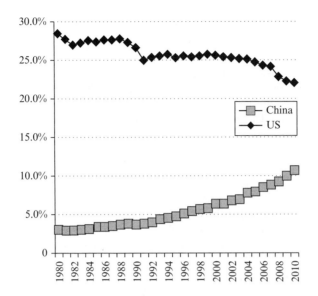

Source: Index Mundi (n.d.).

Figure 11.4 Shares of the world crude oil demand, US and China

imports will increase to over 60 percent of the total supply in 2015 (Zhao 2011).

China's demand and consumption for crude oil affects the forecasts of the world demand and consumption. In June 2011, the International Energy Agency (IEA) raised its forecast for global crude oil demand annual growth to 1.3 percent from 2012 to 2016 on the basis of economic expansion in China. World consumption will increase to 95.3 million barrels a day, with China accounting for about 41 percent of the gain (Nguyen and Smith 2011).

My baseline forecasts assume that China's demand for crude oil will increase by 5 percent annually before 2020 and 4 percent annually from 2020–2030. By 2030, China's demand will be more than 22 million barrels per day, 20 percent of the total world demand, assuming a 1.3 percent annual growth of the world demand. My estimation shows that without major technical innovation and with no significant change in domestic production, China's petroleum imports will be more than 70 percent of supply in 2030.

The Chinese government's energy policy and environmental policy may change the forecasts of China's petroleum demand and consumption. The downturn of the Chinese economy in 2012 and 2013 may reduce China's demand for crude oil in the short term. The change in demand for crude oil in China is a factor affecting the world crude oil price. The forecasts also depend on the economic reform of large SOEs in the oil industry in the near future.

Besides petroleum, natural gas accounted for 2.9 percent of China's energy production in 1978 and 4.3 percent in 2011. The share in energy consumption of natural gas increased from 3.2 percent in 1978 to 5 percent in 2011 (National Bureau of Statistics 2012a, tables 7-1, 7-2).

Coal

China is the largest consumer of coal in the world and its coal mining industry is the world's largest. According to China's National Bureau of Statistics (2012a, p.409), the confirmed reserves of coal were 216 billion tons in 2011 (National Bureau of Statistics 2012a, table 12-4), 13 percent of the world's proven reserves and the third-largest in the world behind the US and Russia (China Industry Map Editing Committee 2012, p.6). Most of the reserves are located in north and north-west China, especially Shanxi province and Inner Mongolia. At current levels of output, China has 48 years of reserves (BP 2008).

Coal has been the major energy source in China since the 1950s or earlier. China's demand for coal continues to increase. China produced 3.24 billion tons of coal and consumed 3.12 billion tons of coal in 2010 (Table 11.4). The share of coal in total energy production increased from 70.3 percent in 1978 to 77.8 percent in 2011. The share of coal in total energy consumption decreased by 2 percentage points from 70.7 percent in 1978 to 68.4 percent in 2011.

China is the largest coal producer in the world, and 5.2 million people worked in the coal mining industry in 2011 (National Bureau of Statistics 2012a, table14-2). About 80 percent of China's mines were unregulated. China's coal production increased from 1.08 billion tons in 1990 to 3.24 billion tons in 2010; that is, by three times over the period. While imports remain a small portion of the total supply, imports recently surpassed exports. Shanxi Coking Coal Group is China's largest metallurgical coal producer, while Haerwusu in Inner Mongolia is China's largest open-pit coal mine. Transportation of coal from the north-west to seaports on China's coast has overloaded the highways in north China. The coal trucks cause traffic congestion; sometimes travelers have to wait for days to pass through the area between the main coal mines and seaports.

Compared to that in the crude oil sector, the economic reform in coal mining has been advanced and successful, at least in the beginning stage of the economic reform. The industry relaxed its market entry restrictions and allowed non-state-owned companies enter the market in the early stage

Table 11.4   Coal balance sheet, China (10000 tons)

Item	1990	2000	2010
Total energy available for consumption	102221.1	136794.5	319772
Output	107988.3	138418.5	323500
Imports	200.3	217.9	16309.5
Exports (-)	1729	5506.5	1910.4
Stock changes in the year	−4238.5	3664.7	−8127.2
Total energy consumption	105523	141091.7	312236.5
Consumption by sector			
Agriculture, forestry, animal husbandry and water conservancy	2095.2	933.4	1711.1
Industry	81090.9	127806.7	296031.6
Construction	437.6	536.8	718.9
Transport, storage and post	2160.9	882.2	639.2
Wholesale and retail trades, hotels and catering services	1058.3	1314.6	1969.9
Other sectors	1980.4	1161	2006.6
Household consumption	16699.7	8457	9159.2
Consumption by usage			
End-use Consumption	60205.9	55913.1	84350.9
Industry	35773.8	42628	68146.1
Intermediate consumption (consumed in conversion)	41257.8	85178.6	227885.6
Power generation	27204.3	55811.2	154542.5
Heating	2995.5	8794.1	15253.1
Petroleum refineries and coal-to-liquids			213.4
Coking	10697.6	16496.4	47150.4
Gas production	360.4	960	1040.1
Loss in coal washing and dressing	4059.3	3191.2	9484.6
Balance	−3302	−4297.2	17535.5

Source: National Burea of Statistics (2011a, table 7-5).

of China's economic reform. The state's control was relaxed and a large number of private companies have entered the coal production sector. Non-state-owned firms produced half of the coal output in the mid-1990s. The infrastructural investment also comes from multiple sources. The infrastructural investment increased from RMB6.1 million in 1985 to RMB181 million in 1996, while the share of the state's investment reduced from 61 percent to 19 percent. The diversification in investment resulted in diversification of the ownership structure in the coal industry, which was one of the driving forces for the rapid increase in coal production.

After the entry of a large number of small firms in the industry, the government did not provide efficient supervision on the safety of production. Partly because of the accidents and deaths in these smaller private mines, the government drove the small private mining firms out of the industry in 2009, which was referred as '*Guo Jin Min Tui*' or 're-advance of the SOEs and the retreat of the private companies'.

Deaths caused by accidents have been numerous in China's coal mining sector. Thousands of workers die every year in China's coal mines. The death rate per million tons of coal produced was more than 100 times higher than that in the US, and more than ten times higher than that in India in the early twenty-first century. China produced one-third of the world's coal but had four-fifths of coal-related fatalities in that year. Many deaths resulted from gas blasts (Factsanddetails n.d.).

The largest sector of coal consumption is industry consumers, which consume over 90 percent of the coal. The second-largest sector of coal consumption is households, with a much smaller percentage of total coal consumption.

China was a net exporter of coal until quite recently. It is estimated that China's demand for coal will exceed its domestic production in the long term and China will be a net importer. China's coal imports exceeded exports in 2008 and 2009. Vietnam and Australia were the largest suppliers of coal to China in recent years.

Assuming an annual growth of 3.5 percent until 2020 and 0.5 percent 2021–2030, my baseline estimates show that the total demand for coal will be about 4.5 billion tons in 2030, with over 10 percent of that demand fulfilled by imports.

Electricity

Urbanization has also created a huge demand for electricity. Different from petroleum and coal, electricity is produced completely by domestic companies without direct connection with the world market. But there does exist a secondary relationship with the world market, through the demand of crude oil and coal, the fuel of electricity production. China's electricity generation is dominated by fossil fuel sources, especially coal.

China is currently the second-largest electricity consumer in the world, second to the US. Electricity production increased dramatically over the past 20 years (Table 11.5). Electricity generation reached 4207 TWh (terawatt hour), 677 percent more than in 1990. Hydropower amounted to 722 TWh, accounting for 17.2 percent; thermal power amounted to 3332 TWh, accounting for 79.2 percent; and nuclear power amounted to 74 TWh, accounting for 1.8 percent. This structure is expected to remain unchanged

Table 11.5   Electricity balance sheet, China (100 million KWH)

	1990	2000	2010
Total energy available for consumption	6230.4	13472.7	41936.5
Output	6212	13556	42071.6
Hydropower	1267.2	2224.1	7221.7
Thermal power	4944.8	11141.9	33319.3
Nuclear power		167.4	738.8
Imports	19.3	15.5	55.5
Exports	−0.9	−98.8	−190.6
Total energy consumption	6230.4	13472.4	41934.5
End-use consumption	5795.8	12535.7	39366.3
Industry	4438.7	9067.9	28303.5
Losses in transmission	434.6	936.7	2568.2

Source: National Bureau of Statistics (2012a, table 7-6).

in the near future. The total annual generation reached 4693 TWh in 2011. The installed capacity increased from 315 GW in 2000 to 900 GW in 2010 (Wikipedia n.d.-b).[2] In 2006, 77 percent of China's electrical capacity was coal-based (Wikipedia n.d.-b).

About 70 percent of electricity was consumed by the industrial sector in 2009 in China. However, end-user consumption increased much faster than the industrial sector during the period 1990–2010, with a growth rate of over 10 percent..

During the planned period before 1978, China's electric power industry was completely monopolized by the state. Production, transportation and final distribution were all operated by large SOEs. Electricity prices were controlled by the central government. Reform in China 's power industry has been successful, compared with the crude oil sector. The aim of the reform is to end the monopoly of the government control by subdividing the large SOEs. China's State Council dismantled the State Power Corporation, a state-owned monopolist, in December 2002 and set up 11 small companies. The smaller companies comprise two electric power grid operators, five electric power generation companies and four relevant business companies. Each of the five electric power generation companies has less than 20 percent of the market share for electric power generation after the reform. The reform separated the power plants from power-supply networks and allowed private investment in the industry. The reform also encouraged competition among SOEs. A regulatory agency was set up in the late 1990s, which was the only independent regulatory agency for an industrial sector in China until it was removed in 2013.

Electricity supply can be separated into three stages: electricity generation, transportation and distribution to final users. Currently in China, some competition exists in the first two stages, though the final distribution prices are still controlled by the government, which causes many problems. In addition, the price of coal, a major input of electricity generation, has been deregulated, while the consumer price of electricity is still strictly controlled by the central government. The price of coal increased dramatically recently, but the price of electricity did not change much. This greatly reduced the profits of electricity generation companies, which no longer had such incentive to produce electric power, and caused a shortage in the supply of electricity. The price caps also encourage wasteful use of cheap electricity on the consumption side. The price of electric power needs to rise to curb the wasteful consumption in the medium term.

Overall, China's electricity demand in the near future will indirectly affect the world market through the demand for its inputs, coal and crude oil. China's electric power industry is projected to grow 6.6 to 7 percent in the next ten years from 2011 to 2020, slightly slower than the growth of GDP (Wikipedia n.d.-a). Assuming an annual growth of 7 percent before 2020 and 4 percent in 2021–2030, my baseline estimate shows that the electricity demand and output will be more than 12 000 TWh in 2030.

The estimate of China's future demand for electricity depends on the economic reform in China's energy industries. The future reform includes, firstly, the reform of the energy price-setting system. The government needs to relax its control over the price of electricity and refined oil products and let these retail prices be decided by the market. The taxes for using resources need to be raised at the same time. Secondly, further opening of the energy market would let more firms enter the market and reduce the monopoly power of large state-owned firms in the fields of, for example crude oil exploration, production and international trade of oil. And thirdly, improved government supervision in safety and environmental protection is needed.

Future Projections

The US Energy Information Administration (EIA) estimated in September 2011 that world energy consumption will rise from 505 quadrillion British thermal units (Btu) in 2008 to 619 quadrillion Btu in 2020, and 770 quadrillion Btu in 2035, with a growth of 53 percent during the period. Much of the growth comes from countries outside the Organisation for Economic Co-operation and Development (non-OECD countries) including China (EIA 2011a).

According to the EIA's estimates, China's energy need will increase from 68.3 quadrillion Btu in 2005 to 140.6 quadrillion Btu in 2020, and

Table 11.6 Estimation of energy consumption, China

Year	Quadrillion BTU	Annual growth (%)
2020	168	5
2030	205	2

Note: Calculated using EIA's 2005 figures and an assumption of 8 percent growth from 2005 to 2011. The actual growth in SCE was 8.8 percent from 2001 to 2011 (National Bureau of Statistics 2012a). The National Bureau of Statistics of China published energy consumption numbers in SCE.

191.4 quadrillion Btu in 2035, with an annual growth rate of 3 percent (EIA 2011a). Assuming an annual growth of 5 percent in 2012–2020 and 2 percent in 2021–2030, my baseline estimation shows that the total energy demand will be 205 quadrillion BTU in 2030, slightly higher than the EIA's estimation (Table 11.6).

Some fundamental changes have been seen recently in the world energy market. US crude oil production increased dramatically and its imports reduced greatly. The US is going to export in the long run. This may end the shortage of crude oil and related products in the near future. China will benefit from this change in the world energy market.

China's Influence on Energy Prices

From the mid-1980s to 2003, the inflation-adjusted price of a barrel of crude oil on NYMEX, measured in February 2013 dollars, was generally under $25/barrel. The price began to rise in 2004. A series of events led the price to exceed $75 in the middle of 2006. Prices then dropped back to $60/barrel by the early part of 2007 before rising steeply again to $140 in July 2008. The price of oil decreased significantly after 2008 (New York Mercantile Exchange).

The international energy prices are the result of relative movements of supply and demand. As the world's second-largest crude oil consumer, China has some influence on the world crude oil prices. The rapid increase in income and energy demand has made China influential in world energy prices. In 2010, the world oil price rose as a result of growing demand associated with signs of economic recovery, including demand from China. The oil price rose to more than $100/barrel in 2011. In July 2012, oil prices tumbled upon signs of China's economic slowdown (AP 2012).

Energy price changes due to policy vary substantially. The domestic oil product prices in China have been controlled by the central government. On March 26, 2013, the Chinese government changed the crude oil product price adjustment mechanism. When the oil prices of Dubai, Essen and Brent, and the moving average price, change more than 4 percent, the National Development and Reform Commission will adjust the domestic product prices within ten working days (People.com 2013). The oil product retail price adjustment mechanism has changed six times in the past 20 years. Before this policy change, the government adjusted the retail price when the moving average of the international price changed more than 4 percent for 22 working days. Under this mechanism, domestic price adjustment often lagged the international price fluctuation in the international market, and sometimes the domestic price was adjusted downward when the international price was rising.

The Impacts of China's Environmental Issues

According to a Dutch research agency (Brahic 2007; Shah 2006), China is the largest emitter of greenhouse gases in the world, although in terms of per capita emissions, China is still far behind some of the developed countries. China's CO_2 emission levels were 4552 Mt in 2004 and 7217 Mt in 2010, increasing 59 percent from 2004 to 2010 (IEA 2010). See Table 11.7.

China published its first National Action Plan on Climate Change in June 2007. The plan did not include targets for carbon dioxide emissions reduction but estimated that the annual emissions of greenhouse gasses would be reduced by 1.5 billion tons of carbon dioxide equivalent by 2010. The Chinese government published the 12th Five-Year Plan on Greenhouse Emission Control in 2011, as part of the 12th Five-Year Plan. The plan set up the goals of cutting carbon emissions intensity by 17 percent by 2015 and cutting energy consumption intensity relative to GDP by 16 percent. A number of low-carbon development zones and low-carbon residential communities will be constructed according to the Plan, and data on greenhouse emissions will be included in future official statistics. The Chinese government has been moving the coal-fired power

Table 11.7 CO_2 emissions, China

2004	4552 Mt
2010	7217 Mt
Change 2004–2010	59%

Note: Mt = Megaton, which equals 1 million tons.

Source: IEA (2010).

and heating plants out of major metropolitan areas, replacing them with gas-fired stations, in an effort to improve air quality.

Current domestic energy production is causing many environmental problems in China. Any major changes in energy policy will change the future domestic production of energy and therefore change China's imports from the world market.

11.2 CAPITAL GOODS AND RAW MATERIALS

Besides energy, China's urbanization and industrialization created a huge demand for raw materials. A portion of this demand has been fulfilled by imports from the world market and the share of imports in total demand is generally increasing.

Steel

Steel is the basic raw material for construction and industrial goods production, made from ores and recycled materials. It is mostly recycled material and, in developed countries, half of the steel is produced by recycling. A major change that happened in the global steel industry since the 1970s is China's emergence as a main consumer and producer in the world.

The twentieth century experienced a rapid growth of steel production and consumption. World production of steel increased from 31 million tons in 1901 to 1.4 billion tons in 2010. Steel exports increased from less than 10 percent of total production in the first half of the twentieth century to almost 30 percent in 2010 (Wang, J. 2012; World Steel Association 2013; International Iron and Steel Institute 1978, 2011).

The United States was the dominant world leader in steel production. US steel production grew from 0.38 million tons in 1875 to 60 million tons in 1920, with an annual growth rate of 7 percent from 1870 to 1913. During the same period, the annual growth rates were 1 percent for Britain and 6 percent for Germany (Citizendium n.d.). Japan's steel industry experienced rapid growth after the Second World War and Japan became an important steel producer in the world. The world steel industry went into a period of slow growth from 1974, with a growth rate of 1.2 percent in 1975–2000 (Wang, J. 2012).

China's steel industry was small in the first half of the twentieth century. The exception was Anshan Iron-making Place and Showa Steel-making Place, established in 1916 under Japanese rule in north-east China. Under the planned system in 1952–1977, three large iron and steel companies were established or updated in Anshan, Wuhan and Baotou with the technological help of the Soviet Union. The production in these plants was inefficient and some of them never started normal production during the planned period.

In the 1950s, the Chinese government tried to use China's vast population to increase steel production. Zedong Mao, the former leader of the Chinese Communist Party, realized that steel and grain were the key pillars of China's economic development. He set a target that in 15 years, China's steel production would surpass that of the UK. In August 1958, the Politburo of the Communist Party decided that steel production would be set to double within the year, and most of the increase would come through backyard steel furnaces. People stopped their normal work and small furnaces were set up along the roadside and in parks and playgrounds. Government workers, students and farmers worked day and night to produce steel. Smoke covered the sky. Steel output reached more than 10 million tons at the end of the year, twice the production capacity at that time, but half of this 'steel' was useless and left piled at the roadside for years.

Mao's target was realized easily after the economic reform. China underwent rapid industrialization and urbanization under Xiaoping Deng's reforms that took place in 1978. Steel output increased gradually, and China's crude steel output reached 50 million tons in 1986, and 100 million tons in 1996, far beyond Mao's target. China produced 641 million tons of crude iron in 2011. The output of crude steel and rolled steel were 685 million tons and 886 million tons, respectively, in 2011 (National Bureau of Statistics 2012a, table 14-22). The annual growth rate of steel production in the early twenty-first century was slightly less than 20 percent. China accounted for 46.4 percent of world crude steel production in 2009 (Wang, J. 2012).

China was a net importing country for steel in the twentieth century. China imported more than 1 million tons of steel in 1953 and 13.3 million tons in 1984. This compared to the slow increase in steel exports: more than 1 million tons in 1982 and 5.4 million tons in 2000. The pattern of steel trade changed dramatically in the twenty-first century: after reaching a peak of 37 million tons in 2003, China's imports went down to the 17 million tons level. During the same period, China's exports grew rapidly, by more than 100 percent annually in 2004 and 2006. China's steel exports surpassed its imports in 2006. In 2011, China exported 0.87 million tons of pig iron and *spiegeleisen* and 48.9 million tons of rolled steel, and imported 686 million tons of iron ore and 15.6 million tons of rolled steel (National Bureau of Statistics 2012a, tables 6-8, 6-9).

Under the planned system, steel prices were controlled by the central government. A dual-price system was implemented in 1985, under which products within a planned quota sold at a price set by the plan and the extra products sold at market prices. In the 1990s, the price control was further relaxed, and most of the steel products sold at market prices.

The main driving force behind China's steel production and imports is domestic demand. Apparent consumption, the amount of product used domestically, is usually used as a measure of domestic demand. It is calculated as the total domestic production plus imports, minus exports. The apparent consumption of steel and its products is an induced demand of the downstream industries. Much research on steel demand starts from the analysis of demand in the downstream industries. Hogan (1999) estimates China's steel demand in 1997 by subdividing the downstream industries into seven sectors: construction, manufacturing, machinery, transportation, electric equipment, mining and forestry, and petroleum refining. J. Wang (2012) uses more recent data and a longer time period, dividing downstream industries into four sub-sectors: construction, machinery, transportation equipment and light industries.

Demand for steel in the construction sector is directly associated with the process of urbanization. Since the housing reform in 1998 that abandoned the system of linking housing distribution with employment, the housing market has experienced rapid development. The total production and value-added from 1991 to 2009 increased by 22.3 percent and 18.5 percent annually, respectively. The share of value-added of construction in GDP reached 6.7 percent in 2009. Commodity houses – houses sold on the market – became the main part of housing supply. The area of commodity houses sold increased from 42.9 million sq m in 1992 to 947.6 million sq m in 2009.

The construction sector's demand for steel recently increased significantly. Steel consumption by the construction sector increased about three times from 1998 to 2008. The share of steel consumption by the construction sector in total steel consumption reached nearly 70 percent in the early twenty-first century and reduced to about 50 percent from 2006 to 2008.

Machinery is another sector using a large amount of steel. The major outputs of the machinery sector include metal-cutting tools, mining equipment, power generating equipment, tractors, and equipment for petroleum and chemical industries. In 2011, the share of the output of China's machinery industry[3] in manufacturing reached 22.5 percent. There has been a dramatic increase in the outputs of mining equipment and power generating equipment since 2003. The machinery sector's consumption of steel grew six times from 1998 to 2008. Its share in total steel consumption recently increased to nearly 18 percent.

The transportation equipment sector, especially the automobile, shipbuilding and container building industries, consumes a large amount of steel. In 2009, China produced 13.5 million automobiles, ranking number one that year in the world. In 2010, China's finished ships and new orders surpassed those of Korea and it became the number one shipbuilding country in the world. As early as 2003, China built 90 percent of containers in the world. As the output of transportation equipment soars, the consumption of steel in this sector has also risen at an astonishing speed. The steel consumption of the transportation equipment sector reached 10 million tons in 2002, 20 million tons in 2006, and 30 million tons in 2008.

Light industry includes hundreds of thousands of products. Among them, three sub-industries – household electrical appliances, hardware and bicycle industries – use a large amount of steel. The production of household electrical appliances, for example refrigerators and washing machines, grew rapidly after China joined the World Trade Organization in 2001. The steel used in household electrical appliances manufacturing increased to 5 million tons in 2005, and more than 9.8 million tons in 2008, as estimated by J. Wang (2012). The hardware industry consumed 14 million tons of steel in 2005. China's bicycle production currently ranks number one in the world. Its production increased from less than 10 million bicycles to 87.6 million in 2008. The steel consumption of China's light industry was 40–50 million tons, 8–10 percent of total steel consumption in the first decade of the twenty-first century.

Most of China's steel outputs were used for domestic consumption. According to J. Wang's (2012) estimate, during the period of 2002–2008 more than 80 percent of steel demand was domestic. Some of the major steel-consumption industries are export-oriented and driven by foreign demand. For example, most of the containers made in China are exported and 70 percent of ships built in China are exported. But overall, most of China's steel demand is domestic.

China's huge steel production needs a tremendous amount of raw materials. Some of these raw materials rely on imports. Unlike most developed countries that use large amounts of scrap iron to produce steel, China's steel plants use large amounts of iron ore to produce steel. China's basic reserves of iron ore were 19 billion tons in 2011 (National Bureau of Statistics 2012a, table 12-5). The per capita basic reserves are low, 66 percent of the world average, due to the large population. China's iron ore is poor in its iron content. Although domestic output of iron ore increased rapidly and reached 900 million tons in 2009, ranking number one in the world, China is increasingly relying on imports of iron ore. In 2009, 71 percent of domestic crude iron production used imported iron ore. China imported 673 million tons of iron ore from January to November 2012, an increase of 8.2 percent compared with the same period the previous year. The demand for iron ore will increase 4 percent and reach 1110 million tons in 2013, more than 60 percent of it will be imported, by estimation. The total imports of iron ore will be 778 million tons in 2013 (Steel and Iron Warehouse Net 2012).

The world's largest supplier of iron ore is the Brazilian mining corporation Vale, followed by the Anglo-Australian companies BHP Billiton and Rio Tinto Group. The main demand in the world iron ore market comes from China, Japan, Korea, the US and the European Union. China is both the largest consumer and the largest importer in the world.

Iron ore prices have been discussed and decided in closed-door negotiations between the small number of suppliers and purchasers since the 1960s. The first deal reached became the benchmark to be followed by the rest of the companies. Since most other commodities already have a market-based price system, suppliers and purchasers of iron ore want to shift to a short-term pricing system. Short-term contracts allow suppliers and purchasers to enjoy the benefits and risks of price fluctuations. Because of the poor quality of its domestic iron ore, China's imports increased and surpassed those of Japan in 2003, when it became the world's largest importer. China entered the iron ore negotiations for the first time in 2003, and followed the benchmark price of an 18.6 percent rise set by Japan JFE and Rio Tinto. In 2004, China accepted a benchmark price of a 71.5 percent increase. China changed its negotiation strategy at the end of 2006 and talked separately with the three major suppliers, and reached the first-round pricing of a 9.5 percent increase in 2007. In 2008, two long-term contracts were reached between suppliers and purchasers. Japan and Korea signed a contract for a 65 percent price rise with Vale, while China refused to accept the benchmark price and reached a deal of a 95.6 percent increase with Rio Tinto. This means the beginning of a new period of breakdown of the long-term contract. Vale began a quarterly pricing mechanism in 2010 and changed it to a monthly pricing system in 2011.

The experience of developed countries shows that as an economy grows to a certain point, the manufacturing sector will shrink while the service sector will increase. This will reduce the demand for steel. At that point, demand for steel will stop increasing when the urbanization is completed. As the economic growth slows down, the growth in demand for steel will also slow down. Gradually the demand for steel will reach a turning point, and beyond that point the demand for steel will decline. Wang et al. (2007) estimate that China's steel output will reach its peak in 2020 with a maximum production of 1 billion tons, considering the restrictions of CO_2 emissions. This means that the growth rates between 2011 and 2020 will be about 3.7 percent per annum. Rio Tinto, the world's second-largest iron ore producer, projected in August 2012 that Chinese steel demand will peak at around 1 billion tons of crude steel production annually in

Table 11.8   Estimation of steel production and iron ore imports

Year	Crude steel production (million tons)	Iron ore (million tons)
2022	920	910

2030, as a result of China's transition to consumer-led growth (Dow Jones Newswires 2012).

China's steel industry has experienced severe overcapacity for years. China's steel production capacity reached 850–900 million tons, but the actual production of crude steel was only 683 million tons in 2011. The steel production capacity was still expanding in 2012. Twenty-seven new blast furnaces were built in the first half of 2012, which added 35 million tons of iron production capacity. In January and February 2012, China's entire steel industry was in deficit, due to the weak market demand in downstream industries and the high costs of raw materials (Steel Association News n.d.). China's steel output fell in November and December of 2011. The world iron ore prices plunged in October 2011, as a result of China's depressed iron ore demand. The world's 2012 average iron ore prices were expected to fall back to 2008 levels due to China's slow growth in crude steel output growth (Steelhome 2012).

Assuming that growth rates gradually reduce from 4.2 percent in 2013 to 0 percent in 2022, my baseline estimates show that China's crude steel output will reach its peak in 2022. The output of crude steel will be about 920 million tons, while imports of iron ore will follow the same pattern and reach 910 million tons in 2022 (Table 11.8).

To sum up, China is the largest consumer of steel, and its demand for steel is fulfilled mainly by domestic production. However, to keep this large amount of production, China has to import a large amount of iron ore from the world market. China's demand for iron ore has caused the world price for iron ore to increase dramatically. In the near future, China's demand for iron ore and steel will increase at a lower growth rate, until it reaches a turning point.

Aluminum and Copper

In addition to iron ore, many metal resources in China are scarce. According to the Ministry of Land and Resources, only six of the 45 metal resources can meet the demand in China (*China Daily* 2009).

Aluminum is widely used in construction, transportation and electricity transmission. China's urbanization has raised the demand for aluminum dramatically in recent years. To meet the demand, China's production of aluminum increased in the early twenty-first century. In 2006, China's aluminum production reached 8.15 million tons, and China became the number one aluminum producer in the world. In the same year, China consumed over 8 million tons of aluminum, and became the largest aluminum consumer in the world (China Investment Consulting 2007).

In the past 20 years, China has transferred from being a net importer of aluminum to being a net exporter. China's imports of aluminum and related products increased from $2.1 billion in 1999 to $9.8 billion in 2011, while its exports of aluminum and related products increased from $0.8 billion in 1999 to $18.6 billion in 2011 (National Bureau of Statistics 2000a, 2012a, table 6-6).

Copper is another important metal resource needed in the process of China's industrialization and urbanization. Historically, China has been a net importer of copper. In 1999, China imported $3.1 billion of copper and exported $0.6 billion. China's imports of copper and related products rose to $54.2 billion in 2011, while exports increased to only $6.7 billion in the same year (National Bureau of Statistics 2000a, 2012a, table 6-6). In real terms, China's refined copper imports in 2007 totaled 1.49 million tons while copper concentrate imports in 2007 totaled 4.52 million tons (IntFX 2008). China's copper consumption in 2008 is estimated at 5.13 million tons, up 8.1 percent from 2007.

China is also a net importer of nickel, zinc and tin. In 2011, China imported $7.4 billion of nickel, $1.3 billion of zinc and $0.8 billion of tin. China has been a net exporter of lead, but the amount of lead exported declined in recent years, while imports increased. The export of lead declined from $0.25 billion in 1999 to $0.16 billion in 2011, while imports of lead increased from $0.01 in 1999 to $0.14 billion in 2011 (National Bureau of Statistics 2000a, 2012a, table 6-6).

Precious Metal

Rare earths, 17 chemically similar metallic elements, are unrecyclable and widely used in the electronics, renewable energy, aeronautics and defense industries. Companies such as Apple Inc., Boeing Co., or G.M. are among the major users of rare earths.

China is rich in precious metal resources, holding about half of the world's reserves of rare earths in 2011, with 55 million tons, compared with 19 million tons in Russia and 13 million tons in the US. China is the biggest producer of rare earths in the world. China's wolfram, indium and precious earth reserves rank first in the world, and the production accounts for over 90 percent of the world's total, up from 27 percent in 1990 (Freedman 2012).

The massive supply of rare earths from China reduced the world price dramatically. Prices of wolfram, indium and rare earths declined 30–40 percent. The 2005 price for rare earths equaled 64 percent of that in 1990, and the price of indium in the world market is $1000 per kilogram, which is far below a sustainable market price of $3000–$5000 (Hu, Yang 2009).

The Chinese government issued regulations on the exploitation and exports of raw materials in 2009, by setting production caps and quotas on exports of rare earths. The Chinese government is also considering set up a strategic stocking system at the national level. The United States, the European Union and Japan filed a suit with the World Trade Organization (WTO) over China's restrictions on exports of precious metals in 2012 (Wu 2012).

As a result, rare earth prices in the world market soared in 2010. But in 2011, average prices of rare earths fell as the slowing global economy curbed the demand for raw materials. Some US and Canadian producers have estimated that China will become a net importer of heavy rare earths as early as 2014.

Overall, as industrialization and urbanization continue, China is making a transfer from being an exporter of many raw materials to an importer of these materials. This will have a dramatic impact on the world market and prices, which has already been experienced by the rest of the world.

Public Transportation

There is a huge demand for public transportation in the process of urbanization in China, which is correlated to the demand for raw materials. The investment in public transportation is controlled by the central and local governments. It has tremendous secondary impacts on many other sectors, such as construction materials, construction equipment and raw materials. The government-driven campaign of construction in the cities has created a huge demand for many things. For example, a large industry in producing of trees and flowers has been developed to meet the demand as urbanization advances.

As of May 2013, 16 Chinese cities had 64 metro transit lines of 1980 km in distance with 1291 stations. A new wave of subway construction began May 2012, with the state's new policy of 'stable growth', which gives the signal to the municipal governments that the approval of construction projects will be relaxed (Lin and Zou 2013).

On September 5, 2012, the National Development and Reform Committee approved the construction of rail transit systems in 25 cities, including the Hangzhou subway line 1 and the Shenzhen subway lines 7

Table 11.9   Cities with metro transit in operation, May 2013

Rank by mileage	City	Mileage (km)
1	Beijing	443
2	Shanghai	439
3	Guangzhou	229
4	Shenzhen	176
5	Chongqing	131
6	Tianjin	131
7	Nanjing	82
8	Dalian	63
9	Wuhan	57
10	Shenyang	50
11	Hangzhou	47
12	Chengdu	39
13	Changchun	31
14	Suzhou	25
15	Xian	20
16	Kunming	18

Source: Lin and Zou (2013).

and 11. Many construction companies and equipment producers are competing for the projects related to this rail transit construction. The total investment includes: (1) construction, 34–40 percent of the total investment; (2) electrical equipment, 17–24 percent of the total investment; and (3) railroad vehicles, 10 percent of the total investment. Large SOEs and private companies are competing for these projects. In terms of sources of investments, 36 percent come from local government, the rest from domestic banks (Zhou, Qiongyuan 2012). In mid-2013, more than 70 lines were under construction. The total investment was RMB1.5 trillion, including the investment approved before 2012 (Lin and Zou 2013). See Table 11.9

To sum up, the development of the first stage of China's urbanization, the construction of the cities, has created a large demand for energy and raw materials. This has been one of the driving forces of China's economic growth in the past decade. This process will continue in the next decade as long as the city construction continues, even though the growth rate may become slower than in the previous century. This has made a tremendous impact on the world economy and will continue to do so in the next decade. Following this, the second stage of China's urbanization will enlarge the market for consumer goods.

NOTES

1. Standard Coal Equivalent, a measurement of energy given as the mass of coal; 1 kW is equivalent to 0.1229 kg SCE.
2. 1 GW = 1 000 000 000 W.
3. The machinery industry includes the manufacturing of general-purpose machinery, special-purpose machinery, electrical machinery and equipment, communication equipment, computers and other electric equipment, measuring instruments, and machinery for cultural activity and office work.

12. Consumer market

In the not so distant future, the market will be more concerned about what plays in Beijing than what plays in Peoria. Business executives at the biggest multinationals will be more interested in what Chinese consumers are buying than what their counterparts in an aging and – currently declining – America are buying. (Kenneth Rapoza 2011)

The increase in China's consumer market is a possible result of the second stage of China's urbanization. This is closely correlated with the rise in the share of the grassroots society in national income, and depends on the reform of income distribution system. China has had a social structure of strong government and a weak society since the time of the Qin dynasty. The economic reform since 1978 did not change this pattern much. As a result of rapid economic development, great wealth came into the pocket of the government and large businesses. The leadership has realized this and plans to reform the income distribution system. The development of China's consumer market will be heavily dependent on this reform.

If China successfully develops its consumer market, the impact will be worldwide. The large scale of China's domestic market will change the demand structure of the world products and services market and reallocate the world's resources, including natural resources, capital, labor and technology.

The impact of China's urbanization on world markets may follow certain timing patterns. The impact on the world's raw materials and capital goods markets has been significant, as I discussed in the previous chapter. Its impact on the world's consumer goods market has not been as significant so far, but could be much more significant in the near future. This depends on the progress of China's urbanization and the changes in income distribution.

China's domestic markets for many products – cars, computers and designer products – are still in their infancy and are thus capable of vigorous growth in the future. Consumer spending only accounts for 35 percent of GDP, about half the proportion of that in the United States, and offers a lot of potential for further growth.

12.1   URBANIZATION AND PERSONAL INCOME

There has been a significant difference between urban income and rural income, which has been one of the major sources of income inequality in China. Urban income is much higher and is growing at a faster rate. Government transactions have failed to change this situation. Urbanization is a feasible way to raise current rural residents' income, by turning them into urban residents.

Population Trends

In 2010, China's population was over 1.34 billion, the largest country in terms of population in the world. However, China's population growth rate was only 0.48 percent in 2010, ranking 156th in the world. The size and growth rate of population in China may be underestimated, because of the large number of migrants and the illegal second or third children some families have, especially in the countryside, which violated the birth regulation and were not reported to the government. Furthermore, the population data published by Chinese government pertain to Mainland China only, and do not include Hong Kong, Macau and Taiwan.

The government implemented the stringent one-child policy in the late 1970s. Under this policy, married couples were officially permitted only one child. As a result of the policy, China successfully achieved its goal of a much reduced fertility rate. The enforcement of the policy varied considerably. It has been more strictly enforced in urban areas than in the countryside. Two children were allowed in many rural areas in recent years.

Males account for 51.27 percent of China's population and the sex ratio at birth is 118.06 in 2010, compared with 105 in most Western countries, which means future gender disparity. The majority of China's population lives in the eastern coastal area, which causes a geographically unequal distribution of population, and income inequality.

US Census Bureau estimated in 2010 that the population in China will be 1.38 billion in 2020 and 1.30 billion in 2050, while the United Nations (UN) made similar projections in 2010 (United Nations 2010). The US Census estimates China's population will be 1.39 billion in 2025 (Table 12.1). The turning point will be around 2026, according to both projections; after that, China's population will decline (US Census n.d., 2009).

China is entering an era of population ageing, at a rapid rate. The share of the population 60 years and older has increased in both urban and rural areas. This share surpassed 10 percent in 2001, which indicates China's entering into ageing society according to the UN's definition. This shift

Table 12.1   Demographic overview, China

Demographic indicators	1995	2005	2012	2015	2025
Midyear population (in thousands)	1 216 378	1 297 765	1 343 240	1 361 513	1 394 639
Growth rate (%)	1.0	0.5	0.5	0.4	0.0
Total fertility rate (births per woman)	1.8	1.5	1.5	1.6	1.6
Crude birth rate (per 1000 population)	17	12	12	12	10
Crude death rate (per 1000 population)	7	6	7	8	9

Source: http://www.census.gov/population/international/data/idb/region.php.

Table 12.2   Projection of age structure in urban and rural China (%)

Age	2010		2025	
	Urban	Rural	Urban	Rural
0–14	15.81	20.67	15.81	13.75
15–24	29.83	17.46	22.29	20.42
25–39	14.45	17.82	10.34	13.12
40–49	18.01	16.64	16.78	9.82
50–64	14.76	17.51	22.87	24.77
65–	7.13	9.89	11.91	18.13

Source: Hu Ying of the National Bureau of Statistics of China, in Wan and Cai (2012, p. 134).

in the age structure of the population tends to lower both labor force participation and savings rates. One feature of the speed of ageing is that it has been faster in the countryside than in the cities, since more young people migrated from the countryside to the cities and left the older family members at home. (See Figure 4.3 in Chapter 4.)

In the future, the age of the population will increase faster in China's countryside than in the cities. Table 12.2 shows a projection of China's population age structure in urban and rural areas.

As the urban population increases, the share of urban employment rises too. These projections of population will be affected by changes in government policy, especially the birth control regulations. It is quite possible that China will change its population policy in the near future. The China Development Research Foundation, an influential independent think

Table 12.3 Estimation of natural growth rate of population

Year	Natural growth rate of population (%)
2013–2015	0.40–0.25
2016–2020	0.20
2021–2025	0.20–0.40
2025–2030	0.40

tank, published a report on China's population policy in October 2012. The report suggests that the government should change its birth control policy and allow each urban family to have two children from 2015. Next, the government should let the families make their birth decisions freely from about 2020, and encourage families have more children after 2026 (China Development Foundation 2012).

In Table 12.3 I present my estimation of the population growth rate in urban China, assuming a population policy change before 2020. The policy change to relax the restriction on urban families against having a second child, seems quite likely to be implemented soon.

Income and Consumption

The per capita disposable income in urban China increased from RMB343 in 1978 to RMB19109 in 2010, about 54 times. During the same period, the per capita net income in rural China increased 43 times, from RMB134 in 1978 to RMB5919 in 2010 (Table 12.4). The growth in the whole period in urban areas has been higher than that in rural areas. Before 1990, the income growth in rural areas was higher than that in urban areas. But since 1990, the growth in per capita income has been much higher in the cities. Figure 12.1 shows the relative income growth in urban and rural China. The difference in the growth rates between the two areas is significant.

Table 12.4 Urban and rural income (RMB)

	Per capita annual disposable income of urban households	Per capita annual net income of rural households
1978	343	133
1990	1510	686
2000	6280	2253
2010	19109	5919

Source: National Bureau of Statistics (2011a, pp. 355, 332, 330).

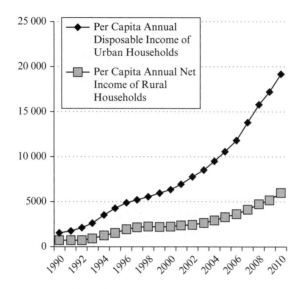

Source: National Bureau of Statistics (2011a, pp. 355, 332, 330).

Figure 12.1 Per capita income in urban and rural areas (RMB)

By using per capita income and population, I calculated the total potential consumer market size in China (Table 12.5). There has been a reshaping of the consumer market between urban and rural areas. The share of the urban consumer market increased to over 70 percent in 2010, as a result of the more rapid growth in urban income and the increase in the urban population.[1]

In 2005, about 35 million urban households had annual incomes ranging from $6000 to $25 000. By 2015, that number will rise to 101 million households by some estimation. The share of the middle class in urban disposable income will increase from 27 percent in 2005 to more than 40 percent in 2015 (Song et al. 2008, in Ryan 2009). The per capita average annual disposable income of 60 percent of the urban households was more than RMB19 000 in 2011, while the lowest 10 percent's per capita income was still lower than RMB7000 (Table 12.6).

I estimated China's per capita urban dispensable income and rural net income. The assumption of growth rates is shown in Table 10A.1 in Chapter 10. Although the growth rates in rural areas are higher than in urban areas, as the estimate shows, the absolute difference between rural and urban per capita income will be larger in 2030.

In the next 10–20 years, the urban share in China's domestic market will continue to increase and make a bigger contribution to China's overall

Table 12.5   China's consumer market, urban versus rural (RMB billion)

	Urban	%	Rural	%
1978	59.2	47.8	64.7	52.2
1990	456.0	45.7	542.3	54.3
2000	2882.9	60.3	1896.0	39.7
2010	12 799.1	72.8	4784.7	27.2

Source: Based on population and per capita income data from National Bureau of Statistics (2011a, pp. 93, 355, 332, 330). Amounts may be underestimated, because the official per capita income may be underestimated, especially in urban areas.

Table 12.6   Distribution of urban household income, 2011

	National average	Lowest 10%	Low 10%	Lower middle 20%	Middle 20%	Upper middle 20%	High 10%	Highest 10%
Per capita disposable income (RMB)	21 810	6876	10 672	14 498	19 545	26 420	35 579	58 842

Source: National Bureau of Statistics (2012a, table 10-7, p. 348).

economic growth. This is under the precondition that the economic and social reform, for example the reform of the *Hukou* system, will continue in the next decade.

12.2   FUTURE DEMAND OF MAJOR CONSUMER GOODS AND SERVICES

China's urbanization in the past ten years has created a large demand not only for raw materials, but also for some consumer goods, such as food and automobiles. But overall, China's consumer goods market is still less developed, compared with consumer markets in other countries and also compared with China's producer goods market, and its influence on the world economy is currently minor. This section will discuss China's demand for some major consumer products and their effects on the world economy currently and in the near future.

Grain

China is one of the largest metals and energy consumers in the world. It is also a top consumer, producer and importer of agricultural products.

Farmland is a scarce resource in China, compared to its large population. According to the official statistics, China's total cultivated land was 122 million hectares in 2008 (National Bureau of Statistics 2012a, table 13-3).[2] About 50 percent of China's population are still employed in agriculture. The average size of a farming family in rural China is four people. The scale of planting activity is extremely small compared with most countries in the world. Currently, the average planting area per family is only 0.4–0.5 hectares. However, China's total production of agricultural products and its share in the world are significant. China's rice production was about 30 percent of world rice production in 2009, from 29.8 million hectares of farmland. China produced 17.2 percent of world wheat in 2009 (Ryan 2009). According the official statistics, China's total grain production was 571 million tons in 2011, including 201 million tons of rice, 117 million tons of wheat, 193 million tons of corn (maize), and 20 million tons of beans (National Bureau of Statistics 2012a, table 13-2).

Grain demand includes edible grain, forage grain, seeds, and grain for industrial uses (Figure 12.2). In China, rice, wheat, corn (maize) and soybean are four major kinds of grain, accounting for 90 percent of grain consumption. Edible grain is the major component of China's grain consumption, over 50 percent of the total. The share of edible grain consumption has been decreasing in the last 30 years. As the consumption of meat, oil and dairy products increased, the consumption of grain went down. The average purchases of grain per capita in China's urban area decreased from 134 kg in 1978 to 77 kg in 2008, down 1.8 percent annually. During the same period, rural residents' crude grain per capita consumption reduced from 257 kg to 199 kg. Although the population is increasing, China's total consumption of grain was stable at around 266 million tons in the period 2004–2008. The share of edible grain consumption decreased from 60.2 percent in 1995 to 51.2 percent in 2008. Forage grain, the second-largest category of grain consumed in China, has been increasing steadily in terms of both absolute amount and share in the total grain consumption. Forage grain consumption went up from 129 million tons in 1995 to 170 million tons in 2008, growing 2.14 percent annually. Its share in total grain consumption increased from 28.5 percent in 1995 to 32.5 percent in 2008. The change in forage grain consumption has become a major component of the increase in grain consumption. The demand for seeds has been declining, from 13 million tons per year in 1995–1999 to 11.6 million tons per year in 2003–2008 (Hu and Guo 2010). The share of

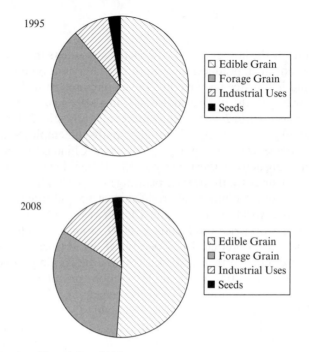

Source: Based on Hu and Guo (2010).

Figure 12.2   Structural change in China's grain consumption (%)

seeds in grain consumption reduced from 2.9 percent in 1995 to 2.2 percent in 2008. In the future, considering the increase in productivity and the scarcity of land resources, the probability of increasing the planting area is trivial, and the demand for seeds will be stable at 11–12 million tons. Grain for industrial uses includes the food, chemical, pharmaceutical and wine industries. China's demand of grain for industrial uses doubled from 38 million tons in 1995 to 74 million tons in 2008, with an annual growth of 5.2 percent. China's subsidy for grain production actually provided cheap raw material for industries. It is estimated that in 2020 the grain demand for industrial use will be about 92 million tons (Hu and Guo 2010).

Using the population forecast of 1.45 billion in 2020[3] and the *Food Guidebook for Chinese Households* by the China Nutrition Society (2007), and assuming the average animal feed conversion ratio is 3.7, Hu and Guo (2010) estimated that human edible grain consumption will be 564 g/day, or 205.9 kg/year. Overall, the grain demand is estimated to be 614 million tons in 2020, including edible grain at 212 million tons, forage grain at 298 million tons, grain for industrial uses at 92 million tons, and seeds at 12

Table 12.7   Forecasts of grain demand, China, 2020

	Million tons	%
Edible grain	212.4	34.6
Forage grain	298.4	48.6
Industrial uses	91.5	14.9
Seeds	11.5	1.9
Total	613.8	100

Source: Hu and Guo (2010).

million tons (Table 12.7). China's demand for forage grain will surpass that for edible grain in just a few years, and become the major driving force of China's grain demand.

In terms of specific categories, rice has been the largest category of China's grain consumption, compared with wheat and corn. Crude rice consumption increased from 128 million tons in 1978 to 195 million tons in 2001, while its share in total grain consumption declined from 47.5 percent to 38.8 percent during the same period. From 2002 to 2011, China's rice consumption increased slightly from 190 million tons to 198 million tons and its share decreased from 38.8 percent to 34.1 percent. From 1978 to 2011, China's wheat consumption increased 53 million tons to 122 million tons. Its share in total grain consumption has been decreasing since 1985, accounting for only 21 percent of grain consumption in 2011. The ranking of wheat in China's grain consumption has changed from second to third place. Corn (maize) is the fastest-growing component in China's grain consumption. China's corn consumption increased more than three times from 48 million tons in 1978 to 191 million tons in 2011. The growth was especially dramatic from 2007 to 2011, when 11.3 million tons consumed were added each year. The share of corn in grain consumption rose from 18 percent in 1978 to 33 percent in 2011. Corn surpassed wheat in the share of grain consumption in 1996 and became the second-largest component in grain consumption. Forage grain accounted for 60 percent of corn consumption, and industrial uses accounted for 30 percent in 2011. Soybeans are mainly used for oil extraction and as forage grain. China's consumption of soybeans increased from 27.7 million tons in 1978 to 70 million tons in 2011, accounting for 12 percent of total grain consumption. Oil extraction accounted for 85 percent of China's soybean consumption in 2011 (Hu and Guo 2010; Cheng 2012). Table 12.8 shows the components of grain consumption by major categories (rice, wheat and corn). It indicates the detailed structure of consumption for each category. For example, it shows that the share of rice in edible grain consumption increased from 2005 to

Table 12.8   China's grain consumption, by major categories

	Year	Edible		Industrial		Forage		Seed	
		Million tons	%	Million tons	%	Million tons	%	Million tons	%
Rice	2005	150.00	81.9	2.60	1.4	23.85	13.0	6.80	3.7
	2011	169.00	85.2	12.00	6.0	16.18	8.2	1.22	0.6
Wheat	2005	87.00	87.1	1.80	1.8	6.90	6.9	4.15	4.2
	2011	83.00	67.9	11.50	9.4	23.00	18.8	4.69	3.8
Corn	2007	13.85	9.5	40.80	28.0	90.00	61.7	1.30	0.9
	2011	16.80	8.8	57.00	29.8	116.00	60.7	1.31	0.7

Source: Cheng (2012, p. 174). The 2011 data are forecast by Cheng.

Table 12.9   China's soybean consumption (million tons)

Year	Total	Edible and industrial	Oil extraction		Seed
			Domestic soybean	Imported soybean	
2005	44.21	7.80	7.40	28.10	0.91
2011	70.40	9.80	3.00	57.00	0.69

Note: The soybean market year is from October to the following September.

Source: Cheng (2012, p. 175).

2011, while the share of wheat in edible grain consumption decreased significantly from 2005 to 2011.

In the mid-term (10–15 years), China's consumption of edible rice and wheat will decrease slowly, while the demand for corn and soybeans will grow, mainly due to their increasing use as forage grain. Using the assumptions of the shares of edible and forage use, Hu and Guo (2010) made a projection of China's grain consumption in 2020 (Table 12.9).

According to Hu and Guo's projection, China's grain demand will be 610 million tons in 2020, 84 million tons higher than that in 2009. This requires an annual growth rate of 1.3 percent. By 2020, China's grain consumption will include 11.5 million tons of seeds, 91.5 million tons industrially used grain, 210 million tons of edible grain, and 298 million tons of forage grain. Forage grain will surpass edible grain and become the largest component of grain demand, accounting for 48.6 percent of the total. In terms of categories, China's grain demand in 2020 will include 140 million tons

Table 12.10   Hu and Guo's projection of China's grain consumption, 2020

	Edible (%)	Forage (%)	Consumption, million tons
Rice	82.6		141.25
Wheat	70.1		90.90
Corn		70	230.19

Source: Hu and Guo (2010).

of rice, 91 million tons of wheat, 230 million tons of corn, and 68 million tons of soybean (Table 12.10). Corn will take over the first place from rice.

Urbanization will change the structure of agriculture production in the countryside. As more migrants leave the countryside, agricultural production will be more land-intensive, which will raise the productivity of agriculture. On the other hand, the total area of agricultural land will reduce due to the expansion of urban areas. A larger share of land will be transferred from planting grain to the use of producing higher-value-added products, for example vegetables. This means that, in the long run, urbanization will cause more imports of agricultural products.

The long-term and mid-term projections of China's food imports will depend heavily upon the assumptions of government policy. Imports will increase dramatically if the government reduces agriculture subsidies and relaxes the monopoly in grain trade. The change in population policy, which will allow urban families have two children, will also increase the demand for grain. If the government keeps the current policy with small revisions, grain imports will increase smoothly. To push the government to change its policy, there needs to be some real pressure, such as a large increase in food prices.

Incorporating more recent information on China's grain consumption, I made some adjustments to the growth rates of different categories and derived the following forecast (Table 12.11). The main differences from Hu and Guo (2010) are a positive growth rate for rice, a zero growth rate for wheat, and a slightly smaller growth rate for corn.

China's grain imports and exports have been controlled by state-nominated grain export and import state-owned enterprises (SOEs). The government issues rations to a limited number of companies, which implement the actual operations.

In most years in the period of 1950–1997, China was a net importer of grain. From 1997 to the early twenty-first century, China was a net exporter. Before 1997, wheat was the main import category. China imported 200 million tons of wheat in the period 1978–1997, which accounted for 81

Table 12.11   Forecasts of China's grain consumption, 2020, baseline

	Growth rate (%)	Million tons	% of total
Rice	0.3	203.8	30.0
Wheat	0.0	122.2	18.0
Corn	3.5	260.5	38.4
Soybean	3.0	91.9	13.5
Total	1.7	678.3	100

Table 12.12   Grain imports and exports, China

		Imports			Exports		
		Cereals and cereals flour			Cereals and cereals flour		
		Total	Wheat	Paddy and rice	Total	Paddy and rice	Maize
2000	Volume (million tons)	3.15	0.88	0.24	13.78	2.95	10.47
	Value (USD million)	593	147	113	1694	561	1052
2011	Volume (million tons)	5.45	1.26	0.60	1.16	0.52	0.14
	Value (USD million)	2043	424	408	753	427	47

Source: Based on National Bureau of Statistics (2002a, 2012a, tables 6-8, 6-9).

percent of grain imports (Food Wealth Net 2008). China's wheat imports accounted for 13 percent of world total in 1989. After 1997, China's wheat imports decreased significantly, and it imported 1.26 million tons in 2011 (Table 12.12), while soybean imports soared. Corn, rice and soybean have been the main export categories. In 1993, China's corn exports accounted for 17.2 percent of the world total. As urbanization progresses, the imports of refined grain of higher quality and grain products may increase in the near future.

Zhang (2012) estimated that in 2020 most of the demand for rice and wheat will be fulfilled by domestic supply, while part of the demand for corn will be fulfilled by imports, fluctuating over time. The soybean demand will rely more and more on imports.

Overall, the grain exports will continue to decrease by my baseline estimation, while the imports will increase in the near future. Based on China's natural resources and the progress of urbanization, China will import more agricultural products. Even though domestic production of rice and wheat will meet the demand in total, China will need to import more high-quality grains.

Meat and Diary

China is the largest pork consumer in the world, and pork counts for more than 60 percent of China's meat market. China's consumption of mutton ranks number one and beef ranks number four in the world. As living standards improved, China's pork consumption increased from 7.8 million tons in 1978 to 48.8 million tons in 2009 (Yz88.com 2013).

China is also the largest producer of meat in the world, producing 79.6 million tons in 2011. China's production of pork increased to 50.5 million tons in 2011 from 45.6 million tons in 2005. China also produced 6.5 million tons of beef and 3.9 million tons of mutton in 2011 (National Bureau of Statistics 2012a, table 13-2). China's share of world meat production has reduced slightly, while the share of beef, mutton and chicken has increased.

Compared with its large production and consumption figures, China's meat exports and imports are trivial. Generally, the world meat trade flows from North America, South America and Australia to Asia and Europe. China exported 1.56 million head of live hogs and 80000 tons of frozen pork in 2011 (National Bureau of Statistics 2012a, table 6-8). In 2009, China exported 40000 tons of beef and imported 20000 tons. China's meat exports mainly went to Japan, Hong Kong and North Korea (Zhu 2010, p. 40), while the imports came from Australia, New Zealand, Brazil and Uganda. Although small in size, China's meat exports and imports have continued to increase. The demand for beef and mutton has caused prices to soar and may increase China's imports from other countries.

According to China Industrial Research Report Net, China's meat consumption will keep increasing in the mid-term, with decreasing growth rates. Urban household meat demand will increase by 2.0 percent, 1.2 percent, 0.3 percent and 0.2 percent annually in the periods 2011–2015, 2016–2020, 2021–2025 and 2026–2030, respectively. Total meat consumption will reach 91.3 million tons in 2020, and 102.9 million tons in 2030. Per capita consumption will be 63.0 kg in 2020, and 68.6 kg in 2030. The shares of pork, beef and mutton, and chicken will be 57 percent, 18 percent and 25 percent, respectively, in 2020 (China Industrial Research Report Net 2012).

China's dairy product consumption lags behind the world average by a large amount. Per capita dairy product consumption is less than 7 kg, far behind the world average of 100 kg (Baidu.com 2012). China produced 38.1 million tons of milk in 2011, up from 28.6 million tons in 2005. Most of the milk produced in China is cow milk of low quality compared with other countries (National Bureau of Statistics 2012a, table 13-2).

As income rises, dairy consumption will increase rapidly. It is estimated that urban households' dairy consumption will increase by 3 percent, 2 percent, 1 percent and 0.5 percent annually in 2011–2015, 2016–2020, 2021–2025 and 2026–2030, respectively, and that rural households' dairy consumption will increase by 5 percent, 3 percent, 2 percent and 1.8 percent during the same periods. Total dairy consumption will reach 50.9 million tons in 2015, 62.1 million tons in 2020, and 78.8 million tons in 2030. The per capita consumption will be 36.3 kg in 2015, 42.8 kg in 2020, and 52.5 kg in 2030 (China Industry Research Report Net 2012).

Housing

China's residential housing market includes two parts, the commercial residential housing market and the low-income housing market. The development of China's residential housing market has been highly correlated with the progress of housing reform since late 1990s, which transferred the welfare-oriented public housing distribution system into a commercial housing market. In gross domestic product (GDP) expenditure accounting, housing is part of investments. Here, I treat it as a consumer product.

The total housing investment was RMB6.2 trillion, including RMB4.4 trillion in residential housing investments in 2011. The total housing construction in that year was 5.1 billion sq m, with 0.9 billion sq m finished. In 2011, residential housing sales reached about 1 billion sq m. From 1998 to 2011 the residential housing sales area increased by 18.4 percent annually. The second-hand housing market has also developed in large cities, with 121 500 and 140 300 units in Beijing and Shanghai, respectively, in 2011. The state-operated residential housing saving system has collected a large amount of funds. Up to November 2011, 93 million people had paid a total of RMB4.0 trillion in deposits under the system and RMB2.2 trillion had been paid out to 14.7 million families (Ren 2012, pp.3, 5).

As an important driving force in the economy, the housing investment has been 20.4 percent of fixed investments in 2011, accounting for 13.1 percent of GDP in 2011. Every RMB100 spent in housing investments created RMB170–220 in related demand, and every RMB100 in housing sales created RMB130–150 in other sales. In 2010, 80 percent of the residential housing was owned by urban residents, a higher proportion than in many developed countries (Ren 2012, p.11). Compared with the self-owned housing, the percentage of rental housing is relatively small.

China's total housing stock in the urban area was about 18 billion sq m in 2010. Per capita housing construction area was about 27 sq m. Assuming area per unit in the urban areas reached 81.4 sq m, there were about 221 million residential housing units in China's urban areas in 2010. In the same year, China had an urban population of 669 million, or 233 million households. The demand for housing units is slightly higher than the supply.[4]

According to the 2010 Census, 669 million permanent residents or 233 million households were living in China's urban areas, and each household had 0.95 units of housing. There is still room for the further development of the residential housing market. It is estimated that, to meet the demand, China needs to build 120 million more resident housing units between 2011 and 2020. If the urbanization ratio reaches 60 percent in 2020, there will be an urban population of 840 million and 312 million urban households (assuming smaller household size). Urban resident housing units will be 327 million, with each family holding 1.05 units of housing in 2020 (Ren 2012, p.21).

As a group of high-income consumers emerges, luxury housing has become a fast-developing market. According to a report, 12 of the 73 projects in the Beijing housing market are active luxury projects. The prices of these houses are RMB50 000–60 000/sq m, and the size of the housing units is 200–300 sq m (Wang, Ying 2012).

Besides commercial residential housing, the Chinese government had provided subsidized housing to 26 million low-income families by the end of 2010; 22 million of these families were in public housing, and the others were in rent-controlled housing. It is estimated that 27 million additional households will need subsidized housing from 2010 to 2015. More than half are non-*Hukou* residents (Ren 2012, p.23).

The urban residential housing price increased by 2.8 times from 1998 to 2011, while the urban disposable income increased by 4.0 times. Currently the average housing price–income ratio is 8 in urban areas, but in some large cities, the ratio is much higher. For instance, the ratio was 21 in Beijing in 2010 (Ren 2012, p. 25). To control the housing prices, the municipal governments put in place various restriction measures under pressure from the central government. In February 2013, the State Council published new regulations for the housing market (*Guo Wu Tiao*). The rules tried to impose a raft of measures aiming to rein in housing prices. Local governments have announced detailed real estate regulations following the central government's recent plan to cool down the market. The local governments have been forced by the central government to announce detailed rules and regulations for their local housing markets. For some considerations, such as local economic growth, the local governments do not want to enforce the rules too much and are playing games with the central government. As a result, in the near future, the local governments will continue the use of these restrictive measures, while relaxing them slightly, for example allowing purchase of a second housing unit under certain requirements or relaxing residential time requirements for purchasing the first house.

Automobiles

China has been the largest automobile producer and consumer in the world since 2009. China's registered cars, buses and trucks (possession of civil vehicles) reached 94 million in 2011 (National Bureau of Statistics 2012a, table 16-24).

Most of the automobiles used in China were produced domestically, by joint ventures of foreign and local companies. China's automobile production started in the 1950s, supported by the Soviet Union. In 1956, First Automobile Works, a large SOE set up by the Soviet Union in Changchun, north-east China, began to produce Jiefang CA-30 trucks. Several other state-owned auto factories were set up in the 1950s and 1960s. For some dozens of years, China's auto production did not exceed 100 000–200 000 per year; most of it was trucks. China produced 5200 passenger cars in 1985. They were almost entirely purchased by the 'working units', government offices and state-owned companies. Private car ownership was virtually unknown at the time. Less than ten people had private cars in Beijing in the early 1960s. One of them was owned by Mr Lianliang Ma, a Peking opera super-star.

After the starting of economic reform in late 1970s, foreign joint ventures were allowed in the auto industry. A large number of foreign auto makers entered China. China's annual auto production capacity first exceeded 1 million in 1992. China's auto market grew by an average of 1 million units per year between 2002 and 2007. In 2007, China's vehicle production capacity exceeded 8 million. China produced 13.8 million automobiles, of which 8 million were passenger cars, in 2009, and surpassed the US as the world's largest auto producer. Both auto production and sales reached 18.3 million units in 2010, and 13.8 million passenger cars sold in that year, the largest number by a single nation in human history (Shanghai Research Center for Automobile Strategy 2011, p.25). The motor vehicle output was 18.4 million in 2011 (Figure 12.3), including 10.1 million cars, 2.3 million buses and 3.2 million trucks (National Bureau of Statistics 2012a, table 14-22).

In 2011, 56 percent of automobiles were produced by joint ventures with

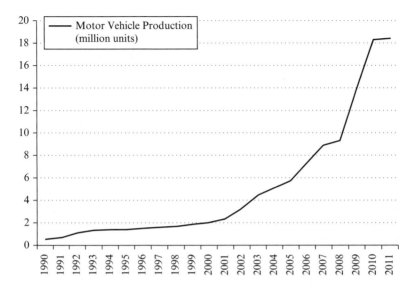

Source: Based on National Bureau of Statistics (2012a, table 14-23).

Figure 12.3 Vehicle production, China (million units)

foreign car makers, for example Volkswagen, GM, Hyundai, Honda and Toyota. In the 1980s, Chinese reformers tried to introduce joint-venture passenger car production. In 1983, American Motors Corporation (AMC, later acquired by Chrysler) signed a contract to produce Jeeps in Beijing. Volkswagen signed a 25-year contract the following year to produce passenger cars in Shanghai.

China has been a net importer of automobiles in recent years. In the 1950s and 1960s, the dominant exporters of cars to China were the Soviet Union and some Eastern European countries, such as Czechoslovakia and Poland. Because of the limit on domestic production, China's imports increased dramatically in the 1980s, despite a 260 percent import duty on foreign vehicles. Japan's vehicle exports to China increased sevenfold in 1984 and China became Japan's second-largest export market in 1985. In 1999, China exported $2.8 billion of vehicles and parts, and imported 2.4 billion. Although the absolute number is small, exports were larger than imports. In 2011, China imported 1 million units or $43.1 billion of motor vehicles (National Bureau of Statistics 2012a, tables 6-8, 6-9). Exports of motor vehicles reached 0.8 million units in 2011 (National Bureau of Statistics 2012a, table 6-8). Most of the exports go to emerging economies such as Algeria, Brazil, Egypt, Iran, Russia or Saudi Arabia, where cars made by Chinese auto makers sell for very low prices. Cars made in China

Table 12.13   Automobile imports, China, 2010

	Number	% of total auto imports
SUV	351 400	
Sedan	343 700	
Minibus	89 900	
SUV, sedan, and minibus		96
Japan	254 800	
Germany	239 300	
Korea	87 400	
US	80 100	
UK	43 300	
Mexico	31 300	
Slovakia	25 300	
Belgium	10 700	
Austria	10 500	
Portugal	6500	
Ten countries together		97

Source: Based on Shanghai Research Center for Automobile Strategy (2011, pp. 31–32).

by multinational joint ventures are generally not for export. In 2010, China imported 813 600 vehicles, from Japan, Germany, Korea, the US and many other countries. Ninety-six percent of them were sports utility vehicles (SUVs), sedans and minibuses (Table 12.13).

China's vehicle ownership reached 78 million in 2010. However, per 1000 people, ownership is only 48, far behind the 600 of developed countries (Shanghai Research Center for Automobile Strategy 2011, p.22). There is still much room for further development. The major obstacles to the development of the automobile market are the vehicle service sector and road construction, especially in the west of the country. At the end of 2010, there were more than 5000 auto rental companies in China, with 200 000 vehicles for rental. A large number of foreign and domestic companies have been investing in the auto repair and service sector. The used-car market is also in rapid development (Shanghai Research Center for Automobile Strategy 2011, p.23).

Although automobile prices in China have been higher than those of the same quality sold in other countries, they have been reduced dramatically in recent years. Compared with housing, cars are relatively cheaper in China, when comparing the services or utility per unit of money paid.

In the future, the development of the auto market will depend on personal income, congestion in cities and government policies. Considering the size of the Chinese cities in the future, it is reasonable to assume that, when China's per capita income reaches the current level in the US, Chinese households will hold fewer cars than those in the US. The number of cars an average Chinese household holds in the future will be close to that in large cities in the US such as New York, or in European cities with well-developed public transportation systems. It is estimated by the China Automobile Industry Association that production and sales of motor vehicles will be 25 million in 2015. Assuming annual growth of 8–10 percent in 2011–2015, and 6 percent in 2016–2020, I estimate that production and sales of motor vehicles will be 25–27 million in 2015, and 33–36 million in 2020.

The government's regulations on car purchasing will have an impact on car sales. The Beijing municipal government set up a rule in 2010 that to buy a car in Beijing, a person needs to have a residential ID and win a lottery. At the end of July 8, 2013, 1 543 743 people and 31 054 firms had applied and were waiting for 53 284 quotas in that month. In 2011, about 240 000 applicants won the lottery (Beijing Car Quota Administration Information System n.d.). Without regulation, 800 000 cars were sold in Beijing in 2010. The quota set for 2011 was one-quarter of the actual sales in the previous year.

Services

In the process of development and urbanization, there has been a shift from the primary and secondary sectors to the tertiary sectors. At the end of the twentieth century, approximately 70 percent of the workforce in the US worked in the service sector, 60 percent of the workforce in Japan, and 50 percent in Taiwan (Ohmae 1990).

As the service demand increases, China will need services provided from the rest of the world. These services will be provided by foreign workers within or outside of China. An example of the former is a Philippine housemaid in China. An example of the latter is a Chinese tourist in the USA who enjoys various services provided by US workers. Both create jobs for foreign countries and can be considered as China's 'imports'. Since China's service market is currently less opened to the world than the manufacturing sectors, this area has only potential influence on the world market.

In China, services represents a large market, which has been under-developed compared with many other countries. China's tertiary sector accounted for 43.4 percent of GDP in 2011, up from 23.9 percent in 1978, 31.5 percent in 1990 and 39 percent in 2000 (calculated using current prices; National Bureau of Statistics 2012a, table 2-2).

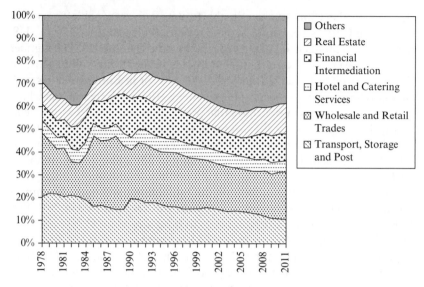

Source: National Bureau of Statistics (2012a, table 2-6).

Figure 12.4   Structure of China's tertiary sector

There are several reasons for China's less-developed service sector. First, the Chinese government paid much less attention to the development of tertiary sector under the planned economy. Second, the slow development of urbanization caused the lag in the growth of the service sector in China. Third, the official statistics underestimated the service sector in the past. There have been some omissions in the statistics of the tertiary industry in the recent past. The National Bureau of Statistics revised the statistics of the tertiary sector in 2005, enlarging the size of service sector.

The current tertiary sector statistics include seven major sub-sectors: transport, storage and post; wholesale and retail trade; hotels and catering services; financial intermediation; real estate; and others. There have been significant changes in the structure of China's service industries (Figure 12.4). In 1978, wholesale and retail accounted for 27.8 percent, followed by transport (20.9 percent), real estate (9.2 percent), and financial services (7.8 percent). In 2010, wholesale and retail accounted for 21.2 percent, transport reduced to 10.7 percent, while real estate and financial services increased to 13 percent and 12.2 percent, respectively. The share of services under the term 'others' increased to 38.4 percent in 2011 from 29.3 percent in 1978 (National Bureau of Statistics 2012a, table 2-7).

Although it is small in size, China's service industry has grown quickly in the last decade. The share of service industries in GDP first surpassed that

Table 12.14   Foreign direct investment in service sector, 2011, actually used (USD million)

Sector	USD (million)
Total	116011
Manufacturing	52101
Services	58253
Real estate	26882

Source: Based on National Bureau of Statistics (2012a, table 6-16).

of the industrial sector in 2001, and has grown steadily larger than that of the industrial sector since 2007. From 2001 to 2010, the service industry added 65 million new jobs, much higher than that in secondary industry (including the industrial sector and construction).

The total foreign direct investment (FDI) in China's service sector has surpassed that in the manufacturing sector (Table 12.14). FDI in housing accounts for almost half of the total FDI in the service sector, while other services – for example education and training, health and culture – have much less FDI as a result of entry regulation.

Brian Linden, an American who first arrived in China in 1984 as a student, and his wife Jeanee, are among a small number of foreign investors who operate boutique hotels in restored properties in China, as reported by the *New York Times*. Guests at the smaller independent hotels like Mr Linden's include wealthy Chinese, but the vast majority are foreigners. More hotels are being built in China than anywhere in the world, including luxury hotels and small boutique hotels like Mr Linden's, which offer tourists more distinctive lodging (Zhou, Xiansheng 2013).

China's service trade increased from \$6.6 million in 2000 to \$28.7 million in 2009, with a larger deficit (Jiang 2012, pp.3, 6). It is expected that China will enlarge the opening of service trade to the rest of the world in the next decade, which will increase the amount and share of service trade. Table 12.15 shows the shares of service exports and imports for detailed service sectors in 2000 and 2009.

Hotels

As a result of market deregulation and the expansion of chain operations, China's hotel industry has developed solidly since the 1990s. The business revenue of designated-size hotels reached RMB326 billion in 2011, with RMB154 billion from hotel rooms and RMB132 billion from meals. Within the hotel industry, the revenue of enterprises with

Table 12.15   China's service trade (%)

	Service exports		Service imports	
	2000	2009	2000	2009
Movie and video	0	0.1	0.1	0.2
Advertisement	0.7	1.8	0.6	1.2
Consultancy	1.2	14.5	1.8	8.5
Patent services	0.3	0.3	3.6	7
Computer and information services	1.2	5.1	0.7	2
Financial services	0.3	0.3	0.3	0.5
Insurance services	0.4	1.2	6.9	7.2
Construction services	2	7.4	2.8	3.7
Communication services	4.5	0.9	0.7	0.8
Tourism	53.8	30.9	36.6	27.6
Transportation	12.2	18.3	29	29.5
Other	23.5	19.2	17.1	11.9

Source: Jiang (2012, p. 8).

foreign investments was RMB24 billion and the revenue of enterprises with funds from Hong Kong, Macao and Taiwan was RMB 32 billion. According to the National Statistical Bureau, the enterprises with foreign investment include joint-venture enterprises, co-operative enterprises, enterprises with solely foreign funding, and shareholding corporations. Enterprises with solely foreign funding account for about one-third of the revenues of foreign-invested enterprises. The Hong Kong, Macao and Taiwan-funded enterprises have a similar structure, with a larger share of joint ventures (National Bureau of Statistics 2012a, table 18-3). Foreign enterprises have had a significant impact on the development of China's hotel industry, introducing high service standards and management experience to China.

The structure of China's hotel industry has not been balanced. The development has focused on luxury hotels so far. The economy hotels have been less developed, accounting for 10–20 percent of the hotel market. It is estimated that economy hotels will face a new round of development, with an annual growth of over 10 percent (Scott 2008).

Catering Services

China's catering service industry has experienced extremely rapid growth in the past 30 years. In 1978, China's catering services had 120000 branches, 1.04 million employees and RMB5.5 billion in sales. Thirty years later, in

2007, the industry's sales reached RMB1.24 trillion, with an annual growth of 20.5 percent (without deducting the inflation effects) (Baidu n.d.). Sales increased to RMB1.80 trillion in 2009 (OCN 2012).

Under the planned system, catering services were in short supply due to the heavy industry-oriented development policy. The catering industry started to grow in the 1980s after the beginning of the economic reform. The market was opened to small private firms and foreign brands. Catering brands grew quickly during this period.

McDonald's, the world's largest fast food chain, opened for business in China in 1990, and developed quickly (*China Daily* 2008). 'We should be opening a restaurant every day in the next three to four years' in China, Peter Rodwell, company president for Asia (excluding Japan, Australia and New Zealand), said in an interview in 2011. McDonald's was opening a restaurant every other day in 2011. According to McDonald's China, the international fast food chain opened 200 new restaurants in China in 2011, marking a new expansion record in the country (Shen and Wong 2012). It aimed to increase its outlets in China from 1300 to 2000 by 2013 (Bloomberg News 2011a).

The 12th Five-Year Plan on National Economy and Social Development (2011–2015) passed by the People's Congress projects that the catering service industry will grow at an annual rate of 16 percent and reach sales of RMB3.7 trillion in 2015 (OCN 2012).

Tourism

China has long been a tourist destination country. As income and living standards rise, China's outbound tourism is booming too. China has become both a popular tourist destination and a tourist source worldwide.

In 2010, the number of overseas tourists visiting China reached 26.1 million, the majority of which came from Hong Kong and Macao. China's history and culture attract tourists from all over the world. Of the 27.1 million foreign tourist arrivals in 2011, more than half were traditional sightseeing tourists; others were tourists for conferences and business. Asia ranked first in terms of visitor-generating sources in 2011, with a market share of 63 percent. Guangdong, Beijing, Shanghai and Zhejiang accounted for 61 percent of the total market share. Inbound tourism generated $48.5 billion in 2011 (National Bureau of Statistics 2012a, tables 18-19, 18-22, 18-13; Scott 2008).

Domestic tourism in China has also developed quickly in the past decade. In 2010, the number of domestic tourists reached 2.6 trillion, with an average annual growth of over 10 percent in the past decade. In 2011, tourists spent RMB1.93 trillion domestically (Zhang et al. 2012; National Bureau of Statistics 2012a, table 18-19).

China's outbound tourism market was trivial until recently, due to the low income levels and the difficulties in applying for passports and visas. More countries became accessible to Mainland Chinese through the approved destination status (ADS) scheme since China's entry into the World Trade Organization (WTO). China's outbound travelers reached 70.3 million in 2011, with an annual growth of 14 percent during the period 2007–2011 (National Bureau of Statistics 2012a). Most of these outbound tourists are urban residents. Popular outbound destinations include the USA, Russia, France, Australia, Japan, Korea and Thailand.

Chinese tourists spend a large amount of money abroad. In 2010, some 1200 Chinese tourists celebrated the Lunar New Year in New York City between February 14 and 20, spending a total of $6 million. According to a report by Global Refund, a company specializing in tax-free shopping for tourists, Chinese tourists spent €155 million ($220.2 million) in 2009, closely followed in terms of total spending by the Russians and the Japanese. In 2011, Chinese tourists spent $69 billion overseas in total (Zhang, Yuqun 2012).

I have witnessed a line of Chinese tourists waiting outside the Galeries Lafayette in Paris before the store opened in the morning. The department store reported that a typical Chinese tourist spent €1000 in two hours in 2009. Purchases made by Chinese tourists represented 15 percent of total spending by tourists in France in 2009, and most of the bills were on fashion items (Xin 2010).

Chinese tourists' shopping spree is due to the following reasons: (1) increasing income and the expectation of future income increases; (2) the price gap for luxury goods sold in China and other countries; (3) the higher transaction cost for some Chinese to go abroad.

The United Nations World Tourism Organization predicts that by 2015 China will become the No.1 tourist-receiving country, and the fourth-largest tourist source country in the world. Domestic travelers will reach 2.8 billion people and outbound tourism will reach 100 million people (Scott 2008). Considering the fact that domestic travelers reached 2.6 billion in 2011, this 2008 forecast of domestic travelers seems somewhat underestimated.

The tourism industry is associated with 109 industries and 39 sectors of the Chinese economy, and the development of related industries will promote the tourism industry to a varying extent. The tourism industry is an important part of stimulating domestic demand.

Education

The education and training industry in China has developed rapidly, accompanying a series of investment and financing activities. Along with the fast development of urbanization, the demand for skilled labor will continue to grow exponentially. College enrollment rose to 6.8 million in 2011, from 0.6 million in 1990, an annual increase of more than 10 percent (National Bureau of Statistics 2012a, table 20-2). Total annual educational spending was RMB2.0 trillion for 2010, including public and private expenditure. The public expenditure on education was about RMB 1.5 trillion in 2010, three-quarters of the total expenditure (National Bureau of Statistics 2012a, p. 776, table 20-39).

China's primary, middle and higher education are dominated by the state-owned colleges and schools. Some private educational institutes have been allowed into the field, but were not given equal conditions to compete with the public schools. It is extremely difficult for private schools to get a license to issue diplomas to graduating students.

Under the planned system, public education at all levels was almost free. After the economic reform, the government could not provide enough funds to support public schools and forced the schools to find their own financial resources. The public schools began to collect extra money from students and their families. In the past 30 years, China's public education has been partially supported by private households. For their children to enter a high-quality public primary or high school, a household usually has to pay a significant amount of money. Households are allocating a higher percentage of their income to education.

China's education market is an underdeveloped market. Public expenditure on education in 1985 and 1990 was 4.8 percent of GDP for all countries, 5.7 percent for high-income countries, 7 percent in the USA, 4.9 percent for mid-income countries, and 4 percent for low-income countries. China's public expenditure on education has been lower than 4 percent for a long time (Wang, Min n.d.). This is a major constraint on China's further development. The Chinese government needs to invest more in education and allow more private investment to enter the field.

Like health care, China's education is a field under criticism and needs fundamental reform. The reform would include: (1) ending the government monopoly on educational activities; (2) allowing private institutes enter the market and giving them equal rights to compete with the state-owned institutes; and (3) allowing foreign institutes to enter the market. These policy changes, if enforced, will change the expected future education market, and exports and imports of education services in China.

Education spending in China grew at an annual rate of 18 percent from

2005 to 2010. China's public expenditure on education was expected to increase to 4 percent of GDP in 2012.

As income and the costs of education rise, many Chinese urban middle-class families are seeking to gain education overseas, especially in the United States. It is estimated that about 220000 Chinese students were studying overseas in 2009 (Liangli de Fengjingxian 2010). The number of undergraduates from China in the US soared to 57000 in 2011, from 10000 in 2006 (Lewin 2012). Compared with the 1980s, more Chinese students are taking undergraduate courses now. Some of the Chinese students in the US start from senior high school. In the 1980s, most of the Chinese students in the US had financial support from US institutes or worked as teaching or research assistants. Now most of the Chinese students are financially supported by their parents.

On the other hand, US universities seek to balance their budgets by charging full tuition fees to foreign students. Higher education is a field of services in which the US has a large comparative advantage, and there is the potential for the US to 'export' to China.

Health Care

Like education, health care is a sector under criticism and in need of fundamental reform. Under the planned system from the 1950s to 1980s, health care was provided by the government and was essentially free in urban areas. SOEs usually covered most of the expenses for their employees. Since almost all firms were state-owned, most of the urban residents were employees of SOEs.

The economic reform abandoned the old welfare system. While most of the major hospitals are still owned by the state, the government dramatically reduced the funding for health care. Hospitals do not have enough funds to pay the doctors. Doctors have to prescribe highly profitable drugs and get commissions to keep their income high enough. Usually, the commission of a doctor is about 30 percent of the total profit. The use of profitable drugs dramatically increases the costs of health care. Soaring costs have made medical services less affordable to ordinary households. Many households set aside large portions of their income for possible health care costs. This is one reason for the high saving rates in China today.

The market structure of China's health care industry is still dominated by a relatively small number of large state-owned hospitals. It is difficult for private hospitals and clinics to obtain permits from the government to enter the market. Patients are crowded into the small numbers of large state-owned hospitals, in which they feel safer.

Although a small number of foreign health care providers have entered the Chinese market by various ways, most of them are still kept out of the market due to government regulation. Many foreign health care providers are preparing to enter the Chinese health care market. The further opening of China's health care market largely depends on the degree to which the Chinese government will open it up.

Total health expenditure in China increased to 2.4 trillion in 2011 from RMB 0.5 trillion in 2000, with an annual growth of 16.4 percent. Within which, 30.4 percent was government health expenditure, 34.7 percent was social health expenditure, and 34.9 percent was private out-of-pocket expenditure. Per capita health expenditure was RMB2695 in urban areas and RMB872 in rural areas (National Statistics Bureau 2012a, table 21-22). Assuming a growth rate of 10 percent, the total health expenditure will be RMB5.7 trillion in 2020.

In this chapter, we have seen some of the impacts of China's urbanization on the world economy; most of them have been correlated with raw materials and production goods in the past. More impacts will be seen in the consumer goods and the service market in the future, if China's urbanization continues. These impacts on the outside world are correlated with the Chinese domestic markets. This is why I have used a large amount of space to discuss the Chinese domestic market. The scale of the secondary, long-run effect on the consumer market depends largely on how the government deals with income distribution and what legal rights the migrant workers can get. This requires fundamental institutional reforms and the redistribution of rights and incomes among social groups in the near future.

NOTES

1. The consumption data in national income account published by the National Bureau of Statistics in 2011 are close to, but not equal to, the numbers in Table 12.5.
2. This is the total of all provinces' cultivated land. From the same source, the cultivated area was much larger in 2011.
3. The assumption seems too high if there are no basic population policy changes.
4. The area per unit is calculated using the urban household survey data, which do not include residents without *Hukou* and could be overestimated. Using area per unit and the total construction area to to calculate the number of units, the latter may be underestimated.

13. Relocation of factors: labor and capital

As urbanization continues, the scale and the structure of China's product market changes, as I mentioned in the previous chapter. At the same time, the capital market, the labor market and the technology used in production have been changing, too.

13.1 CAPITAL MARKET: TWO KINDS OF INVESTMENTS

Physical capital investment has played an extremely important role in China's development in the past decade, accounting for 48 percent of gross domestic product (GDP) in 2011 (Table 13.1). The share of investment in GDP is much higher than that in most other countries in the world. This mode of development is called 'investment-driven' development by many economists. A large portion of this investment is implemented by central and local governments.

Foreign investment accounts for a small portion of total investment, but has an extremely important role in China's economic growth. Foreign investment actually utilized increased from $11.6 billion in 1991 to $117.7 billion in 2011. Due to the large increase in domestic investment, the ratio of foreign investment in fixed assets to total investment in fixed assets

Table 13.1   GDP and physical capital investment, China

	GDP by expenditure approach (RMB trillion)	Gross capital formation (RMB trillion)	Capital formation rate (%)
1978	0.3606	0.1378	38.2
1991	2.2577	0.7868	34.8
2001	10.9028	3.9769	36.5
2011	46.5731	22.5007	48.3

Source: based on National Statistics Bureau (2012a, table 2-17).

decreased from 4.7 percent in 2001 to 1.6 percent in 2011. While the ratio decreased, foreign investments still play an important role in some key areas, such as manufacturing and housing (National Bureau of Statistics 2012a, p.254).

The capital investment in China, especially foreign direct investment, is facing a change from export-oriented to domestic market-oriented. These two kinds of investments have a fundamental difference in their target markets and structure.

Investment with Different Targets

Investments can be subdivided into two categories according to their target market: domestic market-oriented and foreign market-oriented. This is meaningful especially for foreign investments in China: some of them are processing manufacturing investments and target the world market, while others target the Chinese domestic market. From the 1980s to the early twenty-first century, a large portion of foreign investment in China targeted the world market and its products were separated from those of the Chinese domestic market.

China's exports have grown rapidly since the 1990s, at a rate of more than twice the rate of growth of world trade. This growth has been attributed to both domestic and foreign factors: the huge gap in labor costs between China and major developed countries in the world, and the Chinese government's export promotion policies. China set up a processing trade regime that grants firms duty exemptions on imported raw materials or components as long as they are used solely for export purposes. To take advantage of this, many foreign firms moved their labor-intensive final assembly plants to China. The share of processing trade in total exports reached 55 percent in 2005, up from 30 percent in 1988 (Ma et al. n.d.). Processing trade played a vital role in China's economic development, accounting for 50 percent of total exports and creating 30 million jobs in China (Chan 2011).

China's processing trade is heavily reliant on imported inputs from more advanced East Asian countries and areas such as Japan, Korea and Taiwan. After the process of production, the finished products are exported to developed countries, such as the United States and countries in the European Union. This is literally a triangular trade between Japan, China and the US. Considering the complicated relationship of this triangular trade, readers should be careful when reading the trade figures of these countries.

This kind of foreign investment has been correlated with China's urban development. Whether a local government can attract enough foreign investment is crucial to the local economy. To attract foreign investment, the local governments lease land and constructions (buildings) to foreign investors at very low prices.

The investment in processing manufacturing and trade has been extremely important in China's first development stage of economic take-off. As a result of the development of processing trade, as well as many other factors, personal income has increased in China. This has two effects: a rise in labor costs, and growth of a domestic consumer market. Both of these force manufacturers move towards the domestic market. As labor costs increase, firms move their plants out of China to countries with lower labor costs. These low-labor-cost countries include Southeast Asian countries such as Vietnam, and African countries such as Ethiopia. Some firms even move their production back to the developed countries, for example the USA. While this group of firms moves out of China, the other group of firms, which have targeted China's domestic market, will stay in China. The increase in income has created a growing domestic market, ready for firms to explore.

There will be a shift in the target market for capital investments in the near future. Foreign investment targeting China's domestic market will increase, while investment targeting the rest of the world will move out of China. Foreign investment in the automobile industry is an example of investment targeting the domestic market. This kind of investment will stay in China, when some of the processing manufacturing investments retreat from China.

Sector Distribution of Investments

Foreign direct investments are unevenly allocated across China's economic sectors (Table 13.2). About 45 percent have been in the manufacturing sector, the main sector of the export-oriented economy. About 23 percent have been in the real estate sector, which brought high yields due to the booming housing market. Service sectors have been much less invested in, due to government policy or the monopoly of the large state-owned enterprises (SOEs) (such as the financial intermediary, education and health industries).

Within the manufacturing sector, foreign investment firms, including firms from Hong Kong, Taiwan and Macao, concentrated on communication equipment, transportation equipment, chemical and electric machinery industries in terms of value of output (Table 13.3). Foreign investment has entered most industries, with the exception of a small number of industries due to regulations or other reasons.

As urbanization progresses, more capital investment will go into the

Table 13.2   *Foreign direct investment by sector, actually used, 2011 (USD billion)*

Industry	USD billion	% of total
Agriculture	2.009	1.7
Mining	0.613	0.5
Manufacturing	52.101	44.9
Electricity, gas and water	2.118	1.8
Construction	0.917	0.8
Transport, storage and post	3.191	2.8
Information	2.699	2.3
Wholesale and retail	8.425	7.3
Hotel and catering	0.843	0.7
Financial intermediation	1.910	1.6
Real estate	26.882	23.2
Leasing and business services	8.382	7.2
Scientific research and technical services	2.458	2.1
Environment	0.864	0.7
Other services	1.884	1.6
Education	0.004	0.0
Health	0.078	0.1
Culture, sports and entertainment	0.635	0.5
Public management	0.001	0.0
Total	116.011	100.0

Source: Based on National Bureau of Statistics (2012a, table 6-16), percentages calculated by the author.

service sector. Some parts of the service sector in China are less developed, such as the small-scale local banks, private clinics and family doctors, private schools, and many others. Most urban residents do not visit dentists regularly and have problems with their teeth. Children do not visit orthodontist to straighten their teeth. It is also hard to find a family doctor or visit a clinic, which were all eliminated under the planned system. These are extremely large potential markets in this field. The opening of these markets to foreign investors depends on government policy, which in turn depends on pressure from the consumers.

Chinese Investment Outward

After accepting foreign investment at home for 30 years, Chinese firms began to invest overseas. In 2011, Chinese firms' direct investments were seen in more than 100 countries or regions, with total investments of $75

Table 13.3   Output of foreign and Hong Kong, Taiwan and Macao
investment in manufacturing, 2011 (industries output share
over 2%, RMB billion)

	Gross industrial output value	% of total output by foreign invested firms
Total	21 841.7	100.0
Manufacture of communication equipment, computers and other electric equipment	4855.0	22.2
Manufacture of transport equipment	2785.6	12.8
Manufacture of raw chemical materials and chemical products	1592.7	7.3
Manufacture of electrical machinery and equipment	1542.9	7.1
Manufacture of general purpose machinery	920.7	4.2
Processing of food from agricultural products	899.7	4.1
Smelting and pressing of ferrous metals	821.5	3.8
Manufacture of textile	685.7	3.1
Manufacture of special purpose machinery	606.9	2.8
Manufacture of metal products	568.8	2.6
Manufacture of non-metallic mineral products	528.2	2.4
Smelting and pressing of non-ferrous metals	485.2	2.2
Manufacture of apparel and footwear	484.3	2.2
Manufacture of foods	460.6	2.1
Manufacture of plastics	458.7	2.1
Processing of petroleum, coking, and processing of nuclear fuel	458.6	2.1

Source: Based on National Bureau of Statistics (2012a, table 14-14), percentages calculated by the author.

billion. China's cumulative overseas direct investments totaled $425 billion at the end of 2011. In terms of sectors, the largest sectors in China's overseas direct investments are leasing and business services, mining, financial intermediation, manufacturing, and wholesale and retail; followed by transport, real estate and construction (National Bureau of Statistics 2012a, table 6-20). China's most popular investments in developed countries are in the service-trade sector; and in developing countries are in resource extraction and manufacturing (Hunan Business School n.d.). More than 80 percent of China's overseas direct investments are concentrated in Chinese Hong Kong, Australia, the Association of Southeast Asian Nations (ASEAN), the European Union, the USA and Japan. In the past ten years, more and more Chinese firms expanded abroad; more investments took the form of overseas acquisitions, accounting for 40 percent of all Chinese overseas investments. The acquisitions covered the fields of mining, manufacturing, and electricity production and supply. State-owned enterprises accounted for 50 percent of China's overseas investments, followed by private enterprises and foreign investment enterprises (in China).

Not only do the Chinese government and firms invest assets overseas: Chinese families also began to purchase real estate outside of China. Chinese buyers have swarmed into the housing market in California, New York and Florida in the USA, brandishing a large amount of cash. Some Chinese parents bought houses and went back to China immediately, leaving the houses for their children, who attended US colleges. A housing agent showed five houses to a Chinese buyer, according to one story, who did not choose any of them. At the end of the day, the agent said, 'If you are not satisfied, I'll show you more tomorrow.' The buyer said, 'We do not need to do that. I will buy all five.'

Case: China's Investment in Africa and the US

China had 2054 enterprises in 51 African countries at the end of 2011, according to the data of China's Ministry of Commerce (MOC). In recent years, China's annual investment in Africa was $3 billion, and the stock of foreign direct investment (FDI) is more than $20 billion (Zhou, Junan 2013). Recent World Bank research points out that China's Ministry of Commerce data underestimate the scale of Chinese private investment in Africa. A survey of six African countries by World Bank staff shows the reason for the underestimation of the Chinese official data. This is because: (1) the MOC's data are based on projects above $10 million, a threshold which the majority of private projects do not reach; and (2) many private firms which are by law subject to MOC registration try to avoid the procedures of government registration when possible (Shen 2013). The underlying force behind this trend is the pressure of industrial restructuring in coastal China, which has driven some labor-intensive Chinese firms to relocate to Africa.

Chinese investment in the United States increased more than 100 percent annually in 2009 and 2010 (USCC 2011, p.1). Chinese direct investments in the US hit a record level of $6.5 billion in 2012, 12 percent higher than in 2010, according to a report by Rhodium Group (Rhodium Group 2013; *China Daily* 2013). The most appealing US sectors to Chinese firms were oil and gas exploration, advanced manufacturing, and real estate and hospitality. The largest buying activities recently were Dalian Wanda

Group's \$2.6 billion acquisition of AMC Entertainment, and Sinopec Corp's \$2.5 billion investment in a third of Devon Energy's five gas assets. Chinese majority-owned firms in the US employed 29 000 people in 2012. Opposition towards Chinese FDI has become a hotly debated political and security issue in the USA.

China's overseas investments are still small compared with most of the developed countries in the world. This is partly due to the structural imbalance and the large foreign exchange reserves. Some private firms invest overseas because of the poor domestic business environment. It is still difficult for private firms to pass the government approval process and get financial support from the domestic banking system.

13.2   REVERSE FLOW OF LABOR

As capital moves from the export-oriented sectors to the domestic-market-oriented sectors, the labor force will also be redistributed among different sectors of the economy.

Domestic Labor

As long as the urban–rural gap in living standards exists in China, the rural labor force will continue to migrate into the cities over the next two decades. Theoretically, the process of urbanization will stop only when the equalization of the incomes of urban and rural residents is realized, considering all benefits and costs.

Actual urban employment was 359 million in 2011 (National Bureau of Statistics 2012a, table 4-2). Table 10.1 in Chapter 10 shows my forecast of the number of migrant workers in 2020 and 2030. Using the actual urban employment, the assumption of natural growth rate of urban labor force and the forecast of migrant workers, I made an estimation of urban employment in 2020 and 2030, as shown in Table 13.4.

The scale of China's job market is reflected in the Internet recruiting business. Despite the slowdown in 2013, the Chinese economy continues to create jobs, and 2.5 million job opportunities were posted on Zhaopin.

Table 13.4   Estimate of urban employment, China

Year	Urban employment (million)
2020	475
2030	584

Table 13.5   Distribution of migrant workers among selected sectors (%)

	2008	2011
Manufacturing	37.2	36.0
Construction	13.8	17.7
Resident service and other services	12.2	12.2
Wholesale and retail	9.0	10.1
Transport, storage, and post	6.4	6.6
Hotel and catering	5.5	5.3

Source: National Bureau of Statistics (2011c).

com, one of the largest job sets in China, as reported by the *Wall Street Journal* (Orlik 2013).

A further question is which kinds of urban area will the migrants move into: the large cities or small cities and towns? Currently, the largest Chinese cities, such as Beijing and Shanghai, have more restrictions on migration. But the largest Chinese cities are not as large as those in other countries. More migrants will move into these largest cities in the near future, if the government further relaxes the restrictions on migration.

Currently, most of the migrant workers are concentrated in manufacturing and construction, followed by services, and wholesale and retail trade, as shown in Table 13.5.

Within the urban area, more migrants will move into the service sector. Some of them will enter the white-collar workforce in the middle and long term, if the government relaxes correlated regulations. The government, on the other hand, acts only if the society put enough pressure on it. Currently, the government has some incentives to relax the regulation on rural–urban migration. Therefore, I expect labor movement from rural areas to the cities and from the manufacturing to the service sector in the near future.

International Labor Movement

Another potential movement of the labor force is the international migration of labor, which has a direct influence on the world economy. Figures released by the Ministry of Human Resources and Social Security of China showed that 231 700 foreigners were employed in China at the end of 2010 (Rapoza 2011). This is a large number in total, but not large enough if compared with the huge domestic labor force in China.

In the past 30 years, as China opened its door to the outside world, many foreigners came to China and worked in various jobs, including high-level management and consulting jobs, as well as lower-level service jobs such as housing services. Mark Ndesandjo, a half-brother of US President Barack Obama, has been working in Shenzhen, China, for about ten years. He was laid off from his marketing job in Atlanta and decided to reinvent himself by moving to China, a country he had visited with classmates while at Emory University. He has taught English and worked as a business consultant since 2002.

Most foreign workers in China work as: (1) high-ranking managerial personnel of transnational companies; (2) specialists in the fields of finance, technology, production, catering and hotel management; (3) language teachers, professors and editors in culture and entertainment; and (4) self-employed, starting businesses such as language schools, restaurants and consulting firms. Although China has made some progress in opening its labor market to the outside world, there is a long way to go to open its labor market at a large scale and in all fields.

China's demand for foreign workers depends on gaps in the domestic labor supply. The supply of workers in some fields is lacking, and foreign workers are needed to fill the gaps. For example, the legal service sector is completely closed to the outside world and and needs to be opened to foreign specialists. Though partly opened, the financial service sector still needs a large number of foreign specialists. Foreign doctors are also needed under certain conditions. In the future, as urbanization progresses, China will need more foreign workers in the service sectors.

Relative Price of Labor and Capital

China is a labor-abundant country. Due to the large unemployed labor pool in the countryside under the planned system, China's labor costs were extremely low in the past 30 years, until very recently. As the rural labor pool is exhausted, China's wages are going up. Coastal factories are increasing wages to hire quality workers. Foxconn Technology, a Taiwan-based contract electronics manufacturer and maker of Apple iPhones and Dell Computer parts, announced in 2010 that it will double the monthly salaries of many of its 800000 workers in China, to RMB2000 (about $300) per month.[1] The local governments are also raising minimum wage standards (Barboza 2010). Demographic changes and the appreciation of the renminbi are other factors which are raising China's labor costs.

The surplus labor in the rural sector depressed the labor cost in the urban industrial sector, raising the profits of the firms, especially the profits of private firms, since the SOEs usually hire legal urban residents with *Hukou*. Because the firm owners have higher saving rates than ordinary people, this in turn raised the overall saving rates, causing savings to grow faster than investments. As a result, China's economy experienced both an internal imbalance between saving and investment and an external imbalance of current account surpluses (Tao 2013; Lv 2013).

Entering the twenty-first century, the world experienced a large shift in the prices of resources and commodities relative to other goods and services. Resource export prices for Australia increased by 26 percent annually between December 2003 and December 2008, while Australia's prices for manufacturing, agricultural and service exports increased by 2.7, 6.2 and 3.5 percent annually, respectively, during the same period (Cagliarini and McKibbin 2009). According to the International Monetary Fund (IMF), relative to non-durable manufactured goods, energy prices almost tripled and agricultural prices increased more than 50 percent between 2000 and 2008 (IMF 2006).

The profits of Chinese exporters from trading with the US shrank 20–30 percent between 2004 and 2010 as labor costs in China grew and the renminbi kept appreciating, which both have implications for the rest of the world.

Compared with 2000, the energy, mining and agriculture prices were much higher in 2008, while the prices in services and non-durable manufactures in the world increased slightly during the period. The price of durable manufactures went down slightly during the period.

Several factors are responsible for the fluctuation of world prices. First, the changes in productivity in developing countries, especially in China, played an important role affecting the price level. According to the IMF, labor productivity in China has grown by about 6 percent annually since 1979. By the IMF's estimation, total factor productivity (TFP) growth accounts for more than 3 percentage points of this growth, and capital accumulation accounts for nearly 3 percentage points, from 1979 to 2006 (IMF 2006, p.96). The average annual TFP growth in China's manufacturing sector has been 10.5 percent since 1998, which is very high compared with other countries and with China in other periods. As supply-side factors, the increases in productivity have the effect of lowering the world price level, especially for the products China exports in large quantities.

Second, China's industrialization and urbanization is increasing its demand for resources and other goods. In particular, China's energy needs increased significantly in the early twenty-first century. China accounted for 7.5 percent of world energy consumption in 2007, and was responsible for nearly 50 percent of the growth of world energy consumption between 2000 and 2007, compared with North America which was responsible for 5 percent of the growth in world energy consumption (Cagliarini and McKibbin 2009). The increases in relative prices have also been driven by China's demand for certain goods at the early stages of its economic development and urbanization. As I have mentioned earlier in this book, a large portion of China's steel consumption has been in the construction of houses and roads. China's demand for energy and mineral products has also been increasing.

Third, the changes in world relative prices have been a result of the monetary policies of the major countries, such as the United States and China. I will discuss this in detail in the next chapter.

Cagliarini and McKibbin (2009) analyzes the effects of a number of shocks on world inflation and relative price changes. The paper considers the shock to productivity for China. The sectors with strong productivity growth (manufactures) experience falling input costs and lower relative price, while sectors that are not growing quickly (energy and agriculture) are increasingly scarce and their prices tend to rise. Another effect on durable and non-durable goods is that the rise in interest rate reduces the demand for output of the durable good. When the real interest rate rises relative to the real wage, the capital-intensive sectors experience a larger increase in rental costs of capital and will contract relative to the labor-intensive sectors. Cagliarini and McKibbin (2009) projects that the rise in developing-country productivity will raise US consumption and GDP, due to the higher income from investments in developing countries in the short run. But as capital flows into the developing countries in response to higher returns in developing countries, US GDP will drop below the baseline in the medium term. The outflow of capital from the US increases the real interest rates in the US and reduces the investment in the US. In the medium term, the productivity shock will be deflationary for the US due to the lower prices of imported manufactured goods. For Australia, the effect of the capital outflow is partly offset by an inflow of investment into mining for export to the developing countries, due to the demand in these countries for raw materials. In the Cagliarini and McKibbin (2009) model, the initial demand change determines the short-run relative price changes, but over time investment and labor movement across sectors change the supply. In the medium term the demand and supply determine the relative price. In terms of sectors, a productivity shock will increase the relative prices of energy, mining and agriculture compared with manufacturing in the United States. The larger rise in consumption and investment in China will raise the prices of services in China, while the prices of services in the US will be flat. The responses in Australia to the productivity shocks will be similar to the United States in the short run.

The Caglirini and McKibbin (2009) model reflects the situation before the financial crisis in 2008. After 2008, the costs of production rose rapidly and offset the effect of productivity improvement. This will reduce the investments in manufacturing production in China, cause the reverse flow of capital back to the US, and lower the world price level of manufactured goods. On the other hand, as urbanization continues in China, more investment will be put into the energy and mining sectors in China and Australia, causing the world energy price to rise in the short run.

The recent energy technology revolution in the US may further change the direction of capital and labor flow in the world. The decline of energy prices is reducing the cost of production and attracting some manufacturing firms back to the United States. This in turn is bringing more capital and labor to North America. Facing increasing domestic labor costs and lower international energy costs, China has to adjust its production structure and update its industries, which in turn will change labor division and production and the consumption structure in the world.

Overall, China's urbanization not only provides a large market for raw materials and consumer goods, but will also change the worldwide allocation of factors of production. This reallocation will cause worldwide movements of labor and capital and change the prices of these factors of production. The direction of this movement of factors in the near future may be different from that in the past 30 years, as China's urbanization makes further progress and labor costs in China increase.

NOTE

1. Foxconn raised the wage rate but reduced the working hours. As a result, workers' total earnings did not change much.

14. Macroeconomic impacts

As one of the major countries in the world, monetary and fiscal policies adopted in China, combined with those adopted in the United States and other major countries, have large impacts on the world economy.

Under the planned system, most of the firms in China were owned and operated by the government, and the state-controlled production and investment directly by mandatory instructions. For example, there was only one bank in China, the People's Bank of China with many branches all over China, which was completely controlled by the government. Prices and interest rates were also set by the government. The government did not need to collect taxes; it collected profits directly from state-owned enterprises (SOEs).

Since the start of the economic reform in late 1970s, China has made a lot of institutional changes and adopted many modern macroeconomic policies. Following the partial privatization of SOEs, most of the firms in the market are independent from government control to some degree. Most consumer goods prices are determined by the market. Although the major banks are still SOEs, there is some competition among banks. The government collects taxes, which have replaced SOEs' profits as the major source of government revenue.

While learning to use market instruments, the government still retains many administrative measures to control the economy. Sometimes these administrative instruments have been used alongside modern macroeconomic measures. Taxes and government spending are major tools of fiscal policy, but government investment has played an important role in recent macroeconomic policies in China. As a response to the financial crisis in 2008, the Chinese government spent RMB4 trillion in investment, which had some positive effects on Chinese economy, though the investment crowded out some private investments and created many oppertunities for rent-seeking. The central bank, the People's Bank of China, was officially set up in 1983. Its policy instruments include reserve requirements, open-market operations and discount rates. The most frequently used policy instrument, different from that in the developed countries, is reserve requirements, partly due to the sensitivity of changing interest rates and the lack of government bonds available to buy and sell in the market. The foreign exchange rate is determined by the monetary authority, based on market supply and demand, which allows a small amount of floating around the base rate. The banking system treats large SOEs and small private firms differently. The latter receive very limited financial support from the banking system and have to rely on the informal private credit market.

14.1 GROWTH

The primary impact of China's macroeconomic policy on the world economy is China's growth. China accounted for a large part of the growth in the world economy in recent years. In 2009, China played an important role in saving the world economy, by launching an aggressive stimulus program of RMB4 trillion. As China's growth slowed in 2012, the world became worried. When China implements economic stimulation policies, the world pays close attention (NBCNews 2012).

China has been the largest contributor to global growth for several years. In 2011, the country accounted for nearly 10.5 percent of aggregate global gross domestic product (GDP) and 25.1 percent of global growth (calculated from National Bureau of Statistics 2012-a, Appendix table 2-4).

The slowdown of China's economic growth in 2011–2013 has been more severe than expected. This slowdown is the result of several factors, both domestic and international. The weak global environment reduced China's growth in exports. Heavy taxes and lack of financial support made many small businesses retreat from the market. Some of the government policies, such as demand control in the housing market and the automobile market, reduced consumer demand significantly. Finally, the recent campaign against government corruption greatly reduced government expenditures on accommodation and transportation.

The new government led by Mr Keqiang Li which took over in 2013 announced their policy that they would not stimulate the economy to maintain the previous high growth rate. They chose structural reform as their priority and want to change the development strategy: from investment-oriented and export-oriented, to a more balanced development strategy. To realize this target, they may sacrifice the growth rate, to some degree.

14.2 INFLATION

As the future 'world's city', China will be the global inflation generator and will play a role much different from that it played in the past 30 years, exporting inflation to the rest of the world. Urban China may be more productive than the rest of the world, due to the agglomeration economy when resources cluster together. However, competition on the demand side will also bid up the prices of energy, raw materials, land and labor, which increase the cost of production. The large demand for products and services will also make the price for final goods and services soar. Overall, China may have higher inflation compared with the average of the rest of the world.

In the past 30 years, China has been an anchor of global disinflation. The shift to manufacturing in China helped many multinationals to lower the costs and prices of their products. Due to the increase in wages in China, this low-price age will end in the near future. Usually, when raw material prices rise, their costs are passed on to consumers buying finished goods. In the past decade, Chinese manufacturers absorbed some of the cost under the pressure of competition. In December 2003, cotton prices climbed to their highest level, but the price of clothing in US stores was down (Fishman 2006, p.255). As the production costs of the Chinese exporters are rising, the rest of the world has to pay more for goods made in China, resulting in a possible global rise in price levels. Inflation may become China's new export. The high costs have driven some foreign firms out of China. As a result of the shrinking of China's export industry, China's current account surplus fell from 10.1 percent of GDP in 2007 to 2.8 percent in 2011.

The increasing manufacturing prices in China may contribute to global inflation in the short run and result in world consumers spending a larger portion of their incomes to buy products made in China. At the same time, on the supply side, higher production costs in China will allow other countries to increase their shares in world manufacturing. The shift of production out of China will eventually push inflation back to its long-term trend.

The inflation initiated by the higher costs in China may make the monetary policy increasingly difficult to assess and anticipate, since the central banks around the world have to take more into account (Kennedy 2012).

This could be the end of the period of below-average inflation and above-average economic growth for the US if domestic factors in the US are assumed not to change. From 1993 to 2004, annual inflation averaged 2.5 percent in the US, significantly lower than the trend of 3 percent in the period of 1926–2008. This is also well below the above-trend inflation of 4.8 percent of 1980–1992. Nominal interest rates were low during these years due to the low inflation in the US, encouraging businesses and consumers to borrow money to invest.

14.3 MACROECONOMIC POLICY COORDINATION

For some energy products, such as crude oil, the supplier and buyer are in different countries. When the supplier and the consumer cannot communicate with each other about the supply and demand of oil production and transportation, oil prices will jump. Some kind of policy coordination may be needed between the two (or more) countries. But here I am going to discuss policy coordination in a much broader sense.

Global imbalance became a major issue after the financial crisis in 2008. From the income distribution perspective, the share of labor compensation in GDP in China reduced from 48.7 percent in 2000 to 39.7 percent in 2007, while the share of capital returns in GDP increased from 36 percent in 2000 to 45.5 percent in 2007. From the expenditure perspective, the share of consumption in GDP decreased from 62.3 percent in 2000 to 48.6 percent in 2007, while the share of investment increased from 35.3 percent in 2000 to 43.5 percent in 2008, and the share of net exports increased from 2.4 percent to 7.9 percent during the same period (Lv 2013).

The United States and other developed countries have run long-term current account deficits, while China and some other emerging economies have persistently run current account surpluses. The US has been in a borrowing position since the early 1990s, while China is accumulating huge foreign assets. This imbalance is reflected in a falling savings rate in the US, and a rising investment rate in China.

The global imbalances were caused by imbalances within related countries. In China, domestic imbalances include: (1) low labor costs and policies encouraging exports; (2) the large proportion of investment made by the government and the lack of financial resources for private firms; and (3) income distribution between the government and private citizens, which greatly favors the former.

Although the coordination of the governments of related countries plays an important role, the solution to the global imbalance is embedded in the economic forces in the world. China's entering into the world economic system, with its huge cheap labor force, initiated large shocks to the world economy in the late 1990s and early twenty-first century. As time goes by, economic forces gradually adjust towards an equilibrium. When the huge labor pool in China's countryside runs out, China's labor costs will increase dramatically and have a negative impact on its export sector. China's share of exports in GDP has been decreasing, from 35.2 percent in 2007 to 26.2 percent in 2011 (National Bureau of Statistics 2012a, tables 2-1, 6-1), which has significantly reduced China's current account surplus. This is pressuring the Chinese government to change its development strategy, from export-oriented toward domestic demand-oriented. The society may put pressure on the government to reform income distribution, enlarging the share of consumption in GDP.

The renminbi exchange rate was a related issue. The official exchange rate of the renminbi has been undervalued since the early twenty-first century, which favored the Chinese exporters. China changed its policy and has appreciated the renminbi since 2005. Rising labor costs and the appreciation of the renminbi eventually reduced China's trade surplus. Part of the labor-intensive export-oriented sector is moving out of China, to countries with lower labor costs or back to the United States. Now the exchange rate issue has become a less important issue between China and the United States.

Although economic factors played the main role in solving the exchange rate problem, coordination of macroeconomic policies between the two governments was also extremely important. Without government intervention, the global economy will eventually reach its equilibrium. However, it may need longer to realize this equilibrium. Policy coordination cannot change the final destination, but it does change the speed at which the destination is reached.

In the process of reaching global equilibrium, two countries' mid-term macroeconomic policies may have different targets. For example, in the period of 2008–2011, the macroeconomic policy in the US was expansionary, to draw the US economy out of the depression. During the same period, China came out of the recession quickly and inflation became a major risk in 2011. The expansionary policy was right for the US and most of the rest of the world, but not good for China during that period. Coordination among all countries is needed in this kind of situation.

CONCLUSION OF PART II

Overall, China's urbanization will create a huge market, which will attract goods and services, capital and labor from all over the rest of the world. This will change factor allocation and the direction of factor movements in the world. To maintain the world economic order, China will need to coordinate its policies with other countries in the world, especially the United States.

PART III

Choices of China and the world

Globalization may already be turning tailwind to headwind for consumers the world over. (The Economists, in Kennedy 2012)

Facing a changing world economic system and China's urbanization, both China and the rest of the world have to make some fundamental policy changes. China, India and other poor countries used to be the rural area of the world, producing world consumer goods. After their turning points, China and India will be the 'world's cities', with huge urban population and congestion, as well as the tallest buildings and the highest rents, while the US and Europe will be the world's countryside, with large natural resources and a few medium-sized cities. China will have the world's largest cities or city groups, consuming large amounts of raw materials and consumer goods, with higher inflation than the rest of the world. The manufacturing sector in China will still exist, but a large share of its products will be sold domestically. The world's countryside will provide raw materials, some of the manufacturing products, and services for the world's cities. China, as the world's city, will suffer the greatest air and water pollution in the world, traffic congestion on a scale humankind has never seen before, and sky-high land and housing prices matching the height of the buildings in the center of the cities.

To deal with this great change in human history, both the leaders in China and those in the rest of the world need to make some tough decisions.

15. China's choices

The advantages and disadvantages of China's urbanization have placed China at a crossroads. In the past decade, China's reform has been relatively slow and economic growth has been reduced to a historically low rate. To speed up the reform and growth, China needs to find a breakthrough point. A number of tough decisions have to be made.

As I have mentioned before, China is a country with a very strong government and a very weak society. The society has limited means to solve problems itself. In the government bureaucracy, every office is responsible to a higher-level office. The chain of command is from top to bottom. No one cares for the society, which is located at the bottom of the structure, unless the higher-ranked offices give the lower-level office a command to do so. This means that the government, especially the highest-ranked officials, plays a key role in decision-making concerning the benefit of the society, such as in urbanization.

15.1 OVERALL REFORM AND THE WORRIES ABOUT SLOWDOWN

China's economic growth rate has been slowing down during the beginning of the second decade of the twenty-first century. In the past 30 years, China was growing almost 10 percent annually and the average annual growth rate in the past decade was higher than 10 percent annually. However, in 2012, China's growth rate reduced to less than 8 percent. For developed countries this is still a high growth rate, but for China, 8 percent means a significant reduction in growth.

High economic growth has played at least two important roles in the past 30 years. First of all, it gave the current regime the legitimacy that binds the population together. Legitimacy was not a problem in Mao's time. The Communist Party came into the power by military force in 1949 and the population was willing to accept its authority. This support during the early years of the People's Republic was based on people's preference for equality. Since the Communists lost power in the former Soviet Union and Eastern Europe, and since the political incident in 1989, legitimacy became a real problem, and only rapid economic growth gave the regime legitimacy. Second, high growth reduced the political tension in a society where income and wealth are more and more unevenly distributed. Making the cake larger is one way to solve the problem when the government is unable to readjust the income and wealth distribution. The leadership realized this problem and tried to equalize the income distribution and keep the economy growing as quickly as possible.

The slowdown of economic growth was a mixed result of a short-run fluctuation in the world market and a long-run trend. First, the gloomy world market reduced the demand for China's exports. This is temporary and will change in the near future. Second, China's long-run growth mode cannot continue. In the past three decades, this growth was driven mainly by a high level of government investment and a cheap labor supply from the countryside. In the past 30 years, China grew by taking foreign technology and capital and using cheap domestic labor. Eventually, the cheap labor ran out and the capital returns diminished. The income is higher, but the growth is slowing. It is estimated by the World Bank that there existed 400 million unemployed laborers in the Chinese countryside in 2002 (World Bank 2001). This source provided a cheap labor supply to the urban industries in the past 30 years. But now it is almost completely gone.

China's National Bureau of Statistics announced recently that the share of population aged between 15 and 60 fell for the first time in 2012: by 0.6 percentage points, to 69.2 percent (Serdarevic 2013).

The wages for these migrant workers have increased dramatically since 2010, which has raised production costs in the urban areas, especially in the eastern coastal area. The government may continue to provide a high level of investment in the near future, but this is very risky. Many government investments have been financed by borrowing from state-owned banks. A large proportion of local government investments are financed through 'local financing platforms', which are urban China's quasi-market financing platforms which have been fueling local government infrastructure projects ever since the global financial crisis. It is illegal for the local government to issue debt in China. These local governments set up a non-government institute or platform to issue debt. The central government estimated the platform debt at RMB10.7 trillion ($1.72 trillion) nationwide as of late 2010 (Kan and Lu 2013). According to estimates by Administration of Audit in December 2013, the local government debt is RMB 17.9 trillion (Cao 2013). Huge investments, most of them made by the government, also crowded out private investment and consumption, which were considered to be the most important components of aggregate demand in the long run.

The question is whether growth will slow before incomes reach a higher level (ACS 2013). Faced with the slowdown of economic growth, Chinese policymakers and researchers are worrying about the 'middle-income trap', a situation where a country is stuck at certain income level in the process of growth. The middle-income trap appears when manufacturers find themselves unable to compete in export markets with lower-cost producers elsewhere, while they are still behind the advanced economies in higher-value products. The 'middle-income trap' usually ranges from $4000 to $12000 gross national income per person measured in 2010 US dollars. The recent slowdown of China's gross domestic product (GDP) growth indicates the possibility of sticking at a middle-income trap, although it is still only a possibility.

To avoid the middle-income trap, a country needs to introduce new processes and find new markets to maintain economic growth. It also needs to ramp up domestic demand and promote the expansion of the middle class, which can use its increasing purchasing power to buy high-quality products and help drive growth. The Chinese leaders understand that to avoid the middle-income trap they need to do the following: (1) change the current growth mode, which depended too much on government investment; (2) expand the domestic market; and (3) update China's technology and industrial structure.

One way to avoid the middle-income trap that has attracted the Chinese leadership most is through urbanization. Urbanization, by letting peasants into the cities, creates a large group of new urban residents and expands the domestic market dramatically. This could be equivalent to China's entering the World Trade Organization (WTO), which expanded China's export market and gave China ten golden years of double-digit growth. It could be an action of '*Yi Shi San Niao*' (hit three birds with one stone). It can expand the domestic market, maintain the high-speed growth, and solve the problem of uneven distribution of income and wealth.

The new leadership, which took control in 2012–2013, have paid special attention to urbanization recently. They realized that urbanization could be a feasible way out of the middle-income trap. Li Keqiang, China's new Premier, said on November 29, 2012, a couple of days after he was elected as the second most powerful person in China, that China's future development relies on urbanization. He made the comment at a meeting with World Bank President Jim Yong Kim. He said that the biggest development potential lies in the process of urbanization. 'The modernization of 1.3 billion people and the urbanization of nearly 1 billion have never been seen in history,' Mr Li said. 'If China succeeds in the path, it will not only benefit to the Chinese people, but is also our contribution to the world' (Caijing 2012). Li has made many similar comments.

Urbanization is a possible path which can lead China out of the middle-income trap. This is a consensus among the Chinese leadership and researchers. However, currently there is no consensus in the approach to take in order to achieve urbanization, which I will discuss later in this book.

15.2   A COST–BENEFIT ANALYSIS OF CHINA'S URBANIZATION

Is the current pattern of urbanization good for China? What alternative patterns of urbanization can be considered? These are questions must be answered before making decisions.

When some taxi drivers complained online that they could not earn money in large cities due to traffic congestion, an online writer asked them why they did not go back to their hometowns. The taxi drivers stopped complaining immediately, because there is no business in small towns where there are no traffic jams. Everyone needs to calculate benefits and costs before deciding whether to enter a large city. As an economist, let me first do some cost–benefit analysis.

Benefits

One route of development is to gradually speed up the urbanization process and transfer China from an export-oriented economy to a domestic market-oriented economy. There are advantages to following this development route:

1. Large cities will create agglomeration economies, by sharing intermediate inputs, the labor pool and knowledge among firms. Large cities will facilitate specialization in production. All these can reduce the costs of production and increase productivity.
2. Large urbanized areas will become large consumer markets, creating demand much higher than that in the countryside, in terms of both scale and scope. The large-scale demand will foster economies of scale in production and raise productivity.
3. Large cities will become laboratories of new ideas for firms in innovative industries. Innovative high-technology firms share suppliers of intermediate inputs and those that provide product-testing services. The knowledge spillovers in large cities cause firm clustering in these cities.
4. Urbanization is one approach to deal with the income distribution problem. The biggest income disparity in China is the disparity

between urban residents and rural residents, which can be solved simply by letting peasants enter the cities, become legal workers and earn wages similar to those of the original urban residents.

5. Urbanization is a policy that is easy to implement. The government just needs to relax the regulation of urban residency. This is just like the relaxing of farmland ownership regulation at the beginning of economic reform in the late 1970s. Considering the inefficiency of policy implementation, it is extremely important in China to choose a policy that is easy to implement.

Costs

There are also costs of this large-scale urbanization, which cannot be ignored by the decision-makers:

1. Congestion of people and traffic in large cities creates negative externalities and huge costs to society. These externalities become larger as the city size increases. A super-city will create externalities much larger than the increase in its size; to some point the average cost curve will rise as the size of a city increases.
2. The huge demand in super-cities will bid up the prices of housing, transportation, production and services, causing inflation. Inflation has been a major concern of the Chinese government, which has been facing the challenge of maintaining a balance between fast growth with inflation and slow growth with unemployment. Inflation is not welcomed by the Chinese leadership, because it may cause social-political problems and chaos in the society.
3. There is a high probability for large cities to experience social turmoil, due to the clustering of people in the cities, which is an important consideration for the Chinese leadership. As in other countries, most outbreaks of mass unrest in urban areas so far have been difficult for the government to control. This is the worst option for the Chinese leadership.

Equilibrium

Theoretically, it is possible to draw a utility curve for an urban resident/ worker (assuming every resident in a city is also a worker), as in Figure 15.1. This is a utility curve of a representative worker/resident living in the city. As long as agglomeration economies are stronger than the costs, utility increases with city size. When agglomeration economies are weaker than the costs, utility decreases as city size increases (O'Sullivan 2009, p.70). The

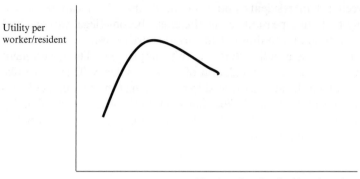

Utility per
worker/resident

Number of workers/residents in a city

Figure 15.1   Utility and city size

urbanization will stop at the city size where the extra benefits of urbanization exceed the extra costs.

Overall, according to current research, the benefits of urbanization
are greater than the costs at the current stage of urbanization in China
(Henderson 2009). China's largest cities are relatively small compared
with its medium-sized cities. Currently, urbanization will bring more net
benefits than costs in China. More urbanization still has extra benefits,
because people are still moving from the countryside to the cities. Not a lot
of people are moving the opposite way, although a small number of people
have moved to other countries in the world. It seems that the decision to
be made is related to the speed of urbanization, not to urbanization itself.

15.3   TOUGH DECISIONS FACING THE CHINESE LEADERSHIP

To some extent, China's leadership has noticed the importance of urbanization. In the past few years, the central government allowed the provincial
and local governments to perform separate experiments in relaxing the
regulations concerning rural–urban migration, urban resident registration and rural land ownership. Some large cities, such as Shijiazhuang
and Zhengzhou, have reduced the restrictions on *Hukou* registration. The
central government passed the Land Rental Law in 2002, giving the peasants land use rights for 30 years. The central government also ordered
the local governments to allow migrants' children enter the urban public
schools (Wan and Cai 2012).

However, overall the leadership has not made up its mind to change the policy of urbanization, especially the *Hukou* regulation, on a national level. The current policy changes are passive reactions, and piecemeal. Without financial support from the central government, the local governments have no incentive to fully implement the central government's policy. China is faced with choices of urbanization in the next decade.

The leadership of the Communist Party and the central government transitioned in 2012. The new leadership will be in office for the next five to ten years, depending on the decision of the next Party Congress in 2017. Barring major accidents, the current leadership will continue for ten years. The new leadership is facing some fundamental policy decisions, concerning China's future path of development. Urbanization is one of these decisions. The leadership needs to make its judgments on the following questions.

How Important is Urbanization?

The first question the leadership needs to answer is whether China needs further urbanization or not. The answers of most Chinese officials and scholars to this question are 'yes'. It is clear that the benefits are greater than the costs at China's current stage of development, which I have discussed in Part I of this book. There is some consensus on the answer to this question.

The next question is how important is urbanization. Some researchers, including myself, think that urbanization is a tool to transfer China from an export-oriented economy to a domestic demand-oriented economy. It will create a huge domestic market, create a middle-income class of minimum size, increase productivity, and solve the problem of income disparity. After the slowdown in the growth of the export-oriented sector, China needs to find another engine of development. Urbanization is one such engine.

The urbanization policy is also easy to implement to some degree. What the government needs to do is just relax the existing regulations. It is much easier to relax an existing regulation than to set up a new regulation. This is just like the rural reform of land use rights in the late 1970s, which was very successful. In that reform, the government did no more than allow peasants to work on their land individually, instead of working collectively. This is extremely important in a country like China, in which the government bureaucracy is not very effective in executing the rules and the people have no habit of following the rule of law.

How Fast Should China's Urbanization Be?

Urbanization is essentially a natural process of migration. The fundamental driving force of this movement is the huge income gap between urban and rural residents. The main resistance is the government regulation on migrants' residency, *Hukou*, and working permissions. Considering the large population in the rural areas and the huge gap between urban and rural households, the speed of urbanization in China will be very fast if government removes all the regulations at once.

The shock of quick urbanization will put great pressure on infrastructure, transportation, housing and employment in the urban areas. To avoid these problems, the leadership needs to consider the graduation of urbanization (Wan and Cai 2012, p.296). This can be done by partially relaxing the residential regulations, for example relaxing the regulations in mid-sized cities and towns first, while keeping the regulations in large cities, and relaxing regulations in large cities as the second step. Ironically, the measures of the old system, for example residency control and working permits, can also be used as tools to control the speed of urbanization. Gradually relaxing these measures may reduce the speed of urbanization and keep the process under the government's control.

Rural Land Ownership and Transaction

The rural–urban migration is closely correlated with the rural land ownership, especially the land ownership in the suburbs of the cities. Currently in China, the lack of a social security system for migrant workers makes the migration partial and incomplete. The migration is temporary because the migrants cannot get the urban residency permits and their children cannot enter the urban public schools. Most of the migrants therefore still have their parents and children living in the countryside. They cannot sell their land in the countryside and leave for the city permanently. As a result, the farmers remaining in the countryside cannot enlarge their farmland and enjoy economies of scale in their agricultural production. To solve this problem, the government needs to implement a reform concerning both urban social security for migrants and the rural land ownership system.

The rural land ownership system should be first identified and clarified at the household level. Currently, the usership of rural land is only defined at the collective (village) level. When rural land ownership is identified and clarified, which is a difficult process, the transfer of the land ownership also needs to be reformed. Urban development needs large amounts of land for new construction, and farmers living in the suburbs of urban areas are willing to sell or rent out their land and housing to city governments and city residents. The problem is that currently in China the only way to transfer land from farmers to cities is by government procurements, in which the government acts as a monopoly. The monopoly of the government in the suburban land market lowers the land retail price and hurts the farmers who sell the land. On the other hand, the local governments resell (rent) the land to the housing developers at a large margin, partly because this is a major income source of the municipal governments. The high reselling prices in turn raise the residential housing prices in the cities and hurt the urban residents. The future reform needs to create a land market to allow farmers sell their land directly to the urban developers. This reform of course will meet resistance from the municipal governments.

The government has been hesitating to reform the land ownership policy. One consideration is the protection of China's farmland. Land is a scarce resource in China, compared with the labor force. For a long period of time since 1949, the Chinese leadership wanted to produce most grain domestically and considered food supply as a strategic problem. The economic reform changed this way of thinking, but it is still in some leaders' subconscious. It is clear that the urbanization process will eventually reduce the area of farmland. Most economists think that comparative advantage does not allow China to produce all the grain it needs by itself. But so far, the government has tried to keep the area of farmland above some critical limit, due to strategic considerations. In the future, the government has to make a trade-off between urbanization and self-reliance in agriculture.

A related problem is the urban land market and residential housing. Housing prices have been increasing dramatically due to: (1) demand created by the large population; (2) the rapid urbanization; (3) the rising income of urban families; and (4) the government's monopoly in the land market. The State Council announced a new regulation on housing prices in 2013, the New Deal. Local governments have announced detailed real estate regulations following the central government's recent plan to cool down the market. It is widely criticized that the market cannot be controlled by the government in the long run. It also hurts the long-run development of the Chinese economy and thus hurts the interests of the local and central governments. To solve the problem, an overall reform is needed, which includes the reform of the central–local government financial relations, the ownership of rural and urban land, and much more.

To solve disputes over the process of land requisition, the government needs to rely on a legislative approach. In other words, the less the government relies on executive power, the more legislative power should be used. Currently in China, land requisition decisions are made by the executive branch of the government. Any objection against a requisition, such as objection to the compensation amount, is raised through the executive process. If the executive decision is in favor of the litigant, the case will go back to the executive institute to make another decision. Some researchers argue that land disputes should be solved through the legislative procedure (Yang 2012).

Changing the rural land ownership system is a tough decision for leadership to make. The central government has let several provincial and local governments to implement experiments with this, but there is no current indication that the leadership wants to reform.

Large or Small Cities? East or West?

Another decision the Chinese government must make is about the scale structure of the urban system. Considering the large size of the population, should China put more resources into building large cities, or focus on a large number of small cities? Should China focus on the development of cities in the remote western area, or the more productive but crowded east coastal cities?

This is not a problem in a complete market economy. In that kind of economy, cities of different sizes will be created automatically by market forces. Central place theory, developed by Christaller in the 1930s, shows how the location patterns of industries combined to form a system of cities. In this system, a small number of large cities coexist with a large number of small cities. This is a natural process of city creation (Christaller 1933).

In China, the story is a little different. Although eventually the economic forces will determine the system of cities, government plays an important role in designing the urban system at least in the short run. Under the planned system, the system of cities was designed and built completely under the control of the government. Since the late 1970s, government control has been relaxed in China. The current system of cities is a combined result of market forces and the responsibilities of different levels of government.

The current scale structure of the system of cities in China is far from equilibrium. The large cities are not large enough, compared with the size-structure of cities in other countries. This is due to the stricter control of migration in the large cities. In the long-run equilibrium, the size of China's large cities relative to medium-sized and small cities will be much greater. Surveys show that more rural residents prefer to live in cities than in the countryside (Lingdian 2010, in Tong 2011, p. 82). The leadership is worried about congestion in large cities and has hesitated to relax migration control in large cities. This is a reasonable consideration in the short run. The old migration regulation could be used to control the speed of urbanization in the process of urbanization, but in the long-run equilibrium, the deregulation in large and small cities should be at the same level, to let the people make their own decisions. If the government keeps controlling migration in large cities, a possible result is the emergence of a new large urban area from small cities or the countryside. The emergence of a large metropolitan area between Hong Kong and Guangzhou from nothing in the past 30 years is a good example. It shows that if an economic necessity exists and the government does not interfere too much, a new urban area will eventually emerge, whether the government wants it or not.

A hot debate during the planned period was over the location of the urban system. Would most of the cities be located in the eastern coastal area, or would they be located in the western interior area? The existing urban system is centered in the eastern coastal area. The government tried to change the existing pattern under the planned system, but failed. Considering the world economic environment, it is efficient to locate the cities in the coastal area, which is closer to the outside world and has high productivity. Given its current political and financial capabilities, the Chinese government cannot change the current pattern of the location of cities, except by making some efforts to prevent the overconcentration of cities in the coastal area (Wan and Cai 2012, p.293).

The design of the urban system in China is not only based on economic and geographical considerations. It also involves the outlook of the Chinese society. Some researchers believe the basic organization of future Chinese society should be built on the county level. This will form a stable foundation for Chinese society and the government bureaucratic system (Jiang 2012). Under this assumption, future China will be organized as a system of 2000 county-level small cities. Other researchers argue that, from the economic viewpoint, a system with super-sized cities is more efficient. According to some other researchers, large cities would also relax the government control of individuals, providing more space for personal development (Tong 2011, p.74). The negative utilities created by super-sized cities may become a more important consideration of the leadership, as pollution and congestion could become serious.

Municipal Government Reform and Central–Local Government Relations

As I have discussed in Chapter 5, since 1994, provincial and local governments have raised a large part of their revenue from selling urban and suburban land. This is referred to as 'land finance'.

The tax reform in 1994 resulted in the local governments facing financial difficulties. The local governments found land requisition to be a source of revenue, by buying rural land and selling (renting) it to city developers. Land requisition has been an extremely important revenue source of local governments. Urban development needs to reform the rural land transaction system, which in turn is closely correlated with local public finance. A precondition of reforming the rural land system is to reform local public finances, which in turn, is connected to the financial relationship between central and local governments. The tax system needs further reform. Currently, no real-estate tax is levied on home owners. Most of the local tax related to housing is levied on housing transaction (buying, selling, and renting), not through ownership of housing. This creates the wrong incentives and needs to be reformed.

A possible reform procedure is as follows. End the monopoly of the local governments in land requisition, and let the rural residents sell their non-farm land to urban developers in the land market. Reform the tax system and change local governments' major revenue source from land requisition to collecting real-estate tax on property ownership. This is also a reform of property-related taxes from collecting in the transaction process to collecting based on the ownership of the real property. The local governments should be allowed to issue debt for long-term construction under a transparent procedure. This is a big operation and needs both the authority of central government and consensus between the central and local governments. Determination is needed by the central government, and time to reach the consensus. Currently in China, real estate tax is levied in a limited number of cities, such as Shanghai, as a policy experiment.

The local tax reform is correlated to the ownership of land. According to the Constitution, land in cities belongs to the state. The state temporarily remises the land ownership to private firms and individuals in return for a land remise fee. The problem is whether it is justified for the state to receive both land remise fees and taxes. It seems that it is acceptable if the amount of remise fees and taxes are reasonable. A more practical problem is that the government does not have enough resources to estimate the value of real property regularly. A large number of specialists, data, and computer programs are needed to value property.

The third problem is the vague property rights existing in Chinese cities, which create tremendous difficulties for implementing the property tax. According to the Constitution, urban land belongs to the state and rural land belongs to the collectives. As the urban areas enlarged, more rural land entered the city limits. However, the ownership of this land is not always clear. To enjoy the benefits of urbanization, the owners of this former rural land have built houses on it, and rent or sell these houses to urban residents or migrant workers. These houses are called 'limited property right housings', which are illegal. There are other kinds of illegal housing. Housing with limited property rights creates problems for levying the property tax. Not only do the owners of the housing built on former rural land have limited property rights, but the owners of housing built on state-owned land also have incomplete property rights. The state just rents the land to private firms and individuals; the longest period of renting is 70 years.[1] When the time expires, the state can take the land back. Of course, the difficulty in the future is how the state will take the land back while leaving the housing on the land untouched.

The financial relationship between central and local governments is one of the key issues that needs to be addressed. In a much broader sense, other fundamental decisions need to be made, including decisions such as to what extent to allow self-governance in the local governments; whether the central government should give the local government more independence; and so on.

Political and Social Problems

The Chinese government faces increasing political and social problems as urbanization continues. One important question is whether the government should impose more state control, or let the market and private firms play a more important role in economic development. It is a question that was already answered by Xiaoping Deng in the 1970s and 1980s. But the situation that has developed in the early twenty-first century has raised the question again. During the past ten years, China's privatization reforms appear to have been reversed in some cases, such as the government use of industrial policies to create state-owned enterprises (SOEs) that dominate important portions of the economy. The tools the government uses to promote the state-owned sectors include direct and indirect subsidies, preferential access to capital, and domestic procurement requirements, among many others. Increasing household consumption and the subsequent emergence of a consumer class may also contradict the policy of keeping economic power in the hands of the state and SOEs.

To promote urbanization and the consumer market, the Chinese government needs to adjust the distribution of income between the government sector and the private sector. The leadership needs to set up constraints on the budgets of the central government's departments and local governments, making the budgets more transparent. The government needs to do more to protect private ownership, reduce tax burdens and establish a better environment for private investments.

There is no indication that China's political system will change fundamentally in the mid-term. China's political system will be significantly different from that in the Western countries for at least the next 30–50 years. This system will coexist with the market economy, with some major conflicts occasionally.

Urbanization and China's Position in the World

China's economic development and urbanization has been one of the most influential events in the history of the twentieth century. As China becomes the second-largest economy in the world, one question that the Chinese leadership must answer is what role China should play in the world.

In the 1980s, Xiaoping Deng defined China's role in the world as to 'hide one's capabilities and bide one's time', which means 'keep a low profile and do not try to be the world leader'. The Chinese government has followed this strategy in the past three decades, accepting the existing world order and the leadership of the United States.

There has been a policy debate in the past few years over whether China should continue this guiding principle of its foreign policy. Most government officials and scholars agree that China's foreign policy should change to a more active one. The focus of debate is whether China should create another set of rules, competing with the existing rules. Some argue that the ultimate goal of China's global strategy should be sole leadership of the world, and China should establish a separate rules system, against the existing system set up by the Western powers. Others think China should join the existing international system and follow the leadership of the USA.

In my opinion, China can be an active and responsible member of the existing international system, playing a more active role in maintaining existing rules and establishing new rules while coordinating with other members of international community. Through cooperation and negotiation, China can express its views, protect its interests and its people, and solve conflicts with other countries. China should be careful in using power and force to deal with international relationships. Urbanization will create many new economic and political relationships between China and other countries, which need to be dealt with using an active and cooperative attitude.

15.4   PATH AND FEASIBILITY

China's urbanization needs a feasible outline, or a clear path map. This is a prerequisite for all reforms, but it is especially important for urbanization, because urbanization is a reform combining several components, or a process including several stages. These stages can be organized in varying orders.

As I have discussed earlier in this book, the major components of China's urbanization include the following. First, reform of the residence control or *Hukou* system. The policymakers have several alternatives to choose from. They can relax the control in all cities, or only relax the control in small and mid-sized cities, depending on the risks of over-crowding of the large cities. After relaxing the residence requirement, the local governments need to provide public services to the new residents. This in turn depends on the financial resources of the local governments, which I will discuss later. Second, reform of the rural land ownership system. The authorities can give the ownership back to the farmers, or only give users' rights to them. The ownership can be held by the farmers, or by the rural collectives (villages). The ownership transfer mechanism also need to be reformed. The policymakers may allow the farmers to transfer land ownership directly to the city developers in a market, or keep the current government monopolized ownership transfer mechanism, or let both co-exist. To reform the land ownership transfer system, the policymakers need to find an alternative financial source for the local government. Third, local and central government financial reforms. The reform designers need to find a feasible financial resource for the local governments. The resource will replace land-selling revenues with alternative sources. A possible alternative source is a property tax. To implement a property tax, many details need to be addressed, such as who determines the rate of the property tax, how the local and central governments share the tax, how to estimate the housing value, and many other issues. Will the central government give some financial support to aid the local government to carry out this reform? This will further connect the local financial reform to the central–local financial relations and the reform of the central government itself. How to ensure that the local governments provide enough public services to the new citizens is another problem that needs to be solved.

Urbanization reform is extremely difficult to implement, because all these components of the reform are interconnected. Any problem in one component will affect the whole reform. The designer of the reform should estimate all possible problems and make detailed plans beforehand. It is not to the advantage of the Chinese policymakers to use their skill, based on their experience in the past 30 years. What the Chinese reformers used to do was to follow a trial-and-error approach. The reform may fail if any party involved is against it. The interest group that has the highest possibility of voting against urbanization could be the municipal governments, which are facing the risk of losing their sources of finance. The following is a road map of China's urbanization summarized by myself.

A Feasible Road Map for China's Urbanization

1. Clarifying rural land ownership in the suburbs of cities. The ownership of farmland and the land upon which farmhouses are built should be clarified by the local government at the collective (or village) level. To clarify the land ownership at the household level is better, but less feasible. The land should be measured and title deeds for land should be issued by the local government. The government should help the collectives to clarify the shares of the ownership of individual members of the collective. Based on the clarified ownerships, the land should be allowed to be transferred in a market set up by the local government. As a first step, homesteads should be allowed to be transferred for urban use in the market. For the farmland, the government should first create a land equivalent standard, which measures the food productive capacity of the land. Based on this standard, the old policy of 'holding 1.8 billion mu of farmland fixed' should be changed to that of 'holding 1.8 billion mu equivalent production capacity fixed'. Farmland can be transferred to other uses if the equivalent rule holds (Zhou, Chengjun 2013). For example, if the agricultural productivity increases, some of the farmland should be allowed to be sold to urban developers.

2. Gradually giving migrant workers and their families urban *Hukou* and equal social benefits, as a citizen should have. It is expected that as soon as the *Hukou* system is relaxed, most people will move to the largest cities, where they will have much higher benefits. To avoid this situation, the government may divide all cities into two groups: the super-cities and others. As a first step, the *Hukou* is relaxed in all cities except the largest ones. The largest cities remain under *Hukou* control while smaller cities give every newcomer *Hukou*. It is expected to take seven years (until 2020) to give *Hukou* to the migrant workers and their families already in the cities, and 100–200 million newcomers during the period. Then if everything goes smoothly, in the next ten years as the second step, the super-cities will open their doors and issue *Hukou* to 100–200 million more newcomers, including those already having *Hukou* in small and middle-sized cities. Within each step, the local government can first reduce some requirements for getting a *Hukou*, and then remove all requirements for getting a *Hukou*. Migrant workers should be included in the low-income housing system and health care system. The children of migrant workers should also be allowed to enter the local public schools without any additional requirements. One precondition for local governments to reform the *Hukou* system is that they have to collect enough resources to provide additional public

services to every new resident in their city; in other words, cities need reforms in public finances.

3. Local public finance reform. (a) Clarify the financial relation between the central government and the local governments by redefining the functions and duties of the two levels of government. When the central government shifts more functions to local governments, corresponding financial resources must also shift to the local governments. Functions related to urbanization shared between central and local governments include primary and middle education, part of low-income housing and part of social benefits. (b) Creating long-term reliable financial resources for local governments. The main financial burdens of urbanization must shift from land finance to property tax and other taxes. The local governments should lower their land leasing revenues to reduce the land prices, and collect property tax for house ownership. The real property related taxes currently collected at the transaction stage should be reorganized and simplified. (c) Create a municipal government bond market as a major financial source of long-term city infrastructure development. Currently, according to law, the local governments have no right to issue debt; they use an informal debt platform to raise money for long-term developments, which involves risk and corruption. The new municipal debt should be based on property tax and other local tax revenues. To guarantee the safety of the municipal debt, a review and supervision mechanism must be set up by the Municipal People's Congresses. The National People's Congress should establish a law of municipal government debt. All revenues of a municipal government, those previously within budget and out of budget, should be included in the budget. A capital budget should be compiled and published. The debt–capital ratio should be set by the law. The municipal government should disclose related budget information and an independent local government debt rating system should be developed. (d) The central government should give earmarked subsidies to local governments to support the local governments' issue of *Hukou* to migrants, based on the number of migrants the city attracts.

4. Reform of the land and housing market. The local governments' monopoly position in urban land supply should be ended. Private land sellers and buyers should be allowed to enter the land market, which will keep land prices at a competitive level and therefore keep housing prices within a reasonable range. Since the local governments are allowed to issue debt for long-term development, they should sell the land at a competitive market price. Because of the competition in the land market, the land price should be reasonable. Adjustment on

both the supply side and the demand side should be used to control housing prices. Direct administrative control of housing prices and transactions should be used very carefully.

5. Developing compact, high-density, intensive city groups. Raise the criteria for density of population in cities on order to use land resources efficiently. Create standards for different city sizes to prevent the population density of cities from being too low. Policy tools should be used to promote systems of cities, in which large and small cities perform different functions.

Of all these steps, gradually issuing *Hukou* to migrants is not the most difficult. Returning the land ownership to individual farmers and the reform of local public finances are the most difficult steps to implement. In the short run, the land leasing power will still be held by the local governments. At the same time, the local governments may collect property taxes from the land owners. The share of land leasing revenue in local government revenue will be reduced, but still remain an important source of local revenue.

It should be noted that this feasible working plan is not the final goal of urbanization; rather, some of the policy suggestions are feasible only in the short run. The Chinese central government is working on a detailed policy package for urbanization, as of the time of writing in August 2013.

Liconomics

Li Keqiang, the first economist-by-training Premier of China, became the head of the Chinese government in 2013. Born in 1955, Li graduated from Peking University (PKU) with a law degree in 1982 and acquired a PhD in economics at PKU under the guidance of Professor Yining Li. After becoming the premier, Li put forward a group of economic policies, which were summarized by researchers as 'Liconomics'. Liconomics sheds light on the future direction of China's economic reform and urbanization.

The three pillars of Liconomics, summarized by researchers, are: (1) no stimulation macroeconomic policies; (2) deleveraging; and (3) structural reform. Mr Li refused to use active monetary and fiscal policies to stimulate the economy to remain a high growth rate in the first half of 2013 when the growth rate reduced dramatically. To reduce the leverage ratio of the banks, the Chinese central bank tightened the money supply in the middle of 2013, resulting in a shortage of liquidity. Structural reform means a more balanced growth by reducing the share of investments and exports and increasing the share of consumption.

Li also put the reform of the interest rate and exchange rate at a high priority. The interest rate for depositing and borrowing at commercial banks has been controlled by the central bank for several decades, and this needs to be reformed. There has been steady progress in these fields in the past few years. The central bank first allowed the interest rates to fluctuate within a narrow limit. Then the limit was enlarged by the central bank in June 2012. The next, and last, step will be removing the limit of fluctuation, which will finish the interest rate reform. The exchange rate is also allowed to fluctuate within a limit, and needs to be relaxed further. It is expected that, due to the strong leadership of Li, the reform of the interest rate and exchange rate will be completed in three years.

Li emphasized simplifying the administrative examination and approval procedures as an important aspect of government reform. In China, many activities need government approval, such as starting a business, investing in a project, getting married or buying a house. Li wants to simplify 600 procedures or delegate approval powers to lower-level governments.

Li insists upon further openness of Chinese cities to the outside world. Under the strong support of Mr Li, the State Council approved Shanghai's free trade zone project in August 2013, after fierce debate. When completed, the project will provide world-class transport and communications facilities and a tax-free environment for domestic and foreign firms.

Li wants to make significant progress in urbanization within his first term. It is reported that the State Council's report on urbanization has drawn a map of future urbanization, including first relaxing *Hukou* in small cities and townships, then opening *Hukou* in middle-sized cities, and then relaxing the residence requirement in large cities and setting reasonable requirements for *Hukou* applications in large cities (Shen 2013).

There is evidence that Mr Li will push the progress of reform, entering into some fields that are very tough to reform, such as the rural land ownership reform, the local government financial reform, medical and health reform, and housing reform. It is good news for China's urbanization, but to make progress in some of these fields is extremely difficult.

15.5 ALTERNATIVE POSSIBILITIES

So far, I have assumed that China's rapid urbanization process will continue in the near future. An alternative possibility is a slow or stagnated urbanization caused by the government's strict control of migration. As mentioned earlier in this book, urbanization is a natural process, but its speed is controlled in China, to some degree, by the central and local governments. If for some reason, such as a social unrest or an internal power struggle, the government decides to retain the control on migration, the process of urbanization will slow down or stop. This may leave China in a middle-income trap or a half-urbanization trap. If this should happen, a large number of migrants would not get full citizenship, and would continue to work illegally and temporarily in cities. They would have a disadvantaged position in negotiating with their employers, and earn wages lower than those of the employees who have full citizenship. They will maintain close relationships with their homes and land in the countryside, which in turn is bad for scale production in agriculture.

A stagnated urbanization will slow down the growth of a consumer market and China's transfer from an export-oriented economy to a domestic market-oriented one. As the costs of production rise and the labor-intensive export-oriented sector perishes, China will be stuck in a middle-income trap.

Wu Jinglian, a major economist in China, has recently repeatedly suggested that China is at a crossroads, facing two alternative roads. One is bureaucratic capitalism or crony capitalism, the combination of government power and financial capital. The other is a market economy with a constitutional government. If the government does not try hard to restrain the already enlarged political power and capital alliance, the first alternative is a real possibility. The second alternative is the continuation of the economic reform started in 1978, which has made great progress but is far from finishing. Currently in China, the government, not the market, is still in a dominant position in resource distribution; the government still owns a large amount of economic resources; state-owned enterprises still have monopoly power in some key industries; the administrative branch of the government, not the judicial branch, has the power to set administrative rules to control market competition. Interest groups behind the government's power have developed, becoming a major obstacle to the economic reform, and a source of corruption. To avoid this possibility, the Chinese people must find some mechanism to limit the power of their government and create well-established rules of the game in which groups can pursue economic freedoms.

This unrestrained government power may ignite social chaos or reaction from the left, which favors a backward movement to Mao's socialist society. This is a another risk that needs to be avoided.

In the short term, the slowdown of China's economic growth in 2012 and 2013 seems serious. The government has repeatedly ruled out a big stimulus plan and argued that China need to change its growth model by relying less on investment. Some economists, business people and government officials are calling for a large stimulus plan like the one in 2008. The government will eventually take some policy measures to prevent the worst situation. After this short-run slowdown, I think, China will enter a new stage of long-term development with a lower growth rate.

Considering all these possibilities, I assume a baseline estimation, in which: (1) the Chinese economy will continue growing, at a lower rate, with some reform toward a market economy; (2) the political system will be fundamentally different from that in the West, which may delay the economic growth to some degree. Besides the baseline, I have also considered the possibility of slower or faster growth paths.

NOTE

1. This is not a problem currently, because the housing reform started about 20 year ago. No rented land has reached the 70-year time limit yet.

16. The choices of the rest of the world

There is no doubt that China's urbanization has had and will have large impacts on the world economy. The future challenge is to figure out how the fundamental changes in the Chinese economy will change the world. Considering the large scale of China's urbanization, this is a new challenge the rest of the world has never before faced. There is big risk involved in having a relationship with China. Can the rest of the world shape a future with China in which everyone prospers? It depends on the foresight of the world leaders and their skills in dealing with China.

Thirty years ago, when China started its reform, US leaders viewed China's reform as the fulfillment of a free-marketeer's dream: 'It is a lovely theory, and it may ultimately be true. There is, however, no evidence upon which to base such a prediction' (Fishman 2006, p. 283). The actual development in China has been quite different from what world leaders had originally thought it would be; also different from what Chinese people had thought it would be at the beginning of the reform. China has become a strange mixture of a controlled economy and a market economy. What lessons can we learn from the experience in dealing with China since China opened its door in the early 1980s?

In the past 30 years, China has followed an export-oriented strategy and exported a large amount of cheap manufacturing products to the rest of the world. This benefited the consumers in the developed world, but also hurt firms and workers in these countries. Consumers in the developed world paid lower prices for these imported goods, but large numbers of workers lost their jobs. As China's urbanization progresses, as discussed in this book, the impacts on the rest of the world may be reversed. For example, the recent increase in China's wage rate may increase the price of consumer goods in the rest of the world. Is this beneficial for the rest of the world? How can the rest of the world adjust to these challenges, which they have never before faced?

16.1 UNDERSTANDING CHINA

About 100 years ago, the US caught up to the UK and became the world's largest economy. Now the Chinese economy is catching up to that of the US, and is becoming one of the largest economies in the world. The two events are quite different. The UK and the US share the same language, culture, and a similar political and economic system. Compared with the US, China represents a different language, culture and political system. The rest of the world, led by the United States, needs to know and to understand China. Understanding is the prerequisite for an appropriate policy.

Compared with the United States and many other developed countries, China has been more advanced in understanding its counterparts in the past 30 years. China has sent more students to the US than vice versa; more Chinese learn to speak English than Americans learn Chinese; more Chinese work overseas than Americans do in China. Of course, these could be results of border controls. The longer you stay in a country, the more deeply you enter the society of that country, and the better you understand that country. Every overseas Chinese knows that: a Chinese person who works in Wall Street and buys a house in Long Island understands America better than a Chinese traveler who visits Manhattan for a couple of days. However, unfortunately, the longer you stay in the US, the better you understand how difficult it is to narrow the misunderstanding between the two great peoples.

China and the US have a lengthy history of miscommunication and misunderstanding. If this gap in understanding is to be narrowed, US politicians and people must recognize how Chinese thought differs from the beliefs that are taken for granted in the West. This can be seen in the reactions of China to the USA's involvement in Korea in 1950. Since China started its open-door policy, the policy of the US has tended towards supporting the development of a market economy in China. However, the American people's greatest misunderstanding of China in the past 30 years is its views on the relation between a market economy and a democratic political system. Americans were under the misconception that a market economy goes together with democracy, and that a market economy will move toward democracy. China's reality in the past 30 years has been a highly developed market economy with a powerful state. The market economy did not create a democratic political system automatically. This misconception comes from a fundamental misunderstanding of Chinese society and China's political system.

When negotiating with Chinese officials, one must keep in mind that China has a different political system and try to understand the incentives of a Chinese government official. Remember that a Chinese mayor is quite different from the Mayor of New York City, because the former is directly responsible to the provincial governor and not the voters.

From dealing with China, the rest of the world may learn many good things from China, such as the hardworking nature of Chinese workers, and the efficiency of Chinese government officials in cases where a problem needs to be solved. All the good and bad characteristics of the Chinese people and their government can be summarized in the Chinese style of production, which is quite distinct from the style of Western developed countries. For example, to produce a car, more machines and less workers are used in the US, but in China more workers and less machines are used and workers work more than 10 hours a day, since China has more people and some of them are migrant workers.

It is extremely important for both China and the rest of the world to understand each other's viewpoints and style. In particular, as the great powers of the world economy, the leaderships of China and the US must understand that the two countries have greater potential to affect the entire world if they have a better understanding of each other's behavior.

16.2   BENEFITS AND COSTS

China's economic development and urbanization will have dramatic impacts on the rest of the world. In general, there will be benefits for China and for the rest of the world, as well as costs for every country in the world.

In the past 30 years, as an export-oriented economy, China exported its cheap labor-intensive manufactured products to the world, especially to the developed countries. This reduced the prices of consumer goods in the developed countries and increased consumers' benefits in these countries. The multinational companies also increased their profits due to the cheap labor used in manufacturing in China. On the other hand, the shift of manufacturing industries to China and other low-labor-cost countries reduced jobs in the developed world. Many small, non-multinational companies were closed due to the competition from the cheap manufactured goods imported from China and other developing countries.

In the future, if urbanization can change China from an export-oriented economy to a domestic demand-oriented economy, there will be some fundamental changes for the developed world. Most of the labor-intensive manufactured production will be transferred to other countries in which production costs are lower than China's, if the capacity of production in these countries is not smaller than China's and therefore can fully supply the world demand. If other developing countries cannot produce all the labor-intensive goods China used to produce, China will continue to produce some products and the export prices of these goods will rise. Other Chinese exports will move up the value chain and the prices of these high-value-added products will not be lower than the market equilibrium price, if competition exists. China's demand for raw materials will also increase the prices of these goods and put pressure on general price levels. All these may reduce the consumers' benefits in developed countries.

China's urbanization, on the other hand, may benefit foreign manu-facturers targeting Chinese domestic markets, if China opens its market further. More of the multinational companies will move to China to produce for Chinese markets, like most of the major auto producers already in China. Other companies will produce in their own countries and export their products to China. In the second case, jobs will be created in other countries as well as in China, such as high-level management jobs, technological and service jobs. In the past, most service jobs were not tradeable. As the world becomes more globalized, more jobs will become tradeable and will be easier to transfer to other countries.

16.3   CHOICES OF OTHER COUNTRIES IN THE WORLD

It is clear that to share the benefits of China's urbanization and its con-sumer market, the rest of the world must enter China's domestic market. China's urbanization is fundamentally determined by economic forces and changes in the political control by the Chinese government. The rest of the world has some limited influence on this process, which is essentially driven by domestic forces. The rest of the world first needs to pay more attention to this process and understand what is happening in China and what the logic of the process is. Based on this understanding, it is possible for the rest of the world to have more influence on China's completion of this process, in a way that will benefit both China and the rest of the world. The following are some choices the rest of the world needs to consider for next two decades, in the face of the growth of the Chinese domestic market and its urbanization.

More Active Participation in China 's Domestic Market

There seems to be no problem among the governments of the rest of the world in terms of their willingness to help their firms enter the Chinese market. But there is still a question of how deeply the rest of the world should be involved in the Chinese market.

Becoming deeply involved in the Chinese market has political and economic risks. China's future development could follow three possible paths: (1) government becomes stronger in China compared with the society and is more aggressive toward the outside world; (2) government becomes less strong, which may lead to chaos inside China, and is less aggressive toward the outside world; (3) a balanced development between the state and the society inside China, and a balanced relationship between China and the outside world. China has been moving towards the third road for most of the past 35 years. However, the past 35 years did not show the movement towards a socio-political system that the Western countries had hoped for in China. The rest of the world has no complete control of the structural change inside China while doing business with China.

Compared with the risks, the benefits of participating in China's domestic market are huge, considering the size of the market and the rapid growth of income and wealth. China's domestic market has been one of the world's three largest markets for several years. Based on more understanding about China, it is worth it for the rest of the world to try to be more active in participating in China's market economy, while keeping alert and being realistic. First of all, it is essentially beneficial for both China and the rest of the world. Second, even though outside forces cannot change the process inside China, influences from the outside world are very helpful for China's internal reforms.

Urging China to Further Open its Domestic Market

China has opened a large part of its market in the past 30 years. However, some sectors are still closed to foreign investments, such as telecommunication. Some policies, such as 'indigenous innovation' policies, guide government procurement to domestically produced goods and services. In some cases, the Chinese government requires technology transfer as a precondition, which is a major cost for foreigners attempting to do business in China.

The governments of the rest of the world should make efforts to urge China to further open its market, especially in the service sector. China's investment policies usually target developing key industries through access to foreign technology and capital. Some foreign investors are encouraged to set up technology-sharing arrangements in exchange for access to China's domestic market. This kind of exchange has actually happened and can be seen every day. It is a hard decision for the rest of the world, especially the developed countries, whether and to what extent to undertake this kind of exchange.

The rest of the world needs to convince Chinese leaders that it is beneficial for China to further open its market, against the background of China's becoming the world's major market. As China's domestic market has become one of the world's central markets, why does China still need to open its market? One answer is efficiency. Even if China were more efficient than the rest of the world in producing all goods, which is not very likely, it is still beneficial for China to specialize in the products that it can produce more efficiently. The second answer is stability. If more firms do business with China, the world will be more stable. A stable world will be mutually beneficial for China and the rest of the world.

In July 2013, China and the USA expressed their intention to enter into substantive negotiation of the China–US Bilateral Investment Treaty (BIT), which could be a milestone for economic relations between the two big countries. This indicated that China had made a public commitment to negotiate market access with the US, which is mutually beneficial for both countries. The draft BIT compiled by the US side demanded *ex ante* 'national treatment'[1] for US investors entering the Chinese market, which the Chinese side did not want to negotiate seriously for a long time, until July 2013. With the BIT, China could benefit from US technology, and move up the production value chain; while the US could benefit from access to the Chinese market, especially in the service sector. It is important for Chinese domestic reform, by borrowing the international standard in Chinese market, so that not only the US firms but also many Chinese private firms can have 'national treatments'. Just like joining the World Trade Organization (WTO) in 2001, the BIT serves as a 'reverse mechanism' to push the stagnant domestic reform in China.

Joining Competition in the Chinese Domestic Market

When many foreign firms are operating in the Chinese domestic market, fair competition will be more important for these firms. As Chinese products move up the value chain, competition between Chinese producers and producers of developed countries will be more severe both in China's domestic market and in the world market.

The current policies promoting the state-owned sector with a variety of industrial policy tools may favor state-owned enterprises (SOEs) over foreign competitors. SOEs may have advantages when competing with foreign firms as well as domestic private firms in the domestic market, due to government subsidies, tax treatments and regulations. As competition intensifies, SOEs have become one of the major concerns of foreign firms in China.

Intellectual property rights are an important factor as far as the competitive environment of foreign firms in China is concerned. Chinese officials have pledged to modify China's innovation policy in response to requests from foreign leaders. There has been some progress, but a lot more still needs to be done.

Government subsidies to Chinese companies are another factor affecting foreign firms. Sometimes the Chinese government's emphasis on industrial upgrading will lead to new subsidies, which may put foreign competitors at a disadvantage.

The difficulty for the rest of the world is that when you want to enter another country's domestic market, you will be in a disadvantaged position in negotiations, unless the other country also wants to enter your market. In this sense, negotiation will be harder for the rest of the world in the second stage of China's development than in the first, when China first entered the world market.

In some cases, the foreign firms in China demand equal treatment by the Chinese government of both foreign and domestic firms, especially when their competitors are large state-owned firms or domestic firms well connected with the government.

Overall, in the long run, China and its urbanization will have a profound impact on the world. The rest of the world and China both need to adjust their policy to face this unprecedented challenge. To coordinate policies and solve conflicts, the rest of the world needs to set up a long-term negotiation mechanism with China, to shape the main features of the China–World economic relationship.

The leadership of China and their counterparts in the United States have been in dialogue with each other for some years. Among these meetings was the Strategic Economic Dialogue led by high-ranking officials of both countries, which is now called the US–China Strategic and Economic Dialogue. The focus of the meetings have been issues such as the response to the economic crisis, ways to cooperate to stem global warming and the proliferation of nuclear weapons, and humanitarian crises. Through this kind of mechanism, the rest of the world maintains a channel through which to express its views and concerns, to discuss urgent and long-term issues, to protect its firms, and influence the Chinese leadership. By exchanging opinions, the rest of the world can provide new ideas in economics and political science to their counterparts, and help China to continue its economic and political reform.

Toward a Balanced Policy and Long-Term Negotiation Mechanism

In the future, the rest of the world, led by the United States, needs a more balanced policy toward China. Here, balance means: (1) a balance between policy measures, insisting upon fundamentals while accepting minor differences; (2) a balance between expectations and reality; (3) a balance between relations with the Chinese government and with the Chinese society, supporting the development of Chinese society while knowing the importance of the role of government and political order in China.

The rest of the world need to understand what has happened in China, and find the logic behind the facts. Most of all, the rest of the world must know that the political and economic process inside China follows its own logic. China and the rest of the world should pay more attention to how each other feels when handling their relations.

The rest of the world needs to build a policy based on understanding of the reality of China, though it should hold onto its principles when the problems are fundamental. The rest of the world should protect its own benefits and its business people, and ensure fair competition in China and in the rest of the world. The rest of the world should help China to continue its economic and political reform, while understanding that China is not able to completely copy the system in the rest of the world.

NOTE

1. '*Ex ante* national treatment' means equal treatment for all foreign firms before entering the market. In other words, they are free to choose which industry to enter.

Conclusions

China's urbanization is an unprecedented event in human history. Several hundreds of millions of people have moved from the countryside to cities during a period half a century, more than the scale of the great migration from Europe to the New World in the nineteenth century. This urbanization will change the fate of hundreds of millions of former peasants and their families in China, create huge demand for products and services for the world markets, and bring work opportunities for workers worldwide.

However, the urbanization that has prevailed in China in the past three decades has been an unfinished urbanization, an urbanization of the government-led physical construction of cities. To complete China's urbanization, the human part of urbanization, the rights of citizenship must be granted to hundreds of millions of migrant workers or former peasants. The scale and importance of this urbanization to China is just like the liberation of slaves in North America in the nineteenth century. If completed, this urbanization will establish a nation based on a solid foundation of equal treatment of all its residents, no matter where they live, which will give China prolonged political stability.

This urbanization in China is an extremely complicated process, a mixture of conflicting factors and processes interlocking with each other. The process involves, as I have mentioned in the first part of this book, the reforms of the residence control system or *Hukou*, rural and urban land ownership, the financial relationship between central and local government, and much more. To solve this puzzle, the Chinese leadership should make overall plans and take all factors into consideration, with high political and economic skill and great courage. The leadership should also minimize the deep social divisions between the farmers, migrant workers, urban residents and local governments in the current environment of a weak society and strong government.

This urbanization will have tremendous impacts on the world economy, changing the markets for capital goods and consumer goods, altering the direction of the movement of factors of production worldwide, and revising the rules of international relations. Confronting this great change, the rest of the world needs to prepare now and take precautions before it is too late.

Considering all the available information and using my understanding of the logic of China's economic development, I have made some rough predictions in this book. My main conclusions are the following:

- China's urbanization will continue over the next two decades. A large percentage of Chinese people will live in the urban areas at the end of this period. As a result, Chinese cities will be huge in terms of both population and constructed area.
- The success of China's urbanization will be determined by the success of a group of intertwined economic and political reforms. These reforms include: (1) change of the residential control system, which will eliminate the different treatments of urban and rural residents; (2) rural land ownership reform, which will return land ownership to farmers at the household level and allow the transition of land ownership; (3) land requisition reform, which will end the monopoly of government in transferring rural land to urban use; and (4) local public finance reform and adjustment of the financial relationships between the central and local governments, which will change the local financial resource foundation from land leasing fees to property taxes and set up a long-term financial resource foundation for local governments, through redivision of the financial responsibilities between central and local governments.
- The possibilities of success in these reforms depend on the vision and determinedness of the leadership; the cooperation or opposition of the local governments; the attitudes of the migrant workers and urban residents; and many other factors. Considering the joint effects of multiple factors, in my baseline forecast, the reforms will be carried out and achieve a degree of success, but not all targets will be fulfilled. Land ownership reform and land requisition reform are examples of the most difficult reforms.
- To some extent, if it succeeds, China's urbanization will solve the problem of inequality between urban residents and a large proportion of the former rural residents in the long run. But in the mid-term, the huge difference between urban and rural residents cannot be completely eliminated. As urbanization advances, a large amount of social problems will be transferred from the rural areas to the cities. At the same time, China's political system will be significantly different from that in the Western countries in the middle to long term – say, for the next 30 to 50 years – which will coexist with the market economy, with some occasional conflicts.
- China's urbanization has changed and will continue to change the world, not only in the factor and product market, but also in the

rules of the international economic and political system and the life style of everyone. These influences include: (1) the urban construction movement that will create a large demand for raw materials and capital goods, which has been seen in the past decade and will continue in the near future; (2) as more migrant workers become city consumers and as urban residents get richer, a huge consumer market will be formed and more consumer goods will be imported; (3) the growth of a domestic market will lead to more domestic market-oriented foreign investments, while export-oriented investments will decrease relatively; and (4) the domestic market will also attract more foreign labor with various skills to China, from the rest of the world.

- From the perspective of welfare, China's urbanization is beneficial for both China and the rest of the world, in general. But from the perspective of a specific person, or country, it is not necessarily good. China's urbanization will ignite the redistribution of income and wealth all over the world.

China's urbanization will create huge energy to fuel the engine of China's development, reshape China's society, and give the world economy a second push, to follow the first push of China's export-oriented development. On the other hand, China and the rest of the world should understand that the problems it creates will equalize the benefits it brings to us. In this great historical event, both China and the rest of the world will enjoy tremendous opportunities and confront unprecedented challenges.

References

ACS (2013). China Approaching the Turning Point. *The Economist*, January 31. Retrieved February 3, 2013 at http://www.economist.com/blogs/freeexchange/2013/01/growth-and-hina?fsrc = scn/li/dc/bl/chinaapproachingtheturningpoint.

AP (2012). Oil Price Drop as China Slow. Norway Strike Ends. July 10. Retrieved July 14, 2012 at http://www.ktvu.com/ap/ap/business/oil-falls-as-china-slows-norway-averts-strike/nPqSj/.

Baidu (n.d.). Development of China's Catering Service Industry. Retrieved August 2, 2012 at http://wenku.baidu.com/view/07e2b89 36bec0975f465e2a3.html.

Baidu Baike (n.d.-a). Housing Subsidy. Retrieved February 18, 2013 at http://baike.baidu.com/view/407842.htm.

Baidu Baike (n.d.-b). Saoziying Village. Retrieved February 19, 2013 at http://baike.baidu.com/view/2305152.htm.

Baidu Wenku (n.d.). The Richest Village in the World. Retrieved March 27, 2013 at http://wenku.baidu.com/view/d18dfc1bb7360b4c2e3f6479.html.

Baidu.com (2012). Per Capita Diary and Mutton Consumption in Inner Mongolia. June 6. Retrieved June 1, 2012 at http://zhidao.baidu.com/question/433804477.html.

Baike Mingpian (2013). Land Finance. Retrieved December 1, 2013 at http://baike.baidu.com/view/2104332.htm.

Barboza, David (2010). As China's Wages Rise, Export Prices Could Follow. *New York Times*, June 7. Retrieved August 5, 2012 at http://www.nytimes.com/2010/06/08/business/global/08wages.html.

BBC (2013). China Media: Wukan Frustration. February 15. Retrieved February 19, 2013 at http://www.bbc.co.uk/news/world-asia-china-21469102.

Beijing Car Quota Administration Information System (n.d.). Results of Allocation. Retrieved August 7, 2013 at http://www.bjhjyd.gov.cn/.

Bloomberg News (2011a). McDonalds to Open a Restaurant a Day in China in Four Years. *Bloomberg News*, July 29. Retrieved August 3, 2012 at http://www.bloomberg.com/news/2011-07-29/mcdonald-s-franchises-to-account-for-up-to-20-of-china-business.html.

Bloomberg News (2011b). China's Affordable Housing Plan to Face Challenge, Cushman Says. March 24. Retrieved on June 24, 2012 at http://www.bloomberg.com / news / 2011-03-24 / china-s-affordable-hous ing-plan-to-face-financing-challenge-cushman-says.html.

BP (2008). BP Statistical Review of World Energy June 2007 (XLS). British Petroleum. Retrieved August 27, 2010 at http://www.bp.com/liveassets/ bp_internet/globalbp/globalbp_uk_english/reports_and_publications/ statistical_energy_review_2008/STAGING/local_assets/downloads/pdf/ statistical_review_of_world_energy_full_review_2008.pdf.

Brahic, Catherine (2007). China's Emissions May Surpass the US in 2007. *New Scientist*, April 25. Retrieved July 10, 2012 at http://en.wikipedia. org/wiki/Energy_policy_of_China.

Brandt, Loren, Jikun Huang, Guo Li and Scott Rozelle (2002). Land Rights in Rural China: Facts, Fictions and Issues. *China Journal*, 47, pp.67–97.

Cagliarini, Adam and Warwick McKibbin (2009). Global Relative Price Shocks: The Role of Macroeconomic Policies. Retrieved August 5, 2012 at http://www.rba.gov.au/publications/confs/2009/cagliarini-mckibbin. pdf.

Cai, Hongbin, J. Vernon Henderson and Qinghua Zhang (2009). China's Land Auctions: Evidence of Corruption. NBER Working Paper 15067, June. Retrieved February 13, 2013 at http://wenku.baidu.com/view/ b26676c158f5f61fb7366696.html.

Caijing (2012). Li Keqiang: Chinuture Development Relies on Urbanization. *Caijing*, November 29. Retrieved January 31 at http:// english.caijing.com.cn/2012-11-29/112322258.html.

Cao, Jing (2013). Audit Result of Government Debt. Guoxin Zhengquan, December 1, 2013. Retrieved February 9, 2014 at http://news.hsw.cn/ system/2013/12/31/051829317.shtml.

Chan, Kam Wing and Li Zhang (n.d.). The Hukou System and Rural–Urban Migration in China: Processes and Changes. Retrieved August 25, 2012 at http://csde.washington.edu/downloads/98-13.pdf.

Chan, Samuel (2011). Processing Trade in China – Profits Tax Implications on Hong Kong Manufacturers. *Highbean*, March 1. Retrieved August 3, 2012 at http://business.highbeam.com/409711/article-1G1-250886457/ processing-trade-china-profits-tax-implications-hong.

Chen, Yingfang (2012). *The Logic of City China*. Shanghai: Shenghuo, Dushu & Xinzhi Bookstore.

Chen, Yunjun, Puqiu Jing and Aimin Chen (2009). *New Views on China's Urbanization*. Beijing: Commercial Press.

Cheng, Guoqiang (2012). *Mechanism and Policy Options for Stabilizing Chinese Grain Market*. Beijing: China Development Press.

Cheng, Mo (2007). How did We Lose the Freedom of Migration? 21ccom. net. August 27, 2012. Retrieved December 1, 2013 at http://www.21ccom. net/articles/zgyj/ggzhc/article_2012082766476_2.html.

China Daily (2008). McDonald's Growing in China. December 5. Retrieved June 2, 2013 at http://www.cctv.com/english/special/opening-up/20081205/112317.shtml.

China Daily (2009). China's Precious Metal Reserves Threatened. July 7. Retrieved July 20, 2012 at http://www.china.org.cn/business/2009-07/07/content_18081707.htm.

China Daily (2013). Chinese Investment in US Hits Record Level. January 1. Retrieved June 9, 2013 at http://english.sina.com/business/2012/1231/543739.html.

China Development Research Foundation (2010). *A New Urbanization Strategy for China: Promoting Human Development*. Beijing: Renmin Press.

China Development Research Foundation (2012). *Changes in the Situation of Population and Adjustments in Population Policy*. Beijing: China Development Press.

China Economy Weekly (2013). Specialists: Local Government Overly Rely on Land Finance. June 25. Retrieved July 30, 2013 at http://finance.sina.com.cn/china/20130625/002815899692.shtml.

China Expat (n.d.). China Housing Bubble. Retrieved June 17, 2012 at http://www.thechinaexpat.com/china-housing-bubble/.

China Industrial Research Report Net (2012). Projections on China's Livestock Products Market Demand. May 28. Retrieved on July 24, 2012 at http://www.chinairr.org/view/V09/201205/28-100230.html.

China Industry Map Editing Committee (2012). *China Energy Industry Map*. Beijing: Social Science Academic Press.

China Investment Consulting (2007). China Has Become the Largest Aluminum Producer and Consumer in the World. July 9. Retrieved July 20, 2012 at http://www.dragonraja.com.cn/20077/22007791293.html.

China News Net (2013). One Quarter of Territory Has Been Shrouded in Thick Fog and Haze. July 11. Retrieved on July 11, 2013 at http://news.sina.com.cn/c/2013-07-11/205627643978.shtml.

China Nutrition Society (2007). *Food Guidebook for Chinese Households*. Retrieved on November 29, 2013 at http://www.cnsoc.org/cn/nutrition.asp?nid=429.

China Weekly (2013). Youth with no Beijing Citizenship was Refused Entry to College Entrance Exam. *China Weekly*. May 22. Retrieved on July 30, 2013 at http://news.sina.com.cn/c/2013-05-22/221127198287.shtml.

China.com (2010). Regional Planning for Yangtze River Delta Region.

June 22. Retrieved September 14, 2013 at http://www.china.com.cn/policy/txt/2010-06/22/content_20320273.htm.

China.com (2012). Chinese Cities Facing Traffic Conjestion. March 13. Retrieved February 4, 2013 at http://news.china.com.cn/2012lianghui/2012-03/13/content_24887703.htm.

ChinaFile (2013). China's New 'Middle Class' Environmental Protests. January 2. Retrieved February 19, 2013 at http://www.chinafile.com/chinas-new-middle-class-environmental-protests.

Christaller, Walter (1933). *Die zentralen Orte in Süddeutschland*. Jena: Gustav Fischer.

Chung, Jae Ho and Tao-chiu Lam (2004). China's 'City System' in Flux: Explaining Post-Mao Administrative Changes. *China Quarterly*, 180, pp. 945–964.

Citizendium (n.d.). Steel Industry, History. Retrieved July 15, 2012 at http://en.citizendium.org/wiki/Steel_industry%2C_history.

Cui, Xu (2013). Research on Rural Collective Economic Organizations. Masters degree thesis, Peking University.

Darwin, Charles (1859). *On the Origin of Species by Means of Natural Selection, or the Preservation of Favoured Races in the Struggle for Life*. London: John Murray.

Department of Comprehensive Statistics of National Bureau of Statistics (1999). *Comprehensive Statistical Data and Materials on 50 Years of New China*. Beijing: China Statistics Press.

Ding, Chengri (2007). Policy and *Praxis of Land Requisition in China*. In Yan Song and Chengri Ding (eds), *Urbanization in China*. Cambridge, MA: Lincoln Institute of Land Policy.

Dingjun (2013a). Competition for Rations of National Level City Group. *21st Century Report*, May 23.

Dingjun (2013b). Number of Small Cities Declined Near 100 in the Past Decade. *21st Century Report*, September 26.

Dong, Jianhong (2004). *History of Urban Construction in China*. Beijing: China Construction Industry Press.

Dongfang Net (2009). History of Hukou Reform in Shanghai. February 23. Retrieved July 25, 2013 at http://news.QQ.com.

Dow Jones Newswires (2012). Rio Tinto Eyes China Steel Demand Peak in 2030. August 8. Retrieved on August 8, 2012 at http://www.foxbusiness.com/news/2012/08/08/rio-tinto-eyes-china-steel-demand-peak-in-2030/.

East Morning News (2011) (Shanghai). 1300 km Road for Home by Motorcycle. January 24.

The Economist (2012). A Dangerous Year. January 28. Retrieved February 19, 2013 at http://www.economist.com/node/21543477.

EIA (2011a). International Energy Outlook 2011. September 19. Retrieved July 14, 2012 at http://www.eia.gov/forecasts/ieo/.

EIA (2011b). World's Total Primary Energy Consumption by Region. International Energy Outlook 2011. Retrieved July 14, 2012 at http://www.eia.gov/oiaf/aeo/tablebrowser/#release=IEO2011&subject=0-IEO 2011&table=1-IEO2011&region=0-0&cases=Reference-0504a_1630.

EIA (2012). China. Country Analysis Brief Overview: China. September 4. Retrieved November 1, 2012 at http://www.eia.gov/countries/country-data.cfm?fips=CH.

Factsanddetails (n.d.). Coal Mine Safty, Deaths and Injuries in China. Retrieved September 8, 2013 at edition.cnn.com/2012/08/29/world/asia/china-miners-blast/.

Finn, Eileen (2010). China's Traffic Problem. *Suite 101.com*, September 12. Retrieved February 4, 2013 at http://suite101.com/article/being-a-pedestrian-in-china-is-dangerous-a291497#ixzz2JqyTTLiU.

Fishman, Ted C. (2006). *China, Inc.* New York: Scribner.

Fleisher, Belton and Dennis T. Yang (2006). Problems of China's Rural Labor Markets and Rural–Urban Migration. *Chinese Economy*, 39(3), pp.6–25.

Fong, Peter K.W. (1989). Housing Reforms in China. *Habitat International*, 13(4), pp.29–41.

Food Wealth Net (2008). History of Grain Trade. December 18. Retrieved July 24, 2012 at http://info.china.alibaba.com/news/detail/v0-d1003662539.html.

Freedman, Jennifer M. (2012). China Could Be Rare Earth Metals Importer by 2014. *Bloomberg*, July 18. Retrieved July 20, 2012 at http://www.renewableenergyworld.com/rea/news/article/2012/07/china-could-be-rare-earth-metals-importer-by-2014?cmpid=rss.

Fukuyama, Francis (2011). *The Origins of Political Order: From Prehuman Times to the French Revolution.* New York: Farrar, Straus & Giroux.

Gu, Chaolin, Taofang Yu and Wangming Li (2008). *China's Urbanization: Pattern, Process and Mechanism.* Beijing: Science Press.

Guo, Jing (2013). Shanghai to Issue Free Plate for Electric Car. Crienglish. com, January 21. Retrieved September 9, 2013 at http://english.cri.cn/69 09/2013/01/21/2743s744561.htm.

Henderson, J. Vernon (2009). Urbanization in China: Policy Issues and Options. China Economic Research and Advisory Programme, November.

Hogan, William T. (1999). *The Steel Industry of China: Its Present Status and Future Potential.* Lanham, MD: Lexington Books.

Home, Andy (2012). China's Raw Materials Imports are (Mostly) Booming.

Reuters, May 24. Retrieved July 7, 2012 at http://business.financialpost. com/2012/05/24/chinas-raw-materials-imports-are-mostly-booming/.

Horsley, Jamie (2009). Public Participation in the People's Republic: Developing a More Participatory Goernance Model in China. Retrieved on June 20, 2012 at http://www.law.yale.edu/documents/pdf/Intellectual_ Life/CL-PP-PP_in_the__PRC_FINAL_91609.pdf.

Hu, Xiaoping and Xiaohui Guo (2010). An Analysis and Projection of 2020 China Grain Demand Structure. *China Rural Economy*, June. Retrieved August 7, 2013 at http://www.doc88.com/p-471422145938. html.

Hu, Xin (2005). *Urban Economics*. Shanghai: Lixin Accounting Publishing House.

Hu, Yang (2009). China's Reserves of Precious Metal Threatened. *China Daily*, July 6. Retrieved May 11, 2013 at http://www.chinadaily.com.cn/ bizchina/2009-07/06/content_8384580.htm.

Hu, Ying (2012). 2000–2008 Estimate of China's Economic Population. In Guanghua Wan and Fang Cai (eds), *China's Road of Urbanization and Development Strategy: Theoretical Inquiry and Empirical Analyses*. Beijing: Economic Science Press.

Hua, Sheng (2013). Real Challenge for China's Financial and Tax Reform. Observation and Exchange 123, Research Center for China and the World, Peking University, Beijing.

Huang, Yuewei, Jingyu He, Tao Liu and Ke Chengyun (2012). Land Reform: From Ownership Clarifying to Land Transferring in Chengdu. China Broadcast Net, November 5. Retrieved February 15, 2013 at http://money.163.com/12/1105/10/8fhq54cm00253b0h_all.html. (in Chinese)

Huangshan Scenic Zone Administration (n.d.). History of Huangshang. Retrieved September 7, 2013 at http://www.chinahuangshan.gov.cn/ huangshanbeautyspot/zjhs/hsjs/ls/A09030102index_1.htm.

Huaxia Jingweiwang (2010). Fifteen Cities Lose RMB1billion Everyday Due to Traffic Jams. December 24. Retrieved July 2012 at http://www. huaxia.com/zt/tbgz/10-078/2231176.html.

Huaxishibao (2013). Local Governments' Anxiety: First Quarter Land Revenue Increased 46.6 Percent. April 20. Retrieved April 27, 2013 at http://finance.sina.com.cn/china/20130420/000715212241.shtml.

Hui, Ning and Li Huo (2007). *Studies on Rural Labor Transfer*. Beijing: China Economic Press.

Hunan Business School (n.d.). Current Situation of China's Overseas Investments. *Baidu*. Retrieved February 2, 2013 at http://wenku.baidu. com/view/32ba0118c5da50e2524d7ff7.html.

IEA (2010). IEA Key energy statistics 2010: country specific indicator. Retrieved December 1, 2013 at www.npconline.co.za/MediaLib/ Downloads/Home/Tabs/Diagnostic/MaterialConditions2/IEA-%20Key %20World%20energy%20statistics%202010.pdf.

IMF (2006). *World Economic Outlook: Financial Systems and Economic Cycles.* World Economic and Financial Surveys. Washington, DC: IMF.

Index Mundi (n.d.). World Demand for Crude Oil. Retrieved July 9, 2012 at http://www.indexmundi.com / energy.aspx?region = xx&product = oil& graph = consumption, http://www.indexmundi.com/energy.aspx?country = cn&product = oil&graph=consumption and http://www.indexmundi. com/energy.aspx?country=us&product=oil&graph=consumption.

International Iron and Steel Institute (1978). Handbook of World Steel Statistics, 1978. Retrieved May 11, 2013 at http://www.worldsteel.org/ dms/internetDocumentList/statistics - archive / yearbook - archive / A - handbook - of - world - steel - statistics - 1978/document/A%20handbook %20of%20world%20steel%20statistics%2019 78.pdf.

International Iron and Steel Institute (2011). Handbook of World Steel Statistics, 2011. Retrieved May 11, 2013 at http://www.worldsteel.org/ dms/internetDocumentList/statistics-archive/yearbook-archive/Steel-sta tistical-yearbook-2011/document/Steel%20statistical%20yearbook%20 2011.pdf.

International Trade @ Suite 101 (n.d.). China's Top Suppliers of Imported Crude Oil by Country in 2010. Retrieved July 9, 2012 at http://suite101. com / article / chinas-top-suppliers-of-imported-crude-oil-by-country-in- 2010-a355760.

IntFX (2008). Copper Consumption in China. March. Retrieved July 20, 2012 at http://www.intfx.com/wiki/Copper_Consumption_China.

Japan's Research Institute of Economy, Trade and Industry (2004). China in Transition, China Surpasses Japan to Become the World's Third-Largest Trader – but the 'Workshop of the World' Is Still Fragile. March 23.

Jiang, Changyun (2012). *China's Service Industry: Development and Reform.* Taiyuan, Shangxi: Shanxi Press & Media Group.

Jiang, Shijie (2010). Infrastructural *Investment and Process of Urbanization.* Beijing: China Architecture and Building Press.

Jiang, Steven and Alexis Lai (2012). China: Haze Isn't Foreign Embassies' Business. CNN, June 6. Retrieved February 2, 2013 at http://www.cnn. com/2012/06/06/world/asia/china-foreign-embassy-pollution-monitor/ index.html.

Jin, Baojie (2013). I Will First Take land in Beijing, Said Ren, Zhiqiang. *21st Century Report,* July 18. Retrieved July 30, 2013 at http://tj.house. sina.com.cn/news/2013-07-18/07422301062.shtml.

Jinghua Times (2013). 200 Million Urban Permanent Residents Have No *Hukou*. July 6. Retrieved July 30, 2013 at http://news.sina.com. cn/c/2013-07-06/034427591550.shtml.

Joint Investigating Group of Ministry of Land and Resources (2007?). Investigating Report of the Purpose and Scope of Land Requisition. 2003. In Yan Song and Chengri Ding (eds), *Urbanization in China*. Cambridge, MA: Lincoln Institute of Land Policy.

Jubal, Jim (n.d.). China's Newest Export: Inflation. Retrieved August 9, 2012 at http://articles.moneycentral.msn.com/Investing/JubaksJournal/ ChinasNewestExportInflation.aspx.

Kan, Huo and Yang Lu (2013). Urban China Platforms in Policy Pressure Cooker. January 23. Retrieved January 31, 2013 at http:// articles.marketwatch.com/2013-01-23/economy/36504155_1_platforms-local-government-government-land.

Kennedy, Simon (2012). China's Export Prowess Fading as Inflation Mounts, Research Shows. July 29. Retrieved August 9, 2012 at http:// www.thestar.com/business/article/1233731--china-s-export-prowess-fad ing-as-inflation-mounts-research-shows.

Kim, M. Julie and Rita Nangia (2008). Infrastructure Development in India and China – a Comparative Analysis. Rand Corporation, August. Retrieved February 16, 2013 at http://www.doc88.com/p-118697820009. html.

Lai, Yaochun (2010). Housing Policy and Cases in China and Other Countries. Mingwang, December 24. Retrieved on June 25, 2012 at http://lunwen.mingmw.com.

Lee, James (2000). From Welfare Housing to Home Ownership: The Dilemma of China's Housing Reform. *Housing Studies*, 15(1), pp.61–76.

Leman, Edward (2006). Metropolitan Regions: New Challenges for an Urbanizing China. World Bank. Chinese version. Retrieved August 29, 2013 at http://wenku.baidu.com/view/b8a2ff29b4daa58da0114a82. html.

Lewin, Tamar (2012). Taking More Seats on Campus, Foreigners Also Pay the Freight. *New York Times*, February 2. Retrieved August 1, 2012 at http://www.nytimes.com/2012/02/05/education/international-students-pay-top-dollar-at-us-colleges.html?pagewanted=all.

Li, Jinlei (2013). National Plan for Development of Urbanization Will Be Published Next Year. Sina.com. December 15. Retrieved December 15, 2013 at http://finance.sina.com.cn/china/20131215/001517636603. shtml.

Li, Lixing (2008). The Incentive Role of Creating 'Cities' in China. Retrieved July 27, 2013 at http://mpra.ub.uni-muenchen.de/8594/.

Li, Peter (n.d.). Housing Reforms in China: A Paradigm Shift to Market

Economy. Retrieved June 17, 2012 at http://www.prres.net/Papers/ Li_Housing_Reforms_In_China_A_Paradigm_Shift_To_Market_Econ omy.pdf.

Liangli de Fengjingxian (2010). The Number of Chinese Students Overseas. April 10. Retrieved August 1, 2012 at http://hi.baidu.com/ liuzhiliangliang/blog/item/4658ba0218b0ef034bfb51b7.html.

Lim, Louisa (2007). Air Pollution Grows in Tandem with China's Economy. NPR, May 17. Retrieved February 5, 2013 at http://www.npr.org/tem- plates/story/story.php?storyId=10221268.

Lin, Justin (2012). *New Structural Economics: A Framework for Rethinking Development and Policy*. Washington, DC: World Bank.

Lin, Xiaozhao and Xin Zou (2013). Hot Spot of Urban Subway Construction. *First Finance and Economics Daily*. May 2.

Liu, Liu (2007). *Dwelling Narrowness*. Shanghai: Yangtse River Art Press.

Liu, Yong (2013). Government Got 60 percent of Housing Price, Difficult to Get Rid of Land Finance. *Huaxiashibao*, April 20. Retrieved April 22, 2013 at http://finance.sina.com.cn/china/20130420/001315212259.shtml.

Lv, Yan (2013). Research on China's Economic Structural Imbalances – Perspective from the Duel Economy. Doctorial thesis, Peking University, June.

Ma, Alyson C., Ari Van Assche and Xhang Hong (n.d.). Global Production Networks and China's Processing Trade. Retrieved August 3, 2012 at http://neumann.hec.ca/pages/ari.van-assche/papers/Hong-Ma-Van%20 Assche-ADBI-090816.pdf.

Ma, Duanlin (1317). *The Wenxian Tongkao* [Comprehensive Examination of Literature].

McCarthy, Lauren (2010). New Regulations Provoke Car Buying Frenzy Across Beijing. *Beijinger*, December 24. Retrieved February 4, 2013 at http://www.thebeijinger.com / blog / 2010 / 12/24 / New - Regulations - Provoke - Car - Buying - Frenzy-Across-Beijing.

McDonald, John and Daniel McMillen (2011). *Urban Economics and Real Estate*. Hobuken, NJ: John Wiley.

Ministry of Environmental Protection (2013). Air Quality Report. Retrieved at http://www.cnemc.cn/.

Ministry of Housing and Construction, Bureau of Planning (2007). China Cities and Their Population Statistics Data.

Ministry of Housing and Urban and Rural Construction (2007). China Urban and Rural Construction Yearbook. Beijing: China Construction Industry Press.

Ministry of Land and Resources (n.d.). 2012 Report of Land and Resources, China. Retrieved April 22, 2013 at http://gz.house.sina.com. cn/news/2013-04-21/07212727782.shtml.

Mokyr, Joel (2000). Editor's Introduction: the New Economic History and the Industrial Revolution. Retrieved August 31, 2013 at http://faculty.wcas.northwestern.edu/~jmokyr/monster.PDF.

Moore, Malcolm (2011). China to Create Largest Mega City in the World with 42 Million People. *Telegraph*, January 24. Retrieved August 31, 2013 at http://www.economist.com/blogs/gulliver/2011/02/development_china.

National Bureau of Statistics (2000–2012-a). *China Statistical Yearbook*. Beijing: China Statistics Press.

National Bureau of Statistics (2004–2011-b). *China City Statistical Yearbook*. Beijing: China Statistics Press.

National Bureau of Statistics (2011-c). Report of a Survey on China Migrant Workers. Retrieved March 3, 2013 at http://www.stats.gov.cn/tjfx/fxbg/t20120427_402801903.htm.

National Bureau of Statistics (2002d). China Rural Labor Employment and Migration, 1997–1998. June 7.

National Bureau of Statistics (2009e). *China Regional Statistical Yearbook*. Beijing: China Statistics Press.

National People's Congress (1982). Constitution of the People's Republic of China. Retrieved August 31, 2013 at http://english.peopledaily.com.cn/constietution/constitution.html.

National People's Congress (1998). Land Administration Law. Retrieved August 31, 2013 at http://www.telegraph.co.uk/news/worldnews/asia/china/8278315/China-to-create-largest-mega-city-in-the-world-with-42-million-people.html.

National People's Congress (2012). Explanation of the Land Administration Law Draft. December. Retrieved August 31, 2013 at http://www.npc.gov.cn/huiyi/lfzt/tdglfxza/node_19554.htm.

Naughton, Barry (2006). *The Chinese Economy: Transitions and Growth*. Cambridge, MA: MIT Press.

NBCNews (2012). As China's Growth Slows, the World Worries. July 13. Retrieved August 7, 2012 at http://economywatch.nbcnews.com/_news/2012/07/13/12725060-as-chinas-growth-slows-the-world-worries.

New Beijing Daily (2013). Strached Ten Mile River. May 23.

New Beijing News (2011). Father Waited Three Days and Three Nights for Tickets. January 25.

Nguyen, Lononh and Grant Smith (2011). IEA Increases 2016 Oil Production Forecast, Says $100 Crude a Threat. *Bloomberg*, June 16. Retrieved July 9, 2012 at http://www.bloomberg.com/news/2011-06-16/iea-boosts-2016-oil-demand-forecast-says-100-crude-is-a-threat-to-growth.html.

OCN (2012). Projection of China's Catering Service Investment.

December. Retrieved August 3, 2012 at http://www.ocn.com.cn/reports/2006083canyin.htm.

Ohmae, Kenichi (1990). The Borderless World: Power and Strategy in the Interlinked Economy. Pensacola, FL: Ballinger Publishing.

Orlik, Tom (2013). Chinese Job Site Offers 2.5 Million Openings. *Wall Street Journal*, August 14, B5.

O'Sullivan, Arthur (2009). *Urban Economics*. Boston, MA: McGraw-Hill. Retrieved August 31, 2013 at http://energy.people.com.cn/n/2013/0329/c71661-20958516.html.

People.com (2013). China's Product Price Adjustment Mechanism Becomes Realistic. March 29.

People's Net (2013). Local Government Debts Exceed RMB20 Trillion. People's Net, May 20. Retrieved July 20, 2013 at http://finance.sina.com.cn/china/20130520/045415515458.shtml.

Ping, Xinqiao (2011). Target of China's Low-income Housing Construction. CMRC China Economy Fast Report, November 2. Retrieved August 31, 2013 at http://wenku.baidu.com/view/2941a33543323968011c92be.html.

Rapoza, Kenneth (2011). More Foreigners Moving To China for Work. *Forbes*, October 17. Retrieved August 4, 2012 at http://www.forbes.com/sites/kenrapoza/2011/10/17/more-foreigners-moving-to-china-for-work/.

Ren, Xingzhou (2011). Policy of Indemnificatory Housing Construction, Institution, and Policy. *CMRC China Economic Observer*, 27. November 4.

Ren, Xingzhou (2012). *China's Housing Market: Trends and Policy*. Beijing: China Development Press.

Research Institute for Industrial Economy (2008). *Chinese Academy of Social Sciences. China's Industrial Development Report 2008*. Beijing: Economy & Management Publishing House.

Rhodium Group (2013). China Investment Monitor. Retrieved August 8, 2013 at http://rhg.com/interactive/china-investment-monitor.

Ryan, Leon (2009). Grain Demand and Consumption Trends in the Chinese, Indian and Durum Wheat Markets. October. Retrieved July 22, 2012 at http://nuffieldinternational.org/rep_pdf/1272936398Leon_Ryan_Nuffield_Report_Final.pdf.

Scott, Dana (2008). The Trends of China's Hotel Industry in 2009. Retrieved July 31, 2012 at http://ezinearticles.com/?The-Trends-of-Chinas-Hotel-Industry-in-2009&id=2871326.

Serdarevic, Masa (2013). China's Two Paths to Urbanisation. *FTAlphaville*, January 31. Retrieved February 2, 2013 at http://ftalphaville.ft.com/2013/01/31/1359652/chinas-two-paths-to-urbanisation/.

Shah, Saeed (2006). China to Pass US Greenhouse Gas Levels by 2010.

Independent. November 8. Retrieved July 10, 2012 at http://en.wikipedia. org/wiki/Energy_policy_of_China.

Shanghai Research Center for Automobile Strategy (2011). *Shanghai Automobile Industry Development Report*. Shanghai: Shanghai Social Academy Press.

Shen, Jianguang (2013). Liconomics Will Face Large Resistance. *Sina Finance and Economics*. June 9. Retrieved August 15, 2013 at http:// finance.sina.com.cn/zl/china/20130709/091116059682.shtml.

Shen, Samuel and Jacqueline Wong (2012). RPT-McDonald's Plans to Expand Franchising in China. Reuters, February 28. Retrieved June 3, 2012 at http://cn.reuters.com/article/companyNews/idUKL4E8DR8952 0120228?symbol=YUM.

Shen, Xiaofang (2013). Private Chinese Investment in Africa. World Bank Working Paper 6311, January.

Song, Yan and Chengri Ding (eds) (2007). *Urbanization in China*. Cambridge, MA: Lincoln Institute of Land Policy.

State Administration of Taxation (n.d.). Domestic Taxation Policy Administration. Retrieved September 8, 2013 at http://www.chinatax. gov.cn/n480462/n4273674/n4273693/n4273712/4293866.html.

State Council (1993). Resolution of the Financial Management System of Tax Division, December 15. Retrieved at http://bbs1.people.com.cn/ postDetail.do?view=2&pageNo=1&treeView=1&id=94187171&boar dId=2.

Steel and Iron Warehouse Net (2012). 2012 Domestic Iron Ore Market Review and 2013 Forecast. December 29. Retrieved August 4, 2013 at http://www.yn56.com/news/show-872696.html.

Steel Association News (n.d.). Forecast of Steel Production, the Second Half of 2012. Retrieved November 8, 2012 at http://futures.hexun. com/2012-07-06/143278175.html.

Steelhome (2012). Global Iron Ore Price to Fall in 2012 on Demand. November 1. Retrieved November 8, 2012 at http://en.steelhome.cn/ 2012/01/11/n574820.html.

Tao, Kunyue (2013). Credit Constraint, Surplus Labor and China's Economy Imbalances. Doctoral thesis, Peking University, June.

Tieba (n.d.). Wuwei Housemaid. Retrieved February 12, 2013 at http:// tieba.baidu.com/p/1525428383.

Tong, Dahuan (2011). *Great Migration in the Century*. Beijing: China Development Press.

United Nations (2010). World Population Perspectives, the 2010 Revision. Retrieved November 11, 2012 at esa.un.org/unpd/wpp/unpp/panel_pop- ulation.htm.

US Census (n.d.). Demographic Overview – Custom Region – China.

Retrieved July 21, 2012 at http://www.census.gov/population/international/data/idb/region.php.

US Census (2009). China's Population to Peak at 1.4 Billion Around 2026. Retrieved August 5, 2013 at http://www.census.gov/newsroom/releases/archives/international_population/cb09-191.html.

US Embassy in Beijing (2013). US Embassy Beijing Air Quality Monitor. Retrieved at http://beijing.usembassy-china.org.cn/070109air.html.

USCC (2011). *2011 Report to Congress.* November. Washington, DC: US Government Printing Office.

Van Sant, Shannon (2013). Despite Pollution Worries, China Exeriments with Carbon Trading. *Voice of America*, January 31. Retrieved February 2, 2013 at http://www.voanews.com / content / despite - pollution - worries - china - experiments-with-carbon-trading/1594361.html.

Wan, Guanghua and Fang Cai (eds) (2012). *China's Road of Urbanization and Development Strategy: Theoretical Inquiry and Empirical Analyses.* Beijing: Economic Science Press.

Wan, Guanghua and Yin Zhang (2006). Impacts of Income Growth and Inequality on China's Poverty. *Journal of Economic Research*, 6.

Wang, Haiping (2012). Nanjing Xiaguan Imperial Land was Investigated: One Company Bought 4 percent of Land in the Area. *21st Century Economic Report*, December 25.

Wang, Helen (2010). Opportunities in China's Healthcare Industry. September 1. Retrieved August 1, 2012 at http://thehelenwang.com/2010/09/opportunities-in-chinas-healthcare-industry/.

Wang, Jian (2012). Analysis of China's Steel Industry Development in the New Century. Doctoral thesis, Peking University.

Wang, Ke, Wang Can, Lu Xuedu and Chen Jining (2007). Scenario Analysis on CO_2 Emissions Reducing Potential in China's Iron and Steel Industry. *Energy Policy*, 35, pp.2320–2335.

Wang, Min (n.d.). Research on China's Public Expenditure on Education: Major Contradictions. Retrieved June 5, 2013 at http://wenku.baidu.com/view/2514f3030740be1e650e9a12.html.

Wang, Ruixia (2013). Rental Price Doubled in Five Years in Beijing. *Zhengquan Times*. April 22. Retrieved Jult 30, 2013 at http://bj.house.sina.com.cn/news/2013-04-22/08062116225.shtml.

Wang, Y.P. and A. Murie (1999). *Housing Policy and Practice in China.* London: Macmillan Press.

Wang, Ying (2012). Administrative Controls: Housing Price Start Increase in Second- and Third-Line Cities. *21st Century Economic Report*, October 25.

Watts, Joanathan (2011). Tens of Thousands Protest Against Chemical Plant in Northern China. *The Economist*, August 14. Retrieved February 19,

2013 at http://www.guardian.co.uk / environment / 2011 / aug / 14 / china - protest - against - px-chemical-plant.

Wen, James G., L. Ding and H. Zhou (eds) (2003). *China's Economic Globalization through the WTO*. Aldershot: Ashgate Publishing.

Wen, Jing (2013). Housing Market in the First Half of 2013. Caixin Net, July 18. Retrieved July 29, 2013 at http://special.caixin.com/2013-07-18/100557523.html.

Wikipedia (n.d.-a). Coal in China. Retrieved July 11, 2012 at http://en.wikipedia.org/wiki/Coal_power_in_the_People%27s_Republic_of_China.

Wikipedia (n.d.-b). Electricity Sector in the People's Republic of China. Retrieved July 12, 2012 at http://en.wikipedia.org/wiki/Electricity_sector_in_the_People%27s_Republic_of_China.

Wikipedia (n.d.-c). Gridlock. Retrieved Feb 3, 2013 at http://en.wikipedia.org/wiki/Gridlock_%28traffic%29.

Wikipedia (n.d.-d). Ancient Chinese Urban Planning. Retrieved February 7, 2013 at http://en.wikipedia.org/wiki/Ancient_Chinese_urban_planning.

Wikipedia (n.d.-e). Expressways of China. Retrieved February 17, 2013 at http://en.wikipedia.org/wiki/Expressways_of_China.

Wines, Michael (2010). China's Growth Leads to Problems Down the Road. August 27. Retrieved February 3, 2013 at http://www.nytimes.com/2010/08/28/world/asia/28china.html?_r=2&scp=2&sq=straddling%20bus&st=cse&.

World Bank (1993). *1994 World Development Report*. Washington, DC: Oxford University Press.

World Bank (2001). *2002 World Development Report*. Washington, DC: Oxford University Press.

World Steel Association (n.d.). Annual Crude Steel Production, 2010–2019. Retrieved May 11, 2013 at http://www.worldsteel.org/dms/internet DocumentList/statistics-archive/production-archive/steel-archive/steel-annually/Annual-steel-2010-/document/Annual%20steel%202010-.pdf.

WSJ (2011). Will Law Reforms Reduce Forced Home Demolitions? January 29. Retrieved on June 20, 2012 at http://blogs.wsj.com/china realtime/2011/01/29/will-law-reforms-reduce-forced-home-demolitions/.

Wu, Jinglian (2013). *Restart Reform: Twenty Lectures on China's Economic Reform*. Beijing: Life, Reading, & Knowledge Press.

Wu, Liming (2012). China's Measures on Rare Earth Fair, Legitimate. *English News*, March 14. Retrieved May 11, 2013 at http://news.xin huanet.com/english/indepth/2012-03/14/c_131466960.htm.

Xi, Jinping (2013). Speech on Boao Forum, April 8. Retrieved April 8, 2013 at http://www.dzwww.com/xinwen/xinwenzhuanti/2008/ggkf 30zn/201304/t20130408_8340755.htm.

Xi, Yihao and Fengling He (2012). We Are Not 'The Party of Rice-Cake'. *Southern Weekend*, December 13.

Xiaoxiang Chenbao (2013). Specialists Say Government Earned 30 Trillion from Land Sale in Recent Years. March 25. Retrieved April 21, 2013 at http://news.sina.com.cn/c/2013-03-25/033726627992.shtml.

Xin, Dingding (2010). Chinese Tourists Spend Lots of Money Abroad. *China Daily*, February 25. Retrieved July 31, 2012 at http://www.chinadaily.com.cn/china/2010-02/25/content_9499101.htm.

Xinhua (n.d.). New Rules to Ease Tensions over Forced Demolition. Retrieved on June 19, 2011 at http://www.china.org.cn/china/2011-01/23/content_21799222.htm.

Xinhua Net (2005). Specialist of Ministry of Land and Resources: China's Oil Reserve is Still Increasing. November 10. Retrieved May 2, 2013 at http://news.xinhuanet.com/fortune/2005-11/10/content_3763369.htm.

Xinhua Net (2013). Taxi Rate raised to RMB13 in Beijing. June 6. Retrieved July 30, 2013 at http://news.sina.com.cn/c/2013-06-06/122127330812.shtml.

Xiong, Wei and Chongqing Gu (2011). A Market for Driving Permits. *China's Reform*, No. 4.

Xu, Daosheng (2000). *Guangdong Province Administration Maps*. Guangzhou: Guangdong Province Map Press.

Yang, Junfeng (2012). Accurately Define the Role of Legislative Power to Solve Land Requisition Dispute. *Nanfang Weekend*, October 4.

Yang, Zhijin (2014). Government Debt Risks are Controllable. 21st Century Economic Report, January 1, 2014. Retrived January 2014 at http://finance.qq.com/a/20140101/003549.htm.

Yanzhao Dushibao (2013). RMB80 000 Public Expenditure Needed for each Migrant Worker. April 14. Retrieved April 27, 2013 at http://finance.sina.com.cn/china/20130414/020815139765.shtml.

Yi, Fuxian (2012). Population Policy Should be Adjusted Timely. *Nanfang Weekend*, October 4.

Yi, Xianrong (2012). How to Realize the Transition of China's Housing Market. *Shanghai Security Daily News*, October 25. Retrieved February 17, 2013 at http://finance.ifeng.com/opinion/mssd/20121025/7197635.shtml.

Yu, Wei-Ping, Li-Hua Wang, Da-Li Yu and Hao Jia (2008). Comparison on the Contribution Rate of Infrastructure Investments and Fixed Assets Investment to GDP. *Railway Transport and Economy*, 30(9). Retrieved February 17, 2013 at http://lib.cqvip.com/qk/91777X/200809/28205873.html.

Yz88.com (2013). China's Pork Consumption Data. September 8. Retrieved June 1, 2013 at http://www.yz88.cn/news/58602.shtml.

Zhan, Yijia (2012). Population Inversion in Pearl River Delta. *Liaowang News Week*, January 16. Retrieved September 15, 2013 at http://www.chinanews.com/gn/2012/01-16/3608489.shtml.

Zhang, Cheng (2006). *Multinationals in the Service Sector and China's Economic Development*. Beijing: China Finance & Economics Press.

Zhang, Fan (2011). Solving Traffic Congestion Problems by Using Pricing Mechanism. *Decision Making and Information*, December. http://www.nsd.edu.cn/cn/article.asp?articleid=14051.

Zhang, Jialin (n.d.). China's Slow-Motion Land Reform. *Baidu Wenku*. Retrieved February 13, 2013 at http://wenku.baidu.com/view/67e984345a8102d276a22f93.html.

Zhang, Jun (2008). The 1994 Tax Division. *Economic Observer*, March 9. Retrieved February 16, 2013 at http://finance.sina.com.cn/stock/.

Zhang, L., S.X.B. Zhao and J.P. Tian (2003). Self-Help in Housing and Chenzhongcun in China's Urbanization. *International Journal of Urban and Regional Research*, 27, pp.912–937.

Zhang, Tingwei (2007). Urban Development Patterns in China: New, Renewed, and Ignored Urban Space. In Yan Song and Ding Chengri (eds), *Critical Issues in an Era of Rapid Growth. Lincoln Institute of Land Policy*, Cambridge, MA: Lincoln Institute of Land Policy.

Zhang, Xiaoling (2013a). National 5 Regulations Released Before the Meetings of Congress: The Most Serious Control in the History. *21st Century Economic Report*, March 4.

Zhang, Xiaoling (2013b). Guangzhou Sample of Local Debt: Land Finance Supports High Land Price? 21st Economic Report. June 20.

Zhang, Xiaoyu (2012). Projection of China's Future Grain Supply and Demand. *Agriculture Perspectives*, 2012(3). Retrieved August 7, 2013 at http://www.caitec.org.cn/c/cn/news/2012-07/10/news_3384.html.

Zhang, Yin and Guanghua Wan (2006). The Impact of Growth and Inequality on Rural Poverty in China. *Journal of Comparative Economics*, 34(4), pp.694–712.

Zhang, Yuqun, Na Wang and Minxia Luo (2012). Chinese Tourists Shopping Spree World Wide. *South Weekend*, October 14.

Zhao, Jianhua (2011). China's Petroleum Demand Will Reach 483 Million Tons in 2011. *China News Net*, January 20. Retrieved July 10, 2012 at http://news.sohu.com/20110120/n278996183.shtml.

Zhao, Yinan (2013). Farmers Need Patience for Improved Legislation. *China Daily*, February 26. Retrieved March 6, 2013 at http://usa.chinadaily.com.cn/china/2013-02/26/content_16255512.htm.

Zhou, Chengjun (2013). Understandings and Suggestions for New Urbanization. *First Finance and Economics Daily*, May 29.

Zhou, Junan (2013). The Impact on the Host Country of China's Direct Investment in Africa. June. Masters thesis, Peking University.

Zhou, Qiongyuan (2012). Urban Rail Transit: the Attraction of the RMB840 Million Cake. *Nanfang Weekend*, October 4.

Zhou, Qiren (2012). Land Transfer: Four Steps. Sohu Finance. Retrieved February 15, 2013 at http://business.sohu.com/s2012/8161/s337121818/.

Zhou, Qiren (2013). Urban–Rural China Comments 60: Origin of the Rural Land Use Regulation. *Economic Observer*, August 13. Retrieved August 31, 2013 at http://www.nsd.edu.cn/cn/article.asp?articleid=17102.

Zhou, Shulian, Yanzhong Wang and Zhiyu Shen (2008). Industrialization and Urbanization in China. Beijing: Economy & Management Publishing House.

Zhou, Xiansheng (2013). From Outsiders to Innkeepers in China's Sleepy Countryside. *New York Times*, August 14. Retrieved August 17, 2013 at http://www.nytimes.com / 2013 / 08 / 14 / business / global / in - chinas - countryside - travelers-find - foreigner - run - hotels . html?nl = todayshead lines&emc = edit _ th _ 20130814&pagewanted=all.

Zhu, Zaiqing (2010). *A Study of the Competitiveness of China's Meat Products*. Beijing: Science Press.

Index

steel
  backyard furnaces 128
  consumption 111, 127–132, 174
  demand 112, 127–132
  and economic reform 127–129
  prices 128–129, 132
  production 127–132
  trade 128, 132
strategic economic dialogue 210

tax
  congestion 82–83
  consumption 50–52
  corporation 50–52
  division 49, 50, 197
  housing property related 51, 65, 66,
    194–195, 197, 199
  land-related 99, 51–52, 99
  personal income 50–52, 66
  reform 49, 50–52, 193–195, 197
  security 50
  treatment on foreign firms 209
  value-added 50
taxi 36, 80–81, 186
Ten Mile River 26–27
tertiary sector 155–156
tourism 158, 159–160
trade
  export-oriented manufacturing 15,
    24, 104, 165–166
  grain 147
  meat 149
  retail 156, 171
  service 157–158, 168
  of steel 128, 132
  surplus 180
traffic
  cars 17, 80–84, 118, 137,
    152–155
  congestions 13–14, 26, 79, 80–83, 94,
    120, 154, 181, 186–187, 192
  congestion tax 82–83
  online ticket purchasing system 33
  policy 81–83, 134
  regulation 80–83, 154–155
  safety 81
trial and error approach 197

unemployment
  pool 37–38

rate 38
urban 105, 108, 187
urban
  construction 59, 98–99, 214
  labor markets 35–39
  population 1, 2, 5–7, 8–9, 13, 17,
    21–24, 28, 30–31, 35, 92, 98,
    108–109, 139, 141, 151
urbanization
  aspects of 9–13
  anti- 18
  challenges to 13–15, 76, 204, 214
  development and 15–17, 155, 174,
    206
  human part of 212
  and migration 9, 190
  negative effects of 13
  and new poverty in the cities 73–75
  partial 39
  other problems in 80–87
  in planned period 5–7
  policy 8, 13, 25, 39, 73–75, 93,
    95–98, 105, 108, 187, 189,
    200
  ratio 5, 6, 7, 8, 9, 22, 23, 24, 25, 31, 9
    2, 95, 105, 108, 151
  road map and logic of 15–20
  role of government in 18–20, 211
  role in China's development 15–18
  social aspects of 71–79
  speed of 188, 190, 193
  stagnated 201, 202
urban–rural inequality 72
US
  Chinese investment in 169–170
  embassy in Beijing 84
utility and city size 188

villages within the cities 74–75

wage
  average 36, 38
  difference 36–37
  minimum 172
wheat 143–149
World Trade Organization 15, 24, 118,
  130, 134, 160, 185, 209
Wu, Jinglian 202

Xi, Jinping 104